Academic Chutes & Ladders

The Hidden Curriculum That Makes or Breaks Academic Careers

Edited by
Kerry F. Crawford and Leah C. Windsor

BLOOMSBURY ACADEMIC
NEW YORK • LONDON • OXFORD • NEW DELHI • SYDNEY

BLOOMSBURY ACADEMIC
Bloomsbury Publishing Inc, 1359 Broadway, 12th Floor, New York, NY 10018, USA
Bloomsbury Publishing Plc, 50 Bedford Square, London, WC1B 3DP, UK
Bloomsbury Publishing Ireland, 29 Earlsfort Terrace, Dublin 2, D02 AY28, Ireland

BLOOMSBURY, BLOOMSBURY ACADEMIC and the Diana logo are
trademarks of Bloomsbury Publishing Plc

First published in the United States of America 2026

Cover Design: Sally Rinehart
Cover Image © Kerry F. Crawford

Library of Congress Cataloging-in-Publication Data
Names: Crawford, Kerry F. editor | Windsor, Leah C. editor
Title: Academic chutes & ladders: the hidden curriculum that makes or breaks academic careers / edited by Kerry F. Crawford and Leah Windsor.
Description: New York: Bloomsbury Academic, 2026. | Includes bibliographical references and index. Identifiers: LCCN 2025033554 (print) | LCCN 2025033555 (ebook) | ISBN 9798765164303 hardback | ISBN 9798765164297 paperback | ISBN 9798765164273 pdf | ISBN 9798765164280 epub Subjects: LCSH: College teaching—Vocational guidance—United States | College teachers—United States—Social conditions | College environment—United States Classification: LCC LB1778.2 A23 2025 (print) | LCC LB1778.2 (ebook) | DDC 378.1/2—dc23/eng/20250930
LC record available at https://lccn.loc.gov/2025033554
LC ebook record available at https://lccn.loc.gov/2025033555

ISBN: HB: 979-8-7651-6430-3
PB: 979-8-7651-6429-7
ePDF: 979-8-7651-6427-3
eBook: 979-8-7651-6428-0

Typeset by Integra Software Services Pvt. Ltd.
Printed and bound in the United States of America

For product safety related questions, contact productsafety@bloomsbury.com.

Academic Chutes & Ladders

This book is written for and inspired by everyone who has stared down the chutes, searched for the ladders, and made the journey easier for those who came behind them.

We see you.

You belong here.

Contents

Figures

Introduction

Academic Chutes and Ladders, Explained

Consider the professors you know. Do you know how each one made it to where they are today? Although each completed graduate school and landed a job at a college or university, the similarities probably end there. At the very start of this book, we want to call your attention to the reality that we don't all travel the same path to and through the academic profession. Instead, we navigate twists and turns, setbacks and opportunities. In this book, we shed light on many of the pathways to, through, and even out of the academic profession. This is not an ordinary academic edited volume. In the chapters that follow, we and our contributing authors bring the literature into conversation with lived experiences. Our contributing authors recount their stories in their unique voices. We hope you will catch glimpses of yourself, your colleagues, and your students in this book's pages, because we have one central goal: to help higher education become a profession that embraces the whole scholar.

In our first book together, *The PhD Parenthood Trap: Caught between Work and Family in Academia*, we introduced the metaphor of academic chutes and ladders (Crawford and Windsor 2021, 2–4). For many years, scholars studying issues of demographic representation among faculty and administration in higher education have discussed the "leaky pipeline" through which women leave the academic profession because of the significant barriers to their success, retention, promotion, and ability to thrive (Clark Blickenstaff 2005; Goulden, Mason, and Frasch 2011; Hesli, Lee, and Mitchell 2012; Hancock, Baum, and Breuning 2013; Gasser and Shaffer 2014; Miller and Wai 2015; Windsor and Crawford 2021; Windsor, Crawford, and Breuning 2021; Scalera Elliott et al. 2023). These studies and the discussions they have prompted have led to improved campus policies, formal and informal mentorship networks and initiatives, and greater awareness of the challenges historically excluded scholars face as they navigate higher education and the academic profession.

But the leaky pipeline metaphor fails to capture the reality that each of our trajectories to and through the academic profession is nonlinear: our lived experiences and identities shape how prepared we are for undergraduate and graduate education; some of us arrive as first-year college students or graduate students with caregiving responsibilities or full-time employment; some of us take time between undergraduate and graduate work or between graduate work and the academic job search for a multitude of reasons; some of us spend years in precarious, non-tenure track employment within the academy; and some of us move directly from a graduate program into a tenure-track faculty position.

We are not commodities passing through a singular, linear pipeline. We don't "leak" out passively along the way. Our paths are widely divergent. Much like players in the childhood board game Chutes and Ladders (or Snakes and Ladders), members of the academic profession encounter opportunities and obstacles at all levels of their career trajectory. Some obstacles (or chutes) will end the pathway through the profession. Some opportunities (or ladders) will advance the "player" to the next level or rank. Some obstacles are minor setbacks; some opportunities yield small advancements. And much like in the board game, at times the opportunities may simply be serendipitous, and the obstacles may have little to nothing to do with one's qualifications or hard work. Race, ethnicity, gender, sexuality, parental and caregiving status, nationality, socioeconomic status, and first-generation student status are intersecting identities that compound bias against and create additional obstacles for scholars at all levels, from undergraduate coursework to hiring and promotion in the academic profession.

Each of us encounters different opportunities for success. Each of us encounters different barriers to our success. Many of these opportunities and barriers arise from the same norms, policies, and practices within the academy that have failed to adapt over time to make higher education and the academic profession more diverse, equitable, inclusive, and accessible. We hope to change that. Once we begin to consider the academic career as one that resembles the game of Chutes and Ladders, we can discuss, strategize, draft, and implement transparent, clearly communicated, equitably applied policies on our campuses and in our professional associations so that all students, faculty, and staff understand the rules of the game. Once we begin to observe the chutes and ladders that shape academic progress, we can create supportive, equitable mentorship networks and initiatives for scholars at all levels.

When someone says, "Can I ask a dumb question?," it is likely that they are seeking information about the hidden curriculum. Dumb questions are not dumb, nor are the people asking them. The hidden curriculum necessarily obscures the unwritten rules of the game. Many times, people flail and flounder needlessly because they don't want to show what they don't know. They don't want to identify themselves as an outsider. They don't want people—their peers and colleagues—to think they don't belong. They fear, perhaps, that they are an impostor, and if they ask the "wrong" questions or signal a lack of understanding, everyone else will realize they were never meant to be in this space. Academic norms are too often arbitrary, so it's no wonder they are not intuitive. They are taught, learned, enculturated, and propagated across generations of scholars. The hidden curriculum is the passkey that unlocks *how* things are done—but not necessarily *why*.

Often, there is no good reason for why things are done the way they are—path dependency often lacks logic and defies explanation. Why do we format academic CVs the way we do? Who knows. Why do we take comprehensive exams? Because our advisers did. Why are disciplinary norms so different? Because academic relevancy depends on demonstrating a unique contribution and staking ideological, methodological, and theoretical claims that provide existential justification. The hidden curriculum thrives in siloed ivory towers and depends on the silence and deference of those among the academic ranks. It's when we ask the basic questions and interrogate the underlying assumptions that the hidden curriculum becomes evident.

Throughout the book, we focus on two key efforts that, if implemented broadly and intentionally, will foster a culture of belonging on campuses and in academic disciplines to ensure that scholars have the opportunities they deserve. These key efforts are, first, investments in formal and informal mentorship; and second, dedication to ensuring that policies and processes are clearly communicated, transparent, and equitably applied.

Because we all follow different paths to and through the academy, we need support systems to help us through our career trajectories. We need an academy that embraces—not one that simply tolerates or ignores—the variation in lived experiences, identities, and perspectives of scholars who comprise its ranks or hope to gain entry. Mentorship, we find, is key to plugging the chutes and pointing out the ladders. Both formal and informal mentorship efforts can demystify the hidden curriculum and help scholars learn to write effective grant proposals or research papers, negotiate parental leave or a higher starting salary, use a syllabus or write one, develop new courses or study for comprehensive exams (Allen, Eby, and Lentz 2006; Allen and Eby 2007; Kim 2018; Windsor and Thies 2021; Scalera Elliott et al. 2023).

Further, clearly communicated, transparent, and equitably applied policies create a foundation for an inclusive campus at all levels (Crawford and Windsor 2021). By making policies and expectations accessible to all, institutions of higher education can begin the important work of fostering campus communities that embrace and support scholars from the undergraduate years through the full professor rank. As many of the contributors to this volume describe, however, such efforts are at once urgently needed and far too rare.

The Hidden Curriculum: Chute for Some, Ladder for Others

Success in academia too often depends on an awareness of higher education's unwritten rules. Within and beyond academia, the term "hidden curriculum" refers to rules, norms, expectations for behavior, and implicit values that are conveyed directly or indirectly in a social or cultural environment (Jackson 1968; Snyder 1973; Margolis 2001; Alsubaie 2015). Philip W. Jackson's book *Life in Classrooms* (1968) introduced scholars in education to the idea of the hidden curriculum. The hidden curriculum is comprised of the subtle but all-important lessons we learn from the social interactions we have in an educational setting. Although Jackson's focus is on elementary (or primary) schools, he observes the connections between the environment in these early years and the high-school and college classroom settings (Jackson 1968, xxi). Jackson's discussion of the dual curricula—hidden and overt—is worth including here:

> School is a place where tests are failed and passed, where amusing things happen, where new insights are stumbled upon, and skills acquired. But it is also a place in which people sit, and listen, and wait, and raise their hands, and pass out paper,

> and stand in line, and sharpen pencils. School is where we encounter both friends and foes, where imagination is unleashed and misunderstanding brought to ground. But it is also a place in which yawns are stifled and initials scratched on desktops, where milk money is collected and recess lines are formed. Both aspects of school life, the celebrated and the unnoticed, are familiar to all of us, but the latter, if only because of its characteristic neglect, seems to deserve more attention than it has received to date from those who are interested in education.
>
> (Jackson 1968, 4)

We become aware of the "unnoticed" aspects of school—from preschool through doctoral programs—once we are on the other side. Like kindergarteners entering an elementary-school classroom unaware of the many social lessons they will learn while also developing skills in reading and math, many of us enter undergraduate and graduate programs and the academic profession partly or entirely unaware of the subtler norms and skills we will learn through our interactions in higher education. Benson Snyder's work advanced the discussion of the hidden curriculum in higher education, observing that unwritten and unknown or misunderstood academic and social norms and expectations on campus drive anxiety and conflict on campuses (Snyder 1971). Maria del Carmen Salazar's work on humanizing pedagogy communicates the ways in which educators deny their students' humanity by erasing their cultural identity, language, and history (Salazar 2013).

Work on the hidden curriculum underscores the effects education—at all levels—has on individuals, their communities, and society as a whole (Vallance 1974; Martin 1976). The hidden curriculum is not, of course, hidden to all; further, hidden curricula exist wherever any learning occurs, whether on a college campus or in training for a new job (Martin 1976). The question Jane Martin posed nearly fifty years ago still resonates today: "What do we do with a hidden curriculum when we find one?" (Martin 1976).

Another way to look at the hidden curriculum is through the lens of the four stages of competence (DePhillips, Berliner, and Cribben 1960). Unconscious incompetence refers to the state of unawareness of lacking key skills. Conscious incompetence follows the awareness of these deficits and often involves making mistakes as individuals navigate the process of integrating new skills. Conscious competence refers to the developmental phase when an individual knows how to do something, but the skill requires careful and effortful attention and moderation. Unconscious competence can be understood as fluency or effortless integration of the skills in practice. Those privy to the rules of the academic game of Chutes and Ladders have unconscious competence; those like the scholars in this book who enter with unconscious or conscious incompetence can remind us how nonintuitive the rules of the game can be.

To succeed in academia—using the ability to obtain a stable faculty position and rise through the ranks as a key marker of success—requires knowledge of and familiarity with discipline-specific steps and stages, research and communication skills (written and oral), ability to network with peers and influential members of one's discipline, and the stubbornness and stability to push through years of coursework, training, and job applications. The specific requirements of each discipline vary, and we do not purport to speak here on behalf of the myriad fields and subfields of academia. Instead, we want readers to start here with the understanding that academic success rests on access to insights and opportunities that are not universally or equitably given. This is the essence of the hidden curriculum of higher education.

The presence of a hidden curriculum creates the potential for inequality of opportunities. Some scholars are fortunate to enter college or graduate school aware of the pathways to success, others learn about them through formal or informal mentorship, and still others leave higher education or the academic profession after encountering one or more of the many obstacles to advancement (Windsor and Thies 2021; Windsor, Crawford, and Breuning 2021; Scalera Elliott et al. 2022). The hidden curriculum, in short, perpetuates inequality in academia if it remains obscured to some and obvious to others. Martin emphasizes the importance of awareness: understanding the hidden curriculum is not a substitute for institutional changes designed to promote equity, but it "may be the best weapon" available for individuals harmed by the effects of unwritten rules, norms, and expectations (Martin 1976, 150).

Fortunately, students, faculty, staff, and administrators on campuses have started taking important steps toward institutional reforms that minimize the effects of the hidden curriculum and create a more level playing field for students and scholars. The growing literature on obstacles confronting historically excluded students and scholars provides accounts of policies, practices, and the need for further changes in higher education today (Kezar 2010; Byrd, Brunn-Bevel, and Ovink 2019; Garcia 2019; Calarco 2020). The chapters in sections one through four highlight some of these changes and suggest the need for more, drawing from both the contributing authors' scholarship and their lived experiences as people in higher education.

Creating a Culture of Belonging in Academia

By demystifying the hidden curriculum, we can create a culture of belonging in higher education, one that embraces the whole scholar. As we mentioned previously, one essential effort is the intentional cultivation of mentorship in its many forms. We and our contributing authors discuss mentorship often throughout the book, and with good reason: mentorship makes the unwritten rules visible and helps make sense of them; it helps scholars find the ladders and avoid the chutes; and when undertaken with care, it humanizes students, faculty, and campus leaders. Mentorship is an investment in people and in the future of our institutions and higher education as a whole. Mentorship helps students make it to graduation. It helps students identify the graduate programs that are right for them as individual scholars. Mentorship helps faculty earn tenure, and it empowers bold, courageous leaders who will protect and advance higher education. Everyone needs someone in their corner who believes in them, stands behind them, and serves as their champion.

Mentorship and individual strategies for success can go a long way toward getting into graduate school, completing a dissertation, getting an academic job, and earning tenure. Formal mentorship initiatives and networks—such as those organized by individual campuses, professional associations, or disciplinary affinity groups—bring early career scholars together with mid-career or senior scholars to discuss disciplinary norms, enumerate and explain processes for writing dissertations or compiling job application materials, offer supportive spaces for research presentations and collaboration, or discuss work-life boundaries and protecting one's well-being while navigating the profession. Informal mentorship is less structured and often more organic. A student may visit a professor's office hours to ask questions about graduate school or seek out opportunities for research collaboration. A graduate student may request a coffee meeting with a scholar in their field at a major conference with the goal of building a research network or identifying job prospects. A faculty member may connect their well-regarded student with a colleague from another campus, opening avenues for collaboration, graduate school admission, or a future job. In short, mentorship is a practice that occurs through both formal and informal approaches.

Faculty and campus leaders can establish formal or informal mentorship networks or initiatives on their campus or within their professional association. Affinity groups on campus or sections within professional associations can provide the structure and visibility to cultivate a formal mentorship network. On campus, departments, colleges, and resources such as centers for faculty innovation or student success may have the resources, space, and talent to support both formal and informal mentorship efforts.

Mentorship paves over the chutes and shines spotlights on the ladders. Nevertheless, mentorship and individual-level strategies or hacks cannot ensure that the game is fair for everyone. With this in mind, we also call for systemic change. It's incumbent upon academic leaders to ensure that the rules and processes guiding all aspects of academia are clearly communicated, transparent, and equitably applied. "Academic leaders" is a category we use to refer to the senior administrators on campus (presidents, chancellors, provosts, deans), the leaders of departments or centers, and undergraduate or graduate program directors. Where can academic leaders begin the effort to assess policies and processes to ensure that they are visible, fair, and conducive to a culture of belonging? Here we offer a few:

- Graduate program admissions policies and application processes
- Graduate student recruitment sessions and new-student welcome events
- Hiring guidelines that outline processes through which search committees and hiring managers identify, interview, and make an offer to candidates for faculty positions
- New faculty welcome workshops, trainings, and events
- Policies governing faculty annual reviews and tenure and promotion
- Codes of conduct and constitutions governing professional associations and their meetings

Beyond policies and processes, academic leaders can work to create physical spaces that communicate an intention to include all scholars. For example, an early career scholars' lounge or a new parents' room at an academic conference signals to graduate students, junior faculty, and scholars with nursing infants or young children that they are welcome and permitted to take up space. A lactation room in a campus building sends the message that an academic program understands the caregiving needs of students, staff, and faculty. Study spaces for international students or first-generation students on campus recognize the importance of solidarity and shared experiences. These are low-cost, high-reward efforts that can help ensure scholars feel supported and stay in the game.

We're Still Here: Why?

As an author team, we have collaborated extensively and supported each other through the processes of growing our families, applying for jobs, navigating a pandemic, and taking on leadership positions. But as individuals, we each took our own path to the academic profession and have encountered but persisted in the face of unique obstacles.

Kerry's "Why," in Her Words

I was a first-generation college graduate, but the allure of books and classrooms drew me in at a very young age. See, neither of my parents attended a four-year college after high school, but my mother began working toward her Bachelor of Arts degree when I was in preschool, taking one class per semester (or less often, depending on finances) with the intention of setting an example for me. On teacher workdays and snow days that conflicted with her classes, I would go to class; I sat at a desk that was far too big for me and drew pictures while listening to the lectures. These early days in college classrooms created an idyllic image of the academy, even if they did nothing to make sense of the practical realities of higher education. I chose a college that was in-state, affordable, and would accept my Advanced Placement credits and perhaps overlook my less-than-impressive SAT scores. I entered as a music major but promptly switched to political science because I enjoyed my required general education Introduction to Political Science course, and I found that the classes offered me the tools to help me make sense of the post–9-11 world as the United States-led war in Iraq raged on. I confided in my political science professor that I was a little bored and didn't find college as challenging as I'd hoped, and she recommended that I start taking her upper-level courses the next semester (spring of my first year) and perhaps add some extra classes to take a heavier course load. In short, my path to the political science professoriate was hardly preordained, but a professor noticed me and shared advice that was just unconventional enough to be perfect for *me*.

I graduated a year early, overloading my class schedule for the five semesters after my first semester, both to minimize the cost of my degree and to challenge my mind. My plan was all about saving money and time and proving that I could take twenty-four credits per semester and still pull off a 4.0 (to prove the SAT wrong). *I've always liked a challenge.* The guidance my political science professors offered in class and during office hours helped me discover a passion for asking big questions, writing, and teaching, and as I approached my graduation from St. Mary's College of Maryland, I realized I didn't want to leave … ever. After a gap year at a global nonprofit organization, I began my PhD at George Washington University and promptly focused on two of the most marginalized topics in political science (at least, at the time): gender-based violence in war and gendered injustice in peacetime.

In my first semester as a graduate student, I realized just how little I knew about the process of working toward a doctoral degree. I was acutely uncomfortable networking, didn't trust myself to give presentations without note cards (even when I knew the information well), and felt outnumbered by the effortlessly confident men in my cohort. But I'm stubborn and relentless; once I set a goal, I complete it. Plus, I do like a challenge. Fortunately, these personality quirks are an asset in academia. Through sheer force of will and with the support of mentors and dissertation committee members, I went on the academic job market after five years in my doctoral program, landed a tenure-track job at James Madison University, and completed my dissertation … while pregnant with my first child. My well-timed son was born just two weeks after I defended and filed my dissertation, a true thesis baby. I didn't fall down a chute at that point, as one may expect: my dissertation committee shared their enthusiastic congratulations when I told them I was pregnant; no one questioned my ability to finish my dissertation, and no one suggested that I avoid going on the job market that fall. And you know what? It all went just fine. Five years, two books, and several journal articles later, I submitted my compelling case for early tenure and promotion at James Madison University … one month after giving birth to my twin daughters.

My "why," the reason I persisted through feeling underqualified in those early months of graduate school and striving to balance the competing demands of academic work and a young family, is simple: I entered the academic profession with the deeply rooted beliefs that, first, education opens doors; and second, understanding makes the world a better place. These two core motivations are more important now than ever before, and they ground my research, teaching, and leadership efforts at a time when it is far from easy to be an academic. I centered those beliefs and was fortunate to find and cultivate supportive relationships with academic mentors all along the way. A part of my "why" may also be that I really do like a challenge, especially when one involves breaking down barriers and turning assumptions upside down. Now, as a woman full professor, mother of three young children, and head of a large and complex academic department, I have the privilege of lifting others while I climb.

Leah's "Why," in Her Words

I took a nonlinear path from undergraduate to master's to doctoral degrees. Though technically not first-generation, my rural upbringing left me underprepared for succeeding in the ivory tower. I never had to work hard in high school, and I lacked study skills and discipline (i.e., the soft skills and work hacks that changed my life later at a mentorship conference), which made my work inefficient and frustrating. I was a very mediocre and not memorable undergraduate student, crawling over the finish line in 1998 with a degree in linguistics. College never came naturally to me—from not knowing how to format the word processing program on a hand-me-down computer freshman year (I turned in my first paper in 18-point Courier bold)—to figuring out how to get a job after graduation.

I was a late-in-life professional academic and started my PhD somewhat on a dare. In the late 2000s, I found myself the only person without a PhD at an annual Halloween party in the living room "Chuck-e-Cheese" style ball pit. I had already been considering pursuing a doctoral degree, and being the least degreed friend in the ball pit convinced me to apply and enroll. In graduate school, it took some time before I understood some of the "hidden curriculum"; for example, that journal articles are generally formatted the same way, and that my papers should *also* follow that pattern. Despite not knowing the "rules of the road," I earned my PhD in less than four years, nearly quitting the semester before I defended because I still felt so out of place among my peers, especially at conferences. (How do you ask a question? How do you know what panels to attend? Can you talk to people just by approaching them? How do you present your work?)

I took the first and closest job available—an instructorship—because I was part of a dual career academic partnership, and my partner was tenure track. The promise of a tenure-track job was routinely dangled in front of me, and although I applied to every position, my department never gave me an interview. This is one of the big academic secrets that few people talk about: whatever rank you enter an institution is how you are perceived. If you're not tenure track, it's very difficult to convince people to see you as tenure-track material. Even if you get a million-dollar grant and publish in great places. My chair told me that I would have to "overcome my subpar PhD program"—rampant elitism is another land mine on the Chutes and Ladders game board. So, I had to go on the job market many times to maneuver from being an instructor, to research faculty, to (finally) a tenured professor.

Is it worth it to me? The answer, most days, is mostly. I have tried to create an academic environment that is supportive and where policies are clearly communicated, transparent, and equitably applied. After more than a decade of fighting seemingly uphill battles for recognition and the respect of a tenured position, I have realized the value of playing the long game in academia. The system of higher education is big and storied and inflexible—and although one person can only do so much, what they *can* do can matter tremendously to people in that academic ecosystem. I live by the motto "bloom where you're planted." My work is quite interdisciplinary, and this challenges the traditional academic silos. My "why" is that being in higher education gives me the opportunity to ask interesting questions, work with clever people who are also curious about the world around them, and mentor students who find themselves as puzzled about being in college as I was.

There Is Value in the Work

It is important to note here that at the time of writing, higher education in the United States is under siege, surrounded on and taking hits from multiple sides. At the federal level, the Department of Education faces an effort to dismantle its core functions, including federal funding for colleges and universities, federal student loans, and policies that promote diversity, equity, inclusion, and access. In a growing number of states, colleges, universities, and faculty contend with efforts to reduce funding, curtail academic freedom, and weaken tenure protections. In the United States and globally, faculty must determine how best to navigate the opportunities and challenges created by artificial intelligence. Campuses around the world must grapple with the commodification and "adjunctification" of faculty labor. To varying extents, colleges and universities worldwide face the prospect of demographic shifts that impact student enrollment. Taking these challenges and others into account, there is immense uncertainty in higher education. Still, we believe in the work, and we believe the work is worth pursuing. Higher education is, at its core, a profession that seeks to illuminate the truth, strives to empower future generations of citizens, and fosters a deeper understanding of our world. The faculty on our campuses and the work they do are worth protecting. The students and early career scholars who want to pursue academic careers are worth supporting. With the understanding that higher education matters, we proceed here with a roadmap of the book.

A Road Map for *Academic Chutes & Ladders*

First, a caveat. We do not claim to present a book that has all the answers to academia's problems or to represent all academics' voices or stories. Our contributors speak for themselves, not as representatives of any identity, group, or institution. No single book can represent the full range of perspectives in the profession. We also do not provide an exhaustive list of all the potential chutes (and ladders) for students and faculty to look out for, nor do we provide an exhaustive set of recommendations for how to navigate every situation. No author or team of authors can do that. Instead, we have set out to highlight the reality that each of our paths to and through the academic career is unique. What we hope to do is to spark conversations on campuses at all levels from students to senior leaders. If you can see yourself or your campus in any of these chapters, and you begin to formulate questions and ideas about your path, your student's path, or the future of your department, college, or university, then we have accomplished our mission.

Our goal is to make the academic profession one that not only tolerates but *embraces* the uniqueness of its members, to empower our colleagues to point out the hidden curriculum when they see it, and to share this wisdom with those who need it. We have endeavored to recruit contributing authors from within and outside our home discipline, political science, as you can ascertain from the list of contributing authors' affiliations. We have sought out contributing authors who can speak to the experiences of undergraduate students, graduate students, non-tenure track faculty, tenure-track faculty, and administrators. At the heart of this book on the hidden curriculum are the core values and lessons from *The PhD Parenthood Trap*: namely, that academia is better when things are clearly communicated, transparent, and equitably applied.

The contributing authors represent a range of identities and backgrounds and draw connections between their lived experiences and the obstacles and opportunities they have encountered in academia. Still, we fully acknowledge that we and our contributing authors are not representative of the full range of experiences in higher education. We invite our readers to take the insights, challenges, and best practices shared on the pages of this book and ask the important questions and call for the needed changes on your campuses, in your departments, in your classrooms, or in your professional associations. Their chapters provide entry points for interrogating how academia is not straightforward for everyone.

We seek an academic profession in which campuses do not simply use boilerplate language about inclusivity, belonging, and representation as recruitment tools, but one in which campuses and campus leaders are eager to embrace each student, faculty, and staff member's unique experiences and goals and meet them with compassionate, clear, and flexible policies that accommodate the wide range of experiences and needs. We call on colleges, universities, and professional associations to match in norms, culture, and practice the mission statements and values they paint on their walls and feature on their websites. That work starts with each of us in our daily tasks and interactions, at all stages of the academic career. There's a reckoning that happens when we realize that we can do better; the point of this book is not to place blame but to create opportunities for conversation that can lead to more responsive and healthy working environments for all.

We hope the chapters in this book will help our readers to see more clearly the rules of the game—academic chutes and ladders—so they will be better prepared to make the most of their undergraduate education, graduate education, job search, early career years, tenure and promotion processes, and campus leadership. In other words, if you choose to play the game, we want to help you identify, understand, and improve the rules of the game. We hope to shape our profession into one that is more hospitable and humane for all who want to build a career within it. To that end, we offer this book to a range of readers. We hope it appeals to undergraduate students and their loved ones, graduate students and their loved ones and mentors, non-tenure track faculty, tenure-track faculty, senior faculty, and administrators of colleges, universities, and professional associations. If you, too, hope to see a more diverse, equitable, inclusive, and accessible academia, we and our contributing authors have written this book for you.

The Sections and Their Goals

The book proceeds in four sections. Some readers will find it helpful to progress through the sections in order, reading the book from this introduction to the conclusion. Others will find it helpful to focus on the sections that relate most directly to their identity, current situation, or position within higher education. We have structured the book to make both approaches possible.

Section one, Square One—Starting the Game, focuses on undergraduate students, graduate students, and the academic job market. The chapters written for and about undergraduate students explore different dimensions of the hidden curriculum in undergraduate education and offer best practices and highly practical tips. The graduate school-focused chapters discuss the hidden rules of academia and offer readers diverse perspectives on surviving, thriving, and making the most of graduate school. The job market is a major component of academia's hidden curriculum, and the chapters in this section expose and clarify components of the job search and its implications for aspiring academics. The job market is full of potential chutes and ladders, as well as abundant unwritten rules and unspoken expectations. Accordingly, graduate students and early career scholars on the job market seek out advice from various sources, ranging from faculty mentors to informal or formal professional development networks to virtual strangers on social media. Square One is a guide for early career scholars and those who work with and support them.

Section two, Ascending the Ladders and Rising through the Ranks, highlights the experiences of non-tenure-track faculty, junior tenure-track faculty, tenure and promotion processes, the service, teaching, and research components of the academic profession, and senior faculty. Non-tenure track faculty occupy a particularly vulnerable space in academia. The chapters in this section offer insights into the challenges that non-tenure track faculty face as well as recommendations for leveraging the resources and opportunities available to them.

Junior faculty who are on the tenure track but have not yet cleared the hurdles to achieve tenure face a particular set of written and unwritten rules and expectations. As faculty on the tenure track, they enjoy more job security than graduate students and non-tenure track faculty, but the expectation to publish, produce quality courses, and accumulate service roles before the tenure deadline imposes significant pressure on junior faculty. Due to the nature of the academic job market, new tenure-track faculty are often uprooted from their support networks through long-distance moves and must navigate life in a new region and decipher the norms, rules, and expectations of a new academic community.

Policies surrounding tenure and promotion must be clearly communicated, transparent, and equitably applied to foster inclusivity and close the chutes. The chapters focused on tenure and promotion processes offer perspectives on service demands and the policies and practices related to tenure and promotion in an effort to demystify the process.

In practice, the three pillars of promotion in academia are teaching, research, and service, in different proportions depending on many factors just as the type of institution (liberal arts college versus top-tier research university), professional classification (tenure track versus instructional faculty), and title (junior versus senior scholar). In reality, other dimensions, such as gender, racial/ethnic identity, and family status, can influence teaching and service assignments, which impact scholars' ability to conduct research. The contributors in the service, teaching, and research chapters in this section redefine what this balance means for professional success in the face of long-term medical challenges and as a historically excluded scholar. Making academia a more equitable environment for people with disabilities and ensuring that historically underrepresented scholars are not overrepresented for diversity's sake on committees will help promote a culture of equity and well-being in departments and universities.

Senior scholars play important roles in the profession. Those who have ascended the ranks are not immune to personal and professional chutes. Discussions of the post-tenure slump long predated the COVID-19 pandemic, but the pandemic, economic insecurity, a reckoning with racial injustice, and myriad other social and political drivers of trauma have brought about increased awareness of and heightened the risk of burnout and compassion fatigue. The chapters focused on senior scholars in this section address the chutes senior scholars face and the ladders they can help junior scholars identify and ascend.

Section three, Historically Excluded Groups, features the lived experiences of international students, LGBTQIA+ (lesbian, gay, bisexual, transgender, queer, intersex, asexual, and other/ally) scholars, BIPOC (Black, Indigenous, and people of color) scholars, and first-generation scholars. The chapter contributors who discuss international students' experiences detail the academic, cultural, logistical, and social hurdles that international students at US universities encounter, highlighting the importance of efforts to make campuses more inclusive. In the chapters on challenges facing LGBTQIA+ scholars, contributing authors discuss their lived experiences on campus.

Many institutions have embraced diversity, equity, and inclusion initiatives to be more welcoming and inclusive of historically excluded scholars, such as non-white and gender nonbinary individuals, but in practice, gender nonconforming scholars still encounter specific and systemic problems in their academic lives. Attention to racial inequity in the United States reignited in 2013 with the advent of the #BlackLivesMatter (BLM) movement as a response to a lack of systemic accountability for individual crimes—such as the killing of Trayvon Martin in Florida (2012), Michael Brown in Ferguson, MO (2014), and George Floyd in Minnesota (2020). The sentiments and sympathies that BLM evoked helped to generate systemic policy changes, from the uptake of DEI initiatives to implicit bias trainings to an increase in "racial and ethnic politics" tenure track faculty lines and searches dedicated to increasing diversity and representation of historically excluded scholars. But academic chutes remain, as our contributing authors discuss in this section.

Finally, first-generation scholars, whose socioeconomic identity often intersects with other historically excluded identities, share their experiences navigating the chutes and ladders in this section. First-generation scholars are so important to academia because they force the interrogation of fundamental concepts and practices within the "ivory tower." First-gen scholars reflexively ask, "Why are things done this way?," not necessarily to create change but because the entire academic enterprise is a daily exercise in the hidden curriculum.

Section four, Invisible Workloads, explores the expectations of and constraints on women+ (people assigned female at birth, cisgender women, and transwomen) scholars, caregivers, neurodivergent scholars, and scholars with disabilities. Women+'s academic journeys are often characterized by their dual roles as mother and scholar; however, women+ of all caregiving statuses face repeated, ongoing, systemic, and interpersonal biases that stymie their careers and provide endless sources of stress and frustration. Women+ are held to antiquated gendered stereotypes and standards and punished when they violate them. Despite these challenges, women+ continue to push forward, supporting each other, toward personal and professional successes. The hidden curriculum of caregiving was laid bare during the COVID-19 pandemic when classrooms—from day cares to postdocs—went remote overnight. The academy may better understand and make more space for caregivers in the post-COVID era, but much work remains, as our contributing authors suggest. The genre of disability accommodation has received increased attention since the COVID-19 pandemic; prior to 2020, accommodations were largely the purview of student disability services and took the form of providing alternative note taking or examination formats. Post-pandemic, universities have realized that accommodations can be made with ingenuity and creativity to help a broader range of scholars facing academic challenges.

In the book's conclusion, we offer a call to action for readers, especially those in positions of power such as department heads, search committees, tenure and promotion committees, conference organizers, and administrators who have the authority to make far-reaching, permanent institutional changes. This final section summarizes the key lessons learned and best practices articulated in the preceding sections and pairs them with a set of conversation starters for campus communities, mentorship networks, and professional organizations. We offer suggestions for campuswide strategies to identify types of problems and ways to address them.

We hope *Academic Chutes & Ladders* will leave readers feeling more acutely aware of the hidden curriculum and empowered to help dismantle the systemic barriers to success. A reminder: you haven't picked up a typical academic edited volume. Instead, you are about to read chapters in which we and our contributing authors merge the academic literature on the hidden curriculum and barriers to success in higher education with the earnestly recounted lived experiences of scholars at all stages of the academic journey. We hope you will see yourself, your colleagues, and your students somewhere in this book. Moreover, we hope it will inspire our colleagues to build a better system that supports belonging and creates a thriving community of scholars who are ready to meet the contemporary challenges facing our society and our world.

Guiding Questions

1. What is your "why"? Why did you pick up this book? Why do you want to pursue or remain in a career in academia?
2. How well do you feel you understand the rules of the game? Do academic norms and processes make sense to you, or do you feel like others are on the inside while you are on the outside?
3. If you are a student or early career scholar, who in your life may be well positioned to help you succeed in academia? If you are established in your career, can you offer guidance to a student or early career scholar?
4. What do you hope to learn from this book?

Section One

Square One—Starting the Game (or Entering the Academic Pipeline)

Undergraduate Students, Graduate Students, and the Academic Job Market

The Why

This section focuses on Square One of academic chutes and ladders. In other words, once someone decides they may want to play the game, how and where do they start? It's also possible that when someone starts college, they may not even be aware that it's a game with explicit and implicit rules. The academic profession begins with one's undergraduate education, so we start there and look at the opportunities and pitfalls in those first four years. People choose to go to college for many reasons: to pursue a career in an already identified passion, to learn what they want to be when they grow up, to fulfill family or societal expectations, or to empower themselves with education to earn a good living. The undergraduate experience can inspire young scholars to pursue a puzzling question or aspire to teach future generations of students, and it has not historically been an accessible or achievable goal for everyone. On the other hand, a frustrating, inequitable, dehumanizing, or silencing undergraduate experience can suggest that a person is not welcome on campus or in the profession, discouraging talented scholars from pursuing a career in the ivory tower. Square One, in other words, can be the beginning or the end of the game.

Our goal is not to convince people to join the academic profession. We are not recruiters for academia. Instead, we understand that there will always be people (like us!) who dream of teaching college students, mentoring graduate students, collaborating with colleagues and students on fascinating research, and spending their days on a vibrant campus. Rather than trying to sell the academic profession as a career path, our aim is to ensure that the academic profession is a humane, accessible, and inclusive one for those who decide to pursue it. *In other words: we want to make the rules of the game clearer and make the game itself fairer so that those who want to play can have a chance at winning.* We define winning as having an overall positive, productive experience in college and graduate school, where goals are set and achieved and connections made that will make possible whatever choices follow.

Barriers to access exist at the undergraduate and graduate levels of higher education, which the existing literature and the authors in this section discuss in depth. Coupled with the randomness and idiosyncrasies of the academic job market, the earliest phases of the academic career have proven to be difficult terrain that makes the goal of a secure faculty position untenable for many. To realize an academic profession that makes room for all scholars, we cannot limit our focus to the people who have already ascended some of the ranks. Much of the discussion of the academic chutes and ladders (or the older, less precise metaphor of the *leaky pipeline*) focuses on the tenure-track years; we maintain that a more accessible academic profession begins in the undergraduate years. Success in a well-regarded undergraduate program opens the door to placement in a well-regarded graduate program; success in a highly ranked graduate program, in turn, opens the door to academic job offers. Although this appears to be a clear formula, so much of the process is unwritten, unclear, and unfair. But it doesn't have to be.

College, graduate school, and the job market are three key phases that, first, will teach the unwritten rules of academic chutes and ladders if a student has access to good mentorship; and second, are (often unfairly) shaped by those unwritten rules. If the rules of the game are more transparent, equitable, and clearly communicated from Square One, the academic profession will become more diverse, equitable, inclusive, and humane.

Finding the Hidden Curriculum and Learning the Rules of the Game at Square One

If we want to ensure that higher education is open to all people, the rules of the game must be clearer at every stage. In this section, the chapters focus specifically on the chutes and ladders that arise in undergraduate education, graduate education, and the academic job market. By intentionally demystifying the hidden curriculum and ensuring that the rules, norms, and processes are transparent, clearly communicated, and equitably applied, we can help talented scholars find their way to the ladders instead of falling down the chutes (Crawford and Windsor 2021). Most of us need help finding the ladders and avoiding the chutes—or even realizing they exist in the first place.

Research on the hidden curriculum in education has emphasized that it is not simply unknown to all but hidden intentionally to limit access to education and the resources and outcomes it provides. Snyder's discussion of the hidden curriculum on college campuses articulates two distinct curricula: the substantive curriculum tied to one's coursework within a particular discipline and the hidden curriculum of academic and social norms that enable students to succeed in their coursework (Snyder 1971). Margolis's volume on the hidden curriculum underscores the importance of making clear the inequities on campuses, including research support, biases in admissions processes and testing instruments, and salaries, among other factors. By understanding the hidden curriculum and further, seeing who stands to benefit from its continuation, we can recognize the effects of higher education on societal gender, race, and socioeconomic inequalities (Margolis 2001, 19). Salazar's work builds on the hidden curriculum research to call for a humanizing pedagogy that recognizes the need to transform academic structures and support the whole student (Salazar 2013).

A question that follows from discussions of the hidden curriculum is this: Are all things hidden problematic? Although it is not always the case that unwritten rules are inherently harmful, we as an author team believe that colleges, universities, and everyone on campus functions best when the policies, procedures, and norms are clearly communicated, transparent, and equitably applied. We set up our students, our colleagues, and ourselves for success when we are all working from the same understanding of the game. In short, the keys to success should never be hidden.

Undergraduate Students

In undergraduate courses and campus experiences, students begin to create a picture in their minds of who professors are and what the profession entails. During the undergraduate years, students get their first exposure to the academic profession and, perhaps, its written and unwritten rules. Students learn how to navigate academia in their undergraduate years, assuming that they have access to opportunities that empower them to engage in research, to learn the nuances and processes of academic writing, to give public presentations, and perhaps even provide teaching assistance.

As chapters in this section discuss, research mentorship in the undergraduate years can be a career-shaping experience, one that serves as a "ladder" from undergraduate to graduate school. These opportunities are not always transparent or clearly communicated to all students; they may depend on a student's willingness to approach a professor to ask about research opportunities, or a student's strong performance in an upper-level course. One colleague shared her first experience attending office hours during her freshman year; she showed up, sat down, and the professor asked what she wanted to talk about. She had no idea. She had been told to "go to office hours" without understanding what that meant. The encounter was awkward and did not beget more office hours visits. During office hours, students have the opportunity for one-on-one time with their professors to ask questions about course material and generally get to know the people they are learning from. Our colleague didn't know she could ask her professor about getting involved in research, for example.

In "Attaining and Sustaining Mentorship during College," Clare Brock and Emily Farris provide a clear road map for developing and maintaining mentorships in college. Their discussion touches on the importance of cultivating mentorships, the challenges students may face when approaching potential mentors, and practical tips for ensuring long-lasting mentorships. The authors provide insights intended for undergraduate students, though faculty and other mentors will also benefit from reading it. A mentor—an upper division student even—could have better prepared our colleague for office hours expectations. Mentors don't wear badges or even have official titles—they are often just ordinary people who impart wisdom and share insights about *how things work.*

Jamie Scalera Elliott, Srobana Bhattacharya, Alison Clifton, Sean Giovanello, and Kirsten Taylor's chapter, "Chutes and Ladders in Mentoring Undergraduate Research," looks specifically at the practicalities of advising undergraduate research. Speaking directly to faculty mentors, the authors emphasize that undergraduate research can be a meaningful and effective way for students to learn aspects of the hidden curriculum. Beyond a narrow focus on research activities, faculty-student collaboration can lead to broader mentorship opportunities such as preparing undergraduates for graduate school. Established academics can serve a range of roles in undergraduate research: faculty can integrate student research in the classroom and one-on-one or lab-based collaborative projects. Department chairs are instrumental in cultivating a culture that celebrates and prioritizes undergraduate research and faculty mentorship of undergraduate researchers.

Access to undergraduate education as a whole is far from guaranteed. Tuition is costly, particularly in the United States. In the United States, prospective students must work through complicated financial aid systems and secure need-based assistance or merit scholarships. C. Kelsey Ryan's chapter discusses the alphabet soup of financial aid, how the processes work, and what colleges and universities could do to improve access to aid. In "FAFSAs, EFCs, and COAs, Oh My: Navigating the Realm of Student Financial Aid," Ryan outlines the practical considerations related to financial aid to support undergraduate education. Because cost is an obstacle to many prospective students, providing a clear understanding of financial aid options is a way for colleges and universities to improve access. This chapter speaks most directly to undergraduate students and their families, as well as campus administrators.

Academic units often lament the lack of diversity among candidates for faculty positions, but at this stage, they are looking at the problem too late. Graduate departments should focus their recruitment efforts on undergraduate students, particularly if graduate departments hope to improve representation of historically excluded scholars in their student cohorts. It is crucial to establish and maintain mentorship networks, research funding, presentation venues, and other opportunities that allow young scholars to see themselves in the roles of graduate student and—later—professor. It's hard to be what you can't see.

It is also important to communicate to undergraduate prospective graduate students the pros and cons of pursuing a doctoral education. The long, arduous, and underpaid slog through graduate coursework, comprehensive exams, and dissertation research and writing can take a toll on a person's health and well-being. The job market has tightened considerably, with fewer tenure-track jobs available, in favor of more temporary or contingent positions offering less certainty and lower pay. Of course, with time, persistence, and support, academia can also result in a fulfilling career. Many careers and professional goals do not require a doctoral degree. Undergraduate students and mentors should have thoughtful, deliberate conversations about the potential benefits and pitfalls of pursuing a graduate education so that all students can enter their programs with more awareness of the hidden curriculum.

Graduate Students

First-generation undergraduate students may find the transition to graduate education particularly challenging. Elizabeth Dorssom's chapter, "From First-Generation College Graduate to PhD Student: How to Transition Successfully," discusses the transition from undergraduate to graduate education in clear detail. Her focus is on the challenges first-generation students face throughout this transition and practical recommendations for overcoming those challenges. She also implores readers to determine whether it is best to go directly from undergraduate to graduate school or to take time to explore professional opportunities to fine-tune research and career interests. Dorssom's chapter appeals most directly to undergraduate and graduate students, faculty, and campus administrators.

For those students who decide a doctoral degree is worth the costs (in all senses), gaining familiarity with the rules of the game at the graduate level will help ensure success. Mentorship is just as important for graduate students as it is for undergraduate students, if not more so. The coursework and research in graduate school are more independent than in undergraduate programs, and the opportunities are more individualized to scholars studying specific research questions or issues. The independent nature of graduate school demands effective time management, both to complete coursework or research *and* to ensure healthy work-life boundaries. Jennifer Tatara's chapter, "Live Long and Suffer: The Plight of the Grad Student," observes that the pursuit of work-life balance is often discussed among career academics and other professionals but rarely among or with graduate students. Tatara's chapter underscores the importance of striving for effective time management and balance in graduate school. The graduate school years require diligence and commitment to coursework and research but do not need to entail endless suffering. Graduate students and their faculty mentors will benefit from her insights.

Learning early on about the supports (mentorship networks, funding, conferences and workshops, equipment and resources, policies to protect against discrimination) available to graduate students within the department and on campus more broadly is an important step for those on Square One. Identifying and cultivating supportive professional relationships with mentors is beneficial not only for research projects but also for the eventual job search and overall well-being. One's health and well-being cannot be set aside for the graduate school years, at least not without incurring terrible costs.

In "Ritual Anxieties: Living with and Working through Anxiety in Academia," Rae Summers-Thompson and William Duffy discuss the importance of cultivating a supportive environment in which graduate students can thrive, even amid typical stressors inherent in a doctoral program. Addressing graduate students and their faculty mentors, the authors emphasize the importance of destigmatizing mental health concerns, building a supportive campus environment and faculty-student mentorships, and encouraging individualized and empowering benchmarks that foster agency for graduate students.

Perhaps the most notable (and feared) phase of the graduate program is the dissertation. Academic writing rarely comes naturally, and it can be an immense source of stress. Just like graduate education as a whole, the dissertation process comes with its own set of written and unwritten rules; and students get varying degrees of preparation for this process and its nuances. But this process is the academic equivalent of a coming-of-age ritual: it marks the transition from student to professional scholar. In "The Developmental Dissertation," Leanne Powner discusses the dissertation as a developmental process wherein a student evolves into an independent researcher. By recounting the stages of the typical dissertation and why these stages are structured the way they often are, Powner aims to unpack the process so graduate students can understand the value of the steps and their sequence. Powner's chapter speaks most directly to graduate students and their faculty mentors.

In addition to the chapters contributed to this section, Jessica McCrory Calarco's book *A Field Guide to Grad School: Uncovering the Hidden Curriculum* offers graduate students advice on identifying a graduate program, navigating coursework, publishing research, leveraging conferences, succeeding on the job market, and balancing the dimensions of academic work with one's personal life (Calarco 2020).

Academic Job Market

The academic job market is one of the first major opportunities to encounter chutes or ladders in the academic profession. This is the proverbial crossroads that will force early career scholars to consider their long-term goals and determine whether they will remain in the academic profession or pursue a career outside of the academy. Just as it is crucial for undergraduate students to have meaningful conversations about their professional goals with their mentors, the later years of the graduate program should involve in-depth conversations between graduate students and their mentors. Although it is best *for the graduate program* and its rankings for students to go on to tenure-track positions with prestigious colleges and universities, this is not realistic or desirable for all soon-to-be PhDs. Our focus in this book is on the pathways to and through the academic profession, and so the chapters related to the job market discuss the academic job market and set aside considerations related to public- and private-sector job searches. There is, however, a growing body of literature on alternative career paths for PhDs and we encourage readers investigating career options outside of academia to consult these books (McAlpine and Amundsen 2016; Urban and Linver 2019; Caterine 2020; Goldgeier and Wittes 2023).

For early career scholars on the academic job market, it helps to keep longer term objectives in mind. For many, the objective is not just landing a job but earning tenure. For others, it will be a job in a specific location, whether near loved ones or in a particularly beloved region or city. For all job seekers, formal and informal mentors are incredibly important. Mentors are well positioned to review job application materials (e.g., the curriculum vitae, statement of teaching philosophy, research statement, sample syllabi, and writing samples), to discuss what one might expect in first-round and on-campus interviews, and to provide guidance with assessing a department for its fit *for you* and your goals. We urge academic job seekers to focus their search and account for their professional and personal goals and constraints; a tenure-track job is quite possibly a permanent position, and everyone deserves to build a career in a place where they can thrive not just professionally but personally. We intentionally built our academic careers around our personal lives and goals. Kerry entered her doctoral program knowing she wanted to teach *and* to have children; although a tenure-track job was her goal, the "publish or perish" lifestyle was never of interest. She was fortunate to land a tenure-track job at an institution that prioritizes quality teaching and leaves room for faculty to maintain personal lives off campus.

No matter the long-term goal and ideal institution, the process of applying and interviewing for academic jobs is grueling. The job market is unpredictable even in times of political and economic stability. The supply of tenure-track academic positions is sensitive to external factors such as higher education funding cuts and eroding public trust in universities, as well as to systemic shocks such as economic recession and global pandemics. Availability of positions varies highly across disciplines, with STEM-related positions increasing and positions in the social sciences and humanities declining (Lange and Olejniczak 2023; Wood 2021). Amy Collins and Kaity Prieto write for job seekers and hiring committees alike in their chapter, "Navigating the Affective Component of the Academic Job Search in a Precarious Market." Collins and Prieto, both having recently navigated the academic job market in a time of acute precarity, discuss the challenges job seekers face. They observe that academic job seekers often fall into a trap of equating their job market success with their self-worth, and the expectations of loved ones and mentors can amplify the stress of the job search. They call for search committees to center an ethic of care in their hiring processes.

The job search can be especially treacherous for historically excluded scholars. Irmak Yazici describes the realities of the academic job search in the United States for international scholars in "Navigating the 'Hidden Curriculum' as an International Scholar." Yazici discusses the increased difficulty international scholars face while searching for academic jobs in the United States. Writing for job seekers, hiring committees, and administrators, the author emphasizes the additional barriers created by universities' hesitation to sponsor visas and the discriminatory language in some job ads, despite federal equal opportunity protections. Parents also face unique challenges, as we address in greater depth in *The PhD Parenthood Trap* (Crawford and Windsor 2021). Here, Christine Kugelmann highlights the challenges facing women scholars, particularly as they search for academic jobs while pregnant or with young children in tow. In her chapter, "Scaling the Chute: Academic Job Hunting while Mothering," Kugelmann emphasizes the injustice of continued implicit bias against women, particularly as the academic job market generally coincides with the most common childbearing years. Her chapter speaks to job seekers (particularly, but not exclusively, parents), search committees, and administrators.

We call on academic search committees to take all steps needed to minimize the role of implicit and explicit bias in their review of applications, interviews, and final deliberations. Every faculty, staff, and student participant in a job search should be informed of and—even better—trained in best practices for minimizing discrimination in hiring (Henningsen, Horvath, and Jonas 2022; Rivera 2017; Blair-Loy et al. 2022; Culpepper et al. 2023). Strategies such as advertising open positions in publications with a diverse readership and with professional associations with a diverse membership, conducting cameras-off Zoom interviews for shortlisted candidates, and ensuring diversity among hiring committee members are good first steps.

Takeaway Points and Best Practices

For Undergraduate Students:

As early as possible, find a supportive mentor in your field who shares your academic interests and/or understands your lived experiences. This should be someone you are comfortable talking with about a wide range of topics, and this person should have the time and availability to help guide you through big decisions. Campus organizations often have faculty sponsors, and this can be a good place to make connections with people who have similar interests and can support you.

Learn everything you can about research opportunities, mentorship networks, and scholarships and financial aid. Go to public talks on your campus. Join student organizations in your field or discipline. Ask faculty in your home department if they have any active research projects you can join. The departmental administrative assistant or business officer is often the "keeper of information" and can be a good resource for students. And they may even keep candy at their desks.

Meet with faculty in your field often as you prepare to apply to graduate school. Don't rely solely on published rankings of programs; ask faculty mentors to read your application materials and recommend graduate programs that specialize in your research interests and offer a supportive intellectual community.

For Graduate Students

As early as possible, find a supportive mentor in your field who shares your academic interests and/or understands your lived experiences. This should be someone you are comfortable talking with about a wide range of topics, and this person should have the time and availability to help guide you through big decisions. Sometimes these mentors will approach you at a conference after your presentation or at a poster session. If someone is interested in your work, follow up with them and keep in touch. Mentor-mentee relationships don't develop overnight, and they require nurturing and communication.

Learn everything you can learn about research opportunities, mentorship networks, and scholarships and financial aid. Go to public talks to learn about new research in your field and present your research when you are ready. Disciplinary organizations are increasingly offering professionalization opportunities, such as early career panels, grant writing or publishing workshops, and mentorship cafes. People who care about mentorship have organized these types of events; take advantage of these programs to improve your awareness of the hidden curriculum in higher education and in your specific field.

Build or join support systems on and off campus, not just to help you with your academic progress but also to foster your overall well-being as you navigate graduate school and the job market. You do not need to work all day, every day. In fact, you shouldn't do that. This is the oddest flex in our opinion—loudly announcing (in person or on social media) that you worked all night, or all weekend, or you haven't had a day off in two months. This does not signal progress; it signals inefficiency. You do not need to work all the time to be productive—in fact, it's counterproductive to do that. Log off, close out, and power down regularly. Keep a schedule and build extracurricular activities into it. Your brain needs a break and some fresh air to think clearly!

For Early Career Scholars on the Academic Job Market

Prepare your materials and have your dissertation committee, graduate adviser, and/or mentors outside your committee review them to be sure that the materials convey your strengths, contributions to the field, and potential. If you are in a program that does not prepare its graduate students well for the job market, seek out a surrogate department. Observe and take notes on what others do. Go to job talks in your department and learn what the format is and how people behave.

Attend conferences, workshops, and online seminars in your field to meet scholars outside your home institution; networking can be a powerful tool for those on the job market. It is also an opportunity to be an ethnographer of your own profession. Find the papers you want to read in the conference's online repository—or email the author and ask for a copy. Attend the presentations and treat the experience like a social scientist would. Make observations and look for patterns. Develop theories about why things work the way they do. And most importantly, attend the business meetings, because this is where important decisions are made.

Prepare yourself for the idiosyncratic experience of academic job interviews and know that all you can do is build the best dossier possible and apply for all jobs you can envision yourself accepting. One colleague mentioned that she was told to "just be herself" during the interview, and at the time that felt very generic and unhelpful. After being invited for several job interviews, she found this to be absolutely true.

For Established Faculty, Mentors, and Administrators

Help your undergraduate and graduate students learn to read and write in your disciplinary style and vernacular. Create assignments with intention and focus on the iterative nature of the writing process so that students can grow comfortable with academic writing. Although most undergraduate students will not go on to academic careers, writing is a skill they will use in virtually any profession.

The years in undergraduate and graduate programs, as well as the time on the academic job market, are when mentorship serves as a recruitment tool for the profession and a lifeline for the individual scholar. If your department does not have mentorship supports in place for undergraduate and graduate students, explore options for starting a formal or informal program to pair students with mentors. Programs that pair undergraduate students with graduate students or faculty can help these very early career scholars determine their best path to the profession. Networks that pair graduate students with more advanced graduate students or faculty can support early career scholars through the dissertation research and writing processes, prepare and proofread job application materials, and navigate the job search.

Outreach to historically excluded scholars in undergraduate programs boosts access to graduate programs, which in turn will help create a more representative academic profession. Faculty and campus leaders should take the initiative to connect with students on their campus and on other campuses, employing a recruitment team approach when possible. Departments should *not* assign this task solely to women+ faculty members or those of color but should ensure that recruitment is a responsibility that all faculty members share.

The academic job market needs drastic change. Most immediately, hiring practices should take the necessary steps to root out implicit bias in the review of candidates. At the time of writing, spring of 2025, this is a particularly fraught topic; but we believe that merit-based hiring requires a conscious effort to ensure that no candidate is excluded on the basis of their identity, and that this effort often involves a process of unlearning implicit biases around race, gender, ethnicity, family status, disability, age, or sexual orientation.

At all stages of the academic profession, many rules and norms remain unwritten, unclear, and (often) unfair; recognizing this reality empowers us to change it. Write down the rules and share them—everyone will be better off for it.

Conclusion and Transition

The learning curve to the academic profession is steep. Some of us arrive on campus on the first day of our undergraduate education with the tools needed to scale that curve. Some of us arrive on the first day of our undergraduate education without any awareness of the curve at all, having chosen a school based on affordability and proximity to home. Those of us in a position to change the uneven awareness of the learning curve, the rules of the game, or the hidden curriculum need to do just that.

This section cannot possibly tell every story or highlight every adversity or success at the start of the academic career. Instead, we hope to start conversations on your campus so you can help those starting at Square One navigate the academic trajectory. Whether you are just now at Square One in academic chutes and ladders or whether you are a mentor, a faculty member, or a campus leader, we hope as you read the chapters in this section you will consider the insights and lived experiences shared by each author and how they apply to your campus.

Guiding Questions

For Students:

1. What is it about the academic profession that interests you? Have you interviewed professors at various career stages (early, mid, late) about why they joined academia—and more importantly, why they stay?
2. What puzzles you about the topic you are studying—what are you curious about? How do you foster and engage with curiosity in your field? Is there a professor you can connect with to discuss your ideas?

For Job Seekers:

1. When you picture the various aspects of your life, which are the top priorities? How can your job search ensure that you honor these priorities?
2. What is your overall outlook on the job search? Do you believe "you win or you learn"—and how do you deal with road bumps, hiccups, or outcomes different from what you had hoped?
3. How are you preparing yourself for the job search? Who can you talk with about how to best prepare yourself for job interviews and the search process?

For Faculty, Mentors, and Campus Leaders:

1. How easy is it for students to connect with faculty mentors? Is there a person or group in your department or on your campus who may be capable of and interested in establishing formal or informal mentorship networks?
2. When did your department or campus last revise your hiring guidelines? What has changed in the interim, and how might you improve those guidelines to mitigate potentially flawed processes?
3. What concrete steps are you taking to prepare your students for the job market?

Undergraduate Education

1

Attaining and Sustaining Mentorship during College

Clare R. Brock and Emily M. Farris

Many people, hopefully, will serve the role of mentor throughout your time in college. Here we discuss how to develop high-quality, successful mentoring relationships.

Mentorship, Defined

A mentor can take many forms, but essentially, a mentor is someone who helps support and guide you in your professional development. Mentors can play an important role in demystifying the college experience and navigating life in college and beyond, whether that includes postgraduate education or help up a rung on the ladder of early career advancement.

When thinking of mentors in college, you may automatically think of faculty. But there are different types of mentoring relationships to consider, including both relationships with people who are more advanced in their careers and peer relationships with people who are on a shared path and at a similar stage. In addition, you might consider mentors who share your demographics (woman+, BIPOC, LGBTQIA+, etc.) and may be able to speak to lived experiences; mentors who have expertise in your interests, or outside them; and mentors in the same or similar institutions who have process-oriented expertise.

Good mentors can help you explore new opportunities, make connections, and particularly for peer mentors, find community. They should be someone you are comfortable asking questions and importantly, someone you trust. A good mentor should listen to you, offer constructive feedback and advice, and encourage you through your journey in college.

Finding a Mentor

Sometimes, a person will become a mentor in your life without much deliberate effort on your part, as they will simply choose to support you. When this happens, appreciate and nurture that relationship. But often, a mentor (or the specific type of mentor you need) will not just fall into your lap. What then?

When looking for a mentor, begin by thinking about what you need help or guidance with. Mentors cannot solve all problems or tell you what to do; rather, they will use their experience and know-how to help you be your best self and to ease your path when possible. Because of this, it is best that you consider your interests and needs prior to setting out to find one.

Once you have identified your purpose in seeking a mentor, list everyone you can think of who might have the relevant knowledge, experience, or skills. This list could include professors, university staff, coworkers, or other students. You may consider peoples' campus involvement, areas of academic interest, or professional experience. When making your list, you should look to see whether there are formal mentoring programs on campus or in professional associations that may help match mentors to mentees. Do your homework: look at people's websites, résumés, publications, experiences, or classes they teach. Then finally, ask which of those people you trust? Consider who has been kind, honest, and genuine in their interactions with you, however limited. Immediately rule out people who do not meet these criteria.

Once you have identified a few potential mentors, reach out to connect. This might send an email introducing yourself, attend office hours, or asking a mutual friend to arrange a meetup. You do not necessarily need to formally say, "I want you to be my mentor" right away. Instead, contact them based on something you have in common. Options might include asking about someone's experience in graduate or law school and for advice on the admissions process; connecting over shared experiences as first-generation students; or mentioning something that they said in a lecture or class that inspired you and asking to discuss it together.

In other words, reach out in ways that feel natural and that work for the relative level of existing relationship you have with this person. If you already know each other well, you may simply need to start asking more questions or soliciting advice when you spend time together. If it is someone that you know less well, you may need a more formal initiation into conversation. Share your goals and set appropriate expectations together once you have connected.

Initial Mentorship Challenges

What if you reach out and the potential mentor does not respond, says no, or agrees to talk to you but then ends up ghosting you? Unfortunately, this may happen. The most important thing is to recognize that mentors might be unable to help for a wide variety of reasons, many of which have absolutely nothing to do with you personally.

The people who you are likely to wish for mentorship from are often people who others would also like to be mentored by. This means those people may be overwhelmed or hit capacity. Other people may say no because they feel that they are not a good fit, they don't know you, or they just don't want to meet up for coffee. Don't let this discourage you.

When a person is unable to offer you mentorship, move on to someone else. You cannot force a relationship, and you want a mentor who is enthusiastic about being a mentor to you as well. Go back to the list of people you identified and reach out to someone else.

Sustaining a Mentoring Relationship

Although mentoring relationships do not need to be formalized, you will want to consider both communication expectations and professional boundaries. Mentors are likely busy people who may not be able to respond immediately to an email or commit to a frequent check-in. You may have to take an active role in initiating conversations and should show respect for their time. To make the most of your meetings, be direct, honest, and open to feedback in your conversations.

Expect mentoring relationships to evolve. You will find that you may need different mentors at various stages of your career. Find and establish relationships with mentors of different kinds—both peers and professionals, especially because no one mentor can be everything for you or solve all problems. And remember, some support is best given by others, such as professionals dealing with mental health.

What if a mentor isn't doing a good job for you? It's OK to realize that someone is giving advice that doesn't work for you and to choose to distance yourself from that person. You don't need to have a dramatic breakup; you can just ask for help less often or not at all.

Although you can't repay your mentors, you can show appreciation by writing a thank-you note or otherwise making it clear that you value your mentor's thoughts, time, and help. You may someday be a mentor, and you will pay it forward by being helpful, generous, and kind to your mentees, assisting others up the ladder of early education and career advancement, just as you were assisted.

RECOMMENDATIONS FOR READERS

1. Mentorship is something that anyone can find and sustain with some thoughtfulness and effort. It doesn't have to be formalized, but you should thoughtfully consider your needs for mentorship.
2. Look for someone who embodies the characteristics, experiences, or skills that you want to emulate or that you share, then ask them for advice or to talk to you about how they climbed the ladder to get where they are.
3. Mentors can be peers or established professionals, and you should have relationships with both. Don't expect any one person to be everything you need; different people have different strengths, allow for that and keep your expectations reasonable.

2

The Chutes and Ladders in Mentoring Undergraduate Research

Jamie Scalera Elliott, Srobana Bhattacharya, Alison M. Clifton, Sean P. Giovanello, and Kirsten L. Taylor

Undergraduate research (UGR) is a strategic focus for many colleges and universities across the United States (Boyer Commission 1998; Taraban and Blanton 2008). UGR can take many different forms: independent projects inside or outside the classroom, honors projects, or students serving as research assistants for faculty.

For students, participating in UGR is a significant cocurricular learning experience that sets them apart and places them at an advantage—offering a ladder to propel them in the next stage of their careers. Undergraduate research can provide insights into the "hidden curriculum" for students by teaching more advanced skills that are otherwise not afforded in the classroom, such as advanced critical thinking skills (Ishiyama 2002), quantitative data skills (Andersen and Harsell 2005), confidence (Cassese et al. 2015), and networking and career development (Koch and Johnson 2000).

Although many academics are familiar with mentoring, unique challenges and opportunities are associated with mentoring undergraduate students. One significant challenge in mentoring UGR is student preparation—or the lack thereof. Few students are introduced to independent research projects in high school, and the COVID-19 pandemic forced many K–12 educators to temporarily lower classroom standards (Wyse et al. 2020).

Consequently, many undergraduates have a weak understanding of research, particularly concepts such as empirical, theoretical, qualitative, and quantitative (Murtonen 2015), which generates fear around the word "research" and can make students hesitant to engage with research in a meaningful way. Empirical research and real data are often associated with hard sciences; however, they are crucial for social sciences as well even if students do not usually make this connection. The mind maps in Murtonen's (2015) study show that at the start of the course, 75 percent of the students hold a problematic conception of research. The mind mapping technique was developed to see how students connect research methodological concepts by relating the concepts to each other. Students in the study were given a set of loose instructions on a piece of paper asking them to draw a map (a mind map or concept map) about "research," and they could use their own concepts along with other concepts such as empirical, theoretical, qualitative, quantitative, and testing of hypotheses and analyzing of data. Of the twenty-eight mind maps analyzed by the researchers, seven were nonproblematic; at the end of the course, fifteen were nonproblematic. The mind maps that were found to be problematic indicated confusion and were underdeveloped, thereby failing to link the research methodological concepts in a meaningful way. Although Murtonen's (2015) research was conducted with master's level students, such issues are also present among undergraduate students. Thus, most undergraduates lack the skill set, the knowledge base, and often the awareness that research is available to them. For students, this represents a problematic chute that can set them back in their academic trajectory.

For academic programs, therefore, it is essential to introduce students early to independent research and to familiarize them with concepts, techniques, and varied approaches. A required introductory research methods course as part of a structured curriculum, particularly in disciplines in the social sciences and humanities, is one simple strategy to accomplish this goal and might provide a meaningful ladder for students interested in further research (Breuning, Parker, and Ishiyama 2001).

Informal or formal research in an upper-level classroom environment is another way to reinforce research skills for undergraduates. Faculty can guide students through the process of framing a research question within the context of substantive material germane to the course. Through classroom readings, faculty can highlight academic sources, such as peer-reviewed journal articles, and useful resources to find quality information, such as journal databases and Google Scholar. Further, a classroom session can focus on how to walk through the structure of academic articles, demonstrating how to "read" them and the formulaic "story arc" that research articles tend to take. Faculty can also encourage students to hone their skills through research papers, presentations, or even more creative outlets such as websites or videos. Using these techniques, students can reinforce their research skills through applying them to major-specific content.

Faculty can further reinforce research skills by discussing their own research in the classroom. For example, faculty can explain the rationale behind selecting from different methodologies, such as quantitative versus qualitative. Faculty can also include visual references and examples from the research process that might be more abstract to students, such as images from field work, original survey instruments, or sample protocols from the Institutional Review Board (IRB). By engaging with these materials, students can better experience the research process.

Sharing research in the classroom has several added benefits for faculty. First, UGR is a well-recognized high-impact practice (HIP) that has been shown to produce higher levels of student learning ("High-Impact Practices" n.d.; McClellan, Kopko, and Gruber 2021). By incorporating research-focused assignments, faculty can easily have their course designated as a HIP course, which can help faculty stand out in teaching evaluations or awards providing a ladder of advancement for teaching-focused faculty.

Moreover, by sharing research projects with students, faculty can invite students to serve as research assistants. For faculty in undergraduate-focused academic departments, undergraduate research assistants can be vital to helping faculty maintain an active research agenda, thereby helping propel them forward in their career trajectory.

Encouraging students to present their research, or even to attend an academic conference, can also be a rewarding experience for students and faculty and provide further ladders along the hidden curriculum. Many colleges and universities have opportunities on campus to showcase student or faculty research, through honors colleges or other programs. If not, faculty can also set up informal presentations within their own departments. Moreover, many professional associations are becoming increasingly more welcoming to undergraduate attendees and presenters, offering poster presentations, undergraduate-focused roundtables, or even welcoming undergraduate students onto the regular program. These opportunities can be a quick, fun way to introduce students to many different types of research programs in a short period of time and be a significant ladder for students and faculty alike. For students presenting their research, these opportunities can provide a unique setting for professionalization and networking as well as another way to showcase oral argumentation skills for a curriculum vitae. For faculty, supervising student research presentations can be a rewarding experience and another clear indication of a faculty member's commitment to student success.

Student availability and attitude pose another challenge for mentoring UGR. Today's students are stretched thin as they balance academics with team sports, work, caregiving, and a variety of other personal and extracurricular responsibilities. Moreover, students today are exhibiting higher levels of stress and anxiety (Lee, Jeong, and Kim 2021; Liu et al. 2022; Ramos et al. 2021). For these students, a challenging task such as independent research can seem even more daunting than ever before, making the risks seemingly outweigh the benefits.

Meaningful faculty-student mentoring relationships might help to overcome these challenges. Relationships are at the core of the undergraduate experience, and building mentoring relationships is vital to successful student research experiences (Morales, Grineski, and Collins 2017; Walkington et al. 2020). The UGR experience allows students to connect and collaborate in meaningful ways with their faculty mentor, calling on skills such as persistence as they pursue a project over the course of one or multiple semesters. Mentors not only teach their mentees new content and skills, but also help them develop as a whole person and envision new possibilities for their future (Walkington et al. 2020).

However, for mentoring relationships to grow and thrive, colleges and universities must value such relationships. For faculty, sinking too much time into mentoring relationships that fail to produce research outputs or garner accolades toward promotion can be a critical chute. Thus, our institutions must intentionally invest resources in building and cultivating an environment that encourages students and faculty to pursue UGR mentoring relationships. In many cases, this responsibility rests first with department chairs.

Department chairs play a crucial role in facilitating all aspects of UGR and in ensuring that the process is positive for both faculty and students; a chair encourages faculty innovation, celebrates success, and helps to develop and deepen a culture where strong mentoring of UGR becomes a signature part of department identity.

A department chair can encourage innovation in UGR beyond existing norms in the department and can support faculty who take a risk in these endeavors, thereby helping them avoid unnecessary chutes. If a department traditionally mentors one-on-one student-centered projects only, a chair can seed or embrace the idea of exploring lab-based research or faculty member-driven research projects (Becker 2020). This process allows faculty to better mentor students in a time-efficient manner while also laying the groundwork for spillover innovation in this or other areas of department life.

In addition, department chairs can highlight individual faculty and student successes in UGR in many ways, ranging from social media to faculty annual evaluations and promotion/tenure dossiers to department strategic plans (Ronnenberg and Sadowski 2011). Doing so celebrates the successes of individual faculty and the department while also strengthening the norm that department mentoring of UGR is central to its mission. In undertaking this work, these efforts highlight to internal and external audiences that UGR is valued while also making clear that it does not happen by accident or coincidence.

RECOMMENDATIONS FOR READERS

1. Cultivate opportunities for undergraduate students to engage in research in a variety of ways early in their academic careers, thereby opening up this area of the hidden curriculum.
2. Support faculty who serve as mentors for undergraduate research by creating intentional ladders, such as teaching awards and research stipends, and by recognizing their service on evaluations.
3. Celebrate undergraduate research and showcase student success for internal and external stakeholders.

3

FAFSAs, EFCs, and COAs, Oh My: Navigating the Realm of Student Financial Aid

C. Kelsey Ryan

Since the mid-nineteenth century, education has been referred to as "the great equalizer." Horace Mann, the first secretary of the Massachusetts State Board of Education, used this term in a report in 1848, stating that education was "the great equalizer of the conditions of men." Since then, the term has been adopted when discussing higher education and around the concept of providing financial aid.

Financial aid policies and expectations have undergone a number of transformations as higher education has grown and changed. Colleges and universities in their original form provided an educational opportunity that was primarily attainable for the elite, who could cover the costs in full. With the creation of financial aid, suddenly the opportunity to continue one's education was no longer out of reach for those not in the upper level of society (Thelin 2019).

From the GI Bill in 1944 to the Higher Education Act of 1965, financial aid changed as the universities and the students they served changed (Kowalski 2016). Now, the federal government offers financial aid "packages" for students, which consist of an assortment of scholarships, federal grants, work-study programs, and low-interest loans. These packages are unique to each student, based on their need and their school choice (Toby 2010).

Many hidden rules and expectations exist in how students pay for college. For students and families who can pay outright, the process is much simpler than for those seeking funding. The various funding sources, including scholarships, grants, and loans, each have distinct rules and agendas.

Navigating the process of obtaining financial aid at a college or university can be a stressful process. When considering which college to attend, it's important for students and their families to sit down and seriously evaluate the financial aid offered by the institutions. This chapter offers tips on how to navigate that process, to help students and their families overcome the hidden chutes associated with the complicated process of funding their education.

Terms To Know

When students are applying for college, they need to consider two important numbers: the institution's cost of attendance (COA) and the student's estimated family contribution (EFC). Based on these two figures, the school can create a financial aid "package" for the student. The financial aid "package" will usually consist of a mixture of grants, scholarships, and low-interest loans, and could also include options such as work-study programs. These packages will be individualized based on the information the student provided in a FAFSA, as well as information from the school.

Figure 3.1 General Cost of Attendance Breakdown. Source: C. Kelsey Ryan.

To determine the institution's COA, the institution takes the average cost of a number of bills to determine how much money the average student would need to attend school (see Figure 3.1). To calculate the student's EFC, the FAFSA uses a number of factors, including tax information provided by the student and their parent(s). According to the 2023 FAFSA website, a student's EFC "is not the amount of money your family will have to pay for college"; however, it shows the following equation: "Cost of Attendance (COA) – Expected Family Contribution (EFC) = Financial Need" is how the system determines the amount of need-based financial aid a student is able to receive.

In addition to need-based aid, merit-based aid is also available for students. Merit-based aid usually exists in the form of scholarships and is awarded to students based on a separate application they submit. These applications look for information that makes the student stand out from their peers and will ask for information such as the student's grade point average (GPA), test scores, volunteer/service hours completed, club and organization participation, leadership roles, and job experiences. There are a lot of scholarships out there, offered from a variety of places. The easiest place to start is with the institution the student plans to attend, but a lot of private companies and nonprofit organizations offer scholarships as well. Examples include religious organizations, activism groups, and national sponsors for high-school clubs. However, the burden falls on the student to seek out these opportunities and then submit the applications by the deadlines.

RECOMMENDATIONS FOR READERS

The following tips are offered from former financial aid professionals to help students (and their families) more easily navigate the complicated process of funding college and start to climb the ladder of securing funding for their education.

Submit the FAFSA every year, as early as you can. The FAFSA is a yearly form, and as such, needs to be completed annually. The FAFSA is used for a full calendar year, meaning it will apply to a student's fall, spring, and summer semesters. During a student's first year in college, they may need to submit two FAFSAs, especially if they are planning to start college in the summer term.

Make an appointment with your school's financial aid office. Once a student has decided where they want to attend college, they should set up an appointment with a representative from the financial aid office. The purpose of the meeting is to go over their financial aid package and the school's COA, to make sure the student has the funding they need and there aren't any hidden expenses they may have missed. Although federal financial aid (the financial aid awarded based on the FAFSA) travels with the student, some financial aid is school-specific. This is an important factor to take into account when considering transferring schools, and it's important to ask about when meeting with the financial aid office.

Read every email, document, and notice sent out. Financial aid offices don't send out junk communication. If a student (or family member) is receiving correspondence from the office, oftentimes there is documentation or paperwork that needs to be completed. Students should make sure to read (and respond to, if necessary) all communication from the office. Missing deadlines or paperwork could delay funding.

Apply for as many scholarships as possible but pay attention to requirements. Students should apply for scholarships during high school but can also continue to apply well into their college career. In fact, some scholarships are reserved specifically for upper-level college students. Even a student who didn't receive a scholarship prior to college can still earn scholarships later in their academic journey. However, when applying, it's important to pay attention to the details and know what is required for each individual award. Some scholarships are offered for multiple years or semesters, while some are for one year and are nonrenewable. Some may require a certain GPA or service hours to renew.

Update financial aid representatives on major family changes. Many things can happen during a student's college career that could have an impact on their financial situation. If events like divorce, job loss, or illness impact finances, the student should notify their financial aid office immediately. A financial aid representative can help the student complete additional documentation, usually in the form of a professional judgment, where they can make financial adjustments even after the FAFSA has been approved.

Research and understand loan repayments and interest rates. Although a portion of students who complete the FAFSA will be offered scholarships and grants, every student who successfully submits a FAFSA will be offered some form of federal loan. It's important to understand what type of loan is being offered, what the interest rate is, and what the repayment expectations are, before accepting the loan. The first time a student accepts a federal loan, they will be required to complete a Promissory Note and Entrance Counseling, to ensure that they understand the terms, before receiving the loan.

Federal loans come in two forms: subsidized and unsubsidized. Subsidized loans are need-based loans sometimes offered to undergraduate students, where the government pays the interest while the student is in school. Unsubsidized loans are offered with every completed FAFSA, and the interest on these loans starts accruing as soon as they are distributed to the student. The interest rate for these loans varies from year to year, so students should always check for updated information from the FAFSA website or their financial aid representative before accepting their loan. Usually, students have a six-month grace period after they graduate, leave school, or drop below half-time status before they have to start repaying their federal loans. However, it's important to note that interest is accruing, even if the student isn't paying the monthly payment.

What If?

It's important to consider the impact on students, schools, and society if students *didn't* have access to financial aid. As the system exists now, financial aid is not available to every student in the United States who wishes to pursue higher education, and additional rules and processes put in place by future administrations could further restrict this access.

Students who are unable to obtain loans through the federal process or through school-specific funds must be creative in their search for funding. Some pursue a career in the military to qualify for the GI Bill. Others pursue careers with private companies that agree to pay for their tuition while employed. Others still delay college and work full-time for a few years, to save up money for tuition and fees, or attend a junior college or trade school, which usually are more affordable. Unfortunately, some students fall victim to predatory lenders and loan scams; others simply forgo attending college as the financial burden is too high.

If financial aid is not available, fewer students will attend college. Universities already expect enrollment to decline in the late 2020s due to lower birth rates in the late 2000s and early 2010s. An additional decrease in enrollment due to lack of funding would be detrimental to many institutions.

Conclusion

Whether to attend college is a serious, deeply personal decision. The decision can have a long-term impact on the individual, not only in terms of potential careers, but also in terms of an individual's personal growth and development. Many students who choose to attend college have an added burden of determining how they will pay the tuition and fees that come with the decision. Although the concept of obtaining an education may be the great equalizer, the process of funding that education is the opposite. However, knowing the steps to take to secure appropriate funding, along with navigating the hidden chutes and ladders built into the funding process, is one step in helping students offset the inequity that exists in the current higher education funding model.

Graduate Students

4

From First-Generation College Graduate to PhD Student: How to Transition Successfully

Elizabeth I. Dorssom

Introduction

First-generation college graduates, or those students who are the first in their family to earn a college degree, face a number of challenges while working on their degrees (Mena 2017).

First-generation students face a steeper learning curve regarding college readiness[1] than their counterparts who receive guidance from their parents who have graduated from college. Approximately only 3 percent of first-generation undergraduate students will pursue doctoral studies (Redford and Hoyer 2017). First-generation students should be encouraged to attend graduate school as they bring a number of assets to higher education including proactivity, optimism, and reflexivity[2] (Garrison and Gardner 2012).

The academic path is often characterized by both "chutes" and "ladders" that shape the experiences of first-generation doctoral students. For first-generation college students, chutes refer to the barriers and obstacles that can create setbacks or make it more difficult for them to succeed in higher education and advance in their careers. These challenges often stem from both personal and systemic factors that first-generation students may face in academia. First-generation students often lack guidance from family members who have navigated higher education themselves. This can result in a steeper learning curve when it comes to understanding academic expectations, navigating the application process, and seeking out resources such as scholarships, internships, or research opportunities.

First-generation students may not have access to mentorship from family members or other academic professionals who are familiar with the academic field. A lack of mentorship can limit their growth, opportunities for networking, and guidance on career and academic choices.

The feeling of not belonging or not being "good enough" is common among first-generation students, especially when they are surrounded by peers whose families have higher education experience. This self-doubt can hold students back from fully engaging in academic or professional opportunities. Without family members or mentors who have firsthand experience in higher education, first-generation students may lack guidance or encouragement when facing challenges. This absence of a strong support system can lead to feelings of isolation and frustration. First-generation students often juggle their academic responsibilities with work and family obligations, which can lead to burnout or difficulty maintaining focus on their studies.

For first-generation college students, ladders are the opportunities or resources that help them overcome barriers and propel them forward in their academic and professional journeys. These "ladders" can provide crucial support, guidance, and motivation that help first-generation students succeed and thrive in higher education. Ladders for first-generation students include gaining research experience, finances especially regarding affording graduate school application fees, and determining whether to enter industry or graduate school first.

Gaining Research Experience

To be successful PhD applicants, it is important for undergraduates to gain research experience. The first way an undergraduate can gain research experience is by connecting with one of their professors and asking if they need a research assistant. Occasionally, professors have projects in which they need assistance and would be willing to have an undergraduate help with some aspect of data collection. Further, professors would also be able to supply undergraduates with other information on how to gain research experience such as the McNair Scholars Program or the Summer Research Opportunity Program.[3]

These professors/mentors can offer tangible, practical assets, including letters of recommendation as well as research skills, potential publications, and advice on programs.

Affording the Graduate School Application Process

Application and GRE fees can be barriers for first generation students who tend to come from lower-income backgrounds. The GRE costs approximately $205 dollars, making it cost prohibitive for low-income individuals. The GRE is required by some graduate programs for admission.[4] The Educational Testing Service (ETS) has a fee reduction program available that will cover 50 percent of the cost for eligible individuals, based on their expected financial contribution (EFC) from the FAFSA.[5]

Another aspect of applying to graduate schools that is cost prohibitive for first-generation, low-income individuals is the sheer cost of applying for graduate school programs. The application fees can vary by university but often vary between $50 and $100. A variety of options are available for individuals who need assistance with

PhD application fees. First, the Big Ten Academic Alliances has a FreeApp fee waiver program[6] that allows individuals who qualify based on set criteria[7] to receive fee waivers to apply for PhD programs at the Big Ten universities. For individuals who want to apply to universities that are not within the Big Ten University Alliance, they should contact the graduate school admissions office to see if they offer application fee waivers.

Graduate School or Industry First?

After deciding to attend graduate school, undergraduates may wonder whether they should attend immediately or gain work experience first. Both decisions have multiple advantages.

For individuals who want to attend graduate school immediately, they will have the benefit of still being in school mode and not having to reorient after a period of not being enrolled in classes. On the other hand, students who begin working on their graduate degree may realize they do not enjoy the field and would rather switch to a different major of study. These students might then begin a new graduate program where their old course credits may or may not transfer.

In addition, gaining work experience after undergraduate allows an individual to learn more about themself as a person before beginning a graduate school program. This work experience can also strengthen graduate school applications as it can demonstrate that the applicant has a clear view of what they want to do after graduation, especially if they have gained experience in that field prior to applying. However, the transition back into school after the "real world" can be difficult. Individuals may have to learn how to balance schoolwork with relaxing extracurricular activities.

Choosing a Graduate School?

Once an individual has decided to attend graduate school, the next step is to choose the right program. One should find a program with professors who can potentially coauthor research projects.[8] Prospective students should also consider university location, particularly the cost of living and the stipend received. The cost of living should be affordable so that a student will not go further into debt in order to earn a PhD.[9] Prospective students should also look at the placement locations of graduates from potential programs.[10] These placements should align with the individual's future plans. For example, an individual who wants to pursue a teaching-focused or research-focused career should look at universities that have had success placing students in these types of careers.

This chapter helped shed light on the hidden curriculum facing first-generation students. By following the recommendations below, students can successfully transition from first-generation college student to successful PhD student.

The Road Not Traveled

The journey of a first-generation college student, as described in this chapter, is often filled with significant hurdles—"chutes"—such as the absence of family guidance, feelings of isolation, and lack of access to a network of mentors. These barriers can contribute to setbacks, making it more difficult for students to stay on the path to PhD completion. If the hidden curriculum were exposed more explicitly to first-generation students, they could avoid some of these pitfalls. For example, students might better understand the implicit expectations for networking, securing internships, and the importance of research experience earlier in their academic careers. Moreover, the feeling of "not belonging," which is common among first-generation students, could be mitigated by early mentorship. Providing targeted mentoring and guidance from the start would allow these students to adjust to the academic environment, foster a sense of belonging, and address self-doubt. In addition, if they had greater access to resources and clearer guidance on how to navigate the application process, such as obtaining fee waivers or understanding how to apply for scholarships, these obstacles might be less discouraging. Mentors could play an instrumental role by normalizing these struggles and offering insights into how they navigated similar challenges. Exposure to the hidden curriculum and strong mentorship can help first-generation students navigate and overcome many of the challenges outlined in this chapter. When mentors guide students through the intricacies of the academic world—offering advice, connections, and reassurance—the path becomes clearer, with fewer chutes and more ladders to ensure their success in higher education and beyond.

RECOMMENDATIONS FOR READERS

1. Undergraduate research is a pathway for future academic success; professors can write letters of recommendation, review your personal statement and CV, and help you gain valuable experience learning about how to do the science of your field.
2. Use the resources available to make the application cost more affordable.
3. Consider and weigh the benefits and drawbacks of going "straight through" from undergraduate to graduate studies versus working or taking time off.
4. Take a holistic approach to selecting a graduate program: cost of living, individualized attention, and ask the graduate studies director and/or current students about their experiences.
5. Decide what your passion or calling is, and market yourself attractively for potential school.

5

Live Long and Suffer: The Plight of the Grad Student

Jennifer H. Tatara

Statistics around graduate student well-being and retention are troubling (Ertem and Gokalp 2022), highlighting the numerous chutes that can derail a person's academic journey. Whereas some choose to leave a program because they no longer see value in that career path, others leave due to burnout. This burnout is largely attributed to antiquated perceptions that lead to a self-fulfilling prophecy of grad students being on the clock 24/7, living in their offices, with ramen noodles as their only source of sustenance. One idea is that graduate student life can be depicted as a triangle with each side representing sleep, social life, and academic success. The catch? Only two can be prioritized. This notion is oversimplistic; life is comprised of more than three sides of a triangle. However, humoring this narrative, a grad student may not always thrive in all three areas at all times, and that is OK. However, burnout in some form or fashion will ensue if one area of the triangle is consistently neglected. The moral: find balance in life as a graduate student and protect that balance.

Graduate programs require a considerable amount of dedication and work. This is not up for debate. What needs reevaluation is the notion that relationships, hobbies, and life outside of academics must be paused, if not sacrificed. The role and job of a grad student can be performed without feeding into the idea that life should be completely consumed and dictated by participation in a program. Administration should clearly set expectations, faculty must make sure graduate students' time is spent wisely, and program directors should allow grad students the voice to speak up if they are not being held to productive and reasonable expectations. Appropriate expectations, structure, and setting safeguards in place will help dispel the dangerous currently accepted image of the overworked, overwhelmed, and self-sacrificing grad student.

If managed correctly, time in a graduate program awards a tremendous gift: a flexible schedule. Although programs may vary on the rigidity of day-to-day schedules, most often, grad students have autonomy in managing their time. This gift comes with a heavy caveat; it must be used wisely. Through trial and error, one must build a schedule that affords balance. No matter the age at which the grad student journey begins, important personal events will arise during the program's duration. Eventually, someone will regret missing out on significant life events if they do not learn how to properly manage time and instead, succumb to the notion that they are not allowed to participate in life outside of academia.

Grad students should and must be encouraged to participate in life outside of academia. Burying oneself in work without proper rest and reset eventually leads to burnout. Implementing work-life balance forces grad students to find ways to work smarter and ultimately makes them more effective scholars. Does this mean grad students should attend every social gathering they are invited to? Of course not. But it means all else considered, they should not have to skip a best friend's wedding, miss a funeral, and they should go out and grab that dinner with friends when their mental health calls for it. Pursuing a graduate degree demands time, energy, and resources. With that said, it does not have to come at the cost of happiness and participation in life. There are tools grad students can use to help keep afloat as they embark on this incredible investment in their life.

RECOMMENDATIONS FOR READERS

1. *Find good mentors.* Work with mentors you respect, and of equal if not greater importance, ensure that a mentor will give you that respect back, serving as a ladder to your academic and personal growth. In grad school interviews with prospective advisers, remember that you are interviewing them just as much as they are interviewing you. This will be your home for the next few years. Choose a place with people who will help you thrive.
2. *Build a strong cohort.* Chances are others are with you in your program. Find peers you trust and share your worries, insecurities, and fears. A strong cohort can act as a ladder, providing support and camaraderie that helps you overcome potential feelings of isolation. Remember, you are not in this alone.
3. *Remind yourself of your "why."* In just a few years, you will be an expert in your chosen field. You are on a path that incentivizes lifelong learning, you have the opportunity to work with incredible mentors, and you will build enduring connections and friendships. Although you might see peers and friends pass milestones you are behind on achieving due to your decision to pursue a graduate degree, this investment will pay off in dividends. Remind yourself of that.
4. *Celebrate all wins, big and small.* Set lofty goals and celebrate their success. If they do not pan out, be flexible in adjusting your expectations. Do not let perceptions of failure define you. Set small goals, and when you meet them, celebrate these, too. Be kind to yourself.
5. *Lastly, have outlets outside of academia.* If you see the benefit of obtaining an advanced degree in your field of interest, do not become a part of that attrition statistic. One of the best ways you can avoid burnout is to dedicate purposeful time to enjoy life. Have fun. Do not feed into the narrative that your life, time with loved ones, and interests are temporarily paused as you pursue a graduate degree. This may require an active and intentional effort to set aside time to explore your hobbies, listen to music, or do whatever brings you happiness.

Although the path requires copious amounts of work (and perhaps caffeine), grad students can employ strategies to protect their well-being. As a prospective graduate student, consider the culture of a program. Do the necessary homework before joining. Talk to current students and faculty. A decision to pursue scholarly endeavors does not mean life has to be put on hold. And no, grad students do not need to work themselves to death. Faculty, administrators, and students must join forces to break down this narrative in hopes that we no longer have to associate graduate studies with pure sacrifice. Academia must find ways to increase motivation and success for those pursuing an advanced degree.

6

Ritual Anxieties: Living with and Working through Anxiety in Academia

Rae Summers-Thompson and William Duffy

If you fail your comprehensive exams, then what?
ADHD makes you a slow writer, and those exams are timed!
Long-Covid is short-circuiting your memory!
If you fail, you might as well give up, because no other grad program will take you!

As a PhD candidate (Rae) and tenured professor (Will), we are familiar with the social pressures of academia. The lines above, for example, represent some of the thoughts that went through Rae's head as she prepared for a call with Will, her adviser, to begin planning for her comprehensive exams. For many graduate students, the comprehensive exams are a defining moment—either a ladder that propels them forward with confidence or a chute that sets them back with self-doubt.

For Rae, these intrusive thoughts needled mercilessly. How was she going to get through the call? And how could she explain this debilitating anxiety to someone whose job it was to advise her academic work, not serve as her therapist? Will assumed that the conversation would follow that of most advising sessions: there would be some small talk, he'd answer questions, and they'd discuss pertinent next steps. He didn't anticipate that he would disclose his own struggles with anxiety and that they would discuss how hard it can be to talk about mental health more generally in academia.

In fact, since that advising session, we've only grown more passionate about this topic while working on Rae's dissertation, a project that develops trauma-informed theory and pedagogy for first-year writing programs. It's not uncommon for students in these spaces to write about personal experience, and if there is or has been trauma in their lives, they might disclose it. Now more than ever, the need is urgent for college instructors to know not only how to respond to such disclosures appropriately but also how to safeguard themselves from vicarious traumatization.

Like many graduate students, Rae has always been driven by new challenges. When she was accepted into a PhD program, she felt confident about her ability to navigate its trajectory, including the comprehensive exams her mind was no longer telling her she could pass. Preparing for that call, Rae had no reason to expect that Will wouldn't listen to her concerns, but she also had no reason to expect that he would understand.

She ran through the responses she was most worried about, advice like "just push through" or "everyone gets anxious about exams" or "don't overthink it."

But that's not what happened. As Rae remembers it, Will's response went something like this: "I understand. I live with anxiety, too. Let's think of ways to make this process work for you." What helped Rae that day was how Will listened compassionately, shared some of his own experience with anxiety, then invited her to set her own path and pace for the exams.

At our department, the comprehensive exam process requires doctoral students to demonstrate mastery in three specialized areas, which they develop in consultation with their advisers. The exam format includes two timed, four-hour written exams and one week-long take-home exam. These traditional structures can feel like chutes for students with anxiety, ADHD, or other neurodivergent experiences. Recognizing this, Will and Rae worked to modify the process within the departmental guidelines, allowing Rae to draft her own questions and engage in ongoing discussions that connected key ideas. This approach offered an alternative to the isolating, high-stakes model often imagined in academia.

High-stakes exams of any type often function as hidden chutes that privilege certain cognitive styles over others. By inviting Rae to take an active role in shaping her exams, Will provided a ladder, one that helped her build confidence, navigate institutional hurdles, and continue her degree progress. Why do those things matter? Fostering a supportive community is especially beneficial to people living with trauma, anxiety, and other neurodiversities. It helps sustain hope or "the perceived capability to derive pathways to desired goals, and motivate oneself via agency thinking to use those pathways" (Snyder 2002, 249). For Rae, a grad student with both ADHD and trauma-based anxieties, experiencing Will's compassionate encouragement helped her feel she could identify with and belong to the same professional circles as other academics. Will helped Rae realize how important it is for novice academics to understand that none of us is completely self-sufficient. "Trauma-informed education experts, researchers, and clinicians agree," says Alex Shevrin Venet, "healing from trauma and building resilience to guard against future trauma happens within the context of strong, supportive relationships" (2021, 83).

Lest anyone think that a supportive community were to mean a *dependent* one, this is not the case. When Will invited Rae to take a more active role in designing her exams, he accomplished two things: he offered the flexibility she needed to process the concrete material of the exams to move past her abstract fears, and he stepped aside to make room for her own autonomy to set the pace and direction of her progress. "The core experiences of psychological trauma are disempowerment and disconnection from others," explains psychologist Judith Herman, so "recovery, therefore, is based upon the empowerment of the survivor and the creation of new connections" (1998, S145). Will's approach enacted just the kind of support, flexibility, and room for autonomy needed to motivate Rae to set manageable goals to function actionably through the examination process. For his part, that conversation and Rae's subsequent dissertation research helped Will understand that one of the most effective ways to destigmatize anxiety is to maintain informal spaces where academics can be open and transparent about their own struggles with it.

RECOMMENDATIONS FOR READERS

1. **Build a Supportive Community**
   Faculty can establish peer mentoring programs and faculty-student discussion groups that normalize conversations about mental health in academia. Administrators can develop policies that prioritize mentorship training and encourage faculty to integrate trauma-informed approaches into their advising practices.
2. **Assess Program Procedures for Accessibility**
   Institutional procedures often create hidden chutes that disadvantage students with different neurological needs. Academic programs should thus regularly conduct surveys or focus groups to understand how departmental policies and procedures impact different student populations.
3. **Identify Small Benchmarks**
   Whether you are a mentor or a student, setting small, achievable goals can create momentum, reduce anxiety, and provide a sense of progress. Breaking large academic milestones into smaller, manageable steps helps make success feel more attainable. Develop habits for celebrating these small victories as a remedy for counteracting feelings of isolation and stagnation.

7

The Developmental Dissertation

Leanne C. Powner

The Dissertation as Developmental Process

In my role as a coach for dissertators, I hear a lot of confusion about why students write their dissertations and what the process is like. First, the most common perception is that it is simply a hurdle to get past, a sort of gauntlet of pain and distress that is a necessary hazing step in the process of becoming a researcher, with few rules or guidelines or even an idea of where the finish line is. The second theme I hear is that they feel "abandoned" by their advisers at some point. The third is that they are often unaware that the dissertation is a developmental process wherein they define their own intellectual program separate from their adviser. The ones who can take a slightly more objective stance—perhaps because they have a more supportive adviser or department culture—see it as a grinding process with a slightly clearer finish line but still no linear path to get there.

Did you ever stop to think, though, about *why* dissertations are organized and administered the way they are? There is a point and a method to this madness. The lack of structure *is* itself a structure, and it's intentional. It's a ladder, not a chute. The goal of the dissertation is developmental: it's to transform a student into an independent researcher.[1] This is the stage at which you stop being a student and become a junior peer. To do so, your adviser must eventually push the baby bird (you) out of the nest so you can learn to fly on your own. The multi-chapter structure of a dissertation allows them to do it a bit more gradually and less abruptly.

The typical academic field dissertation—as opposed to a professional field such as management, nursing, education, or public administration—has three or four pieces of research under a common thematic or theoretical umbrella. This is, as many in my field of political science say, about two-thirds of a book—which is a good thing, because those of us pursuing academic careers in these fields typically need to publish a book, or a book's worth of articles, for tenure. Those writing a "five-chapter" dissertation, essentially one empirical investigation stretched out over five chapters instead of sections, may not experience as strong a developmental process feeling, but it's still there.

The Process of Dissertating

So that's the desired output, the end stage or finish line. Now let's talk process. A typical (American) doctoral program marks three major milestones: comprehensive or field exams, the dissertation proposal, and the dissertation defense. The purpose of comps is to ensure your baseline subject knowledge. Do you understand what we know and how we know it in the fields where you intend to do your research and in your discipline more broadly? The dissertation proposal, on the other hand, is about ensuring that you understand the norms for conducting research in your field: what it looks like, what the goal is, how data is collected and processed, what forms analysis take. The proposal and its defense are about ensuring that you can be trusted to go off and execute a plan that will produce something that is acceptable as a dissertation, both in quality and quantity, in substance and in methods. Your committee is attempting to be sure that you do not run afoul of any major principles or protocols that are relevant to your research and that the final product will meet the standards for acceptance in your department and field.

In my experience, once past the prospectus defense, most students are left generally unsupervised through the data/input collection process. (This is less true in lab-based fields, more so in the humanities.) Your prospectus outlined a plan for data collection, so now that it's been approved, you're expected to execute it. Here is where the process starts to be badly misunderstood and risks becoming a chute out of the process. Your professors aren't being hands-off because they want you to flounder. They want you to finish. They trust that you can reasonably execute your data collection plan on your own or they would not have approved it. This is usually the first time, though, that students have no clear deadline and no defined path for completion; data collection (or reading/processing a corpus) is a unique process that varies from project to project, even for the same scholar. If you're stuck here, the conversation you usually need to have with your chair is how to systematize the process and set viable intermediate goals. It's not, as most suspect, an issue of time management; if you've made it this far, you probably have a mostly workable structure for this. Instead, it's an issue of not knowing how to actualize the process that you envisioned in your proposal, and an experienced researcher can help you do that. How do you track sources? How do you organize notes? How do you ensure that you've covered all the necessary bases and been consistent in your recordkeeping and coding? You're not asking student questions now; you're asking novice researcher questions.

Beyond the Preliminary Steps

As you move into writing chapters, the dynamic changes. Be prepared to receive copious feedback on your first chapter or two, especially if you have little experience writing documents of that form (scholarly paper, literature review, theoretical section/chapter). This is, after all, the first time that almost all graduate students take on writing anything of this length and complexity; many may never have written about or constructed their own theory at all. Most students find that these early chapters require at least two, and often three, complete drafts—as in, starting from scratch—to be acceptable. This is normal as you learn to produce different genres of text. It's also not uncommon at this stage to get feedback that pulls your project in a direction you didn't intend. It's not deliberate; it's probably because the reader doesn't remember the details of your proposal and sees linkages to their own work. You're the only one who knows what changes have been made since the initial proposal, whenever that was. Consult with your chair on how to proceed: incorporate some of the feedback or potentially push back with the consent and support of your chair (their peer), who can also help with justifications.

By the second body chapter, though, the chair (and often the rest of the committee) eases off a bit. You've already gotten thorough input from them on what a body chapter looks like; incorporate as much of that information as is relevant into the new chapter. If you're switching methodologies or conceptual lenses, check in with the committee member whose experience is closest about how this new chapter will differ. Don't be afraid to ask questions. Now that you know what to look for, seek input preemptively to reduce feedback later. You can start to push back if people are pulling you away from your research question. Again, work with your chair, but generally you can be a little more assertive and make the rejection based partly on your own expertise instead of relying on your chair. Feedback needs to be a ladder to growth and success, not a chute to disappointment.

For most students, by the third body chapter, voluntary feedback becomes scarce. It's deliberate. You've learned enough—or nearly enough—to function independently as a scholar. Your chapters look and read like chapters even on the first draft because you know what you're doing now. The feedback you get is mostly specific things you ask for, not blanket criticism and writing advice. So, be specific. Start asking reviewers specific questions related to their area of expertise rather than expecting blanket feedback. If someone tries to pull your project in a different direction now, you normally have enough standing of your own to push back on your own terms (though consulting with your chair is always good form). Your final body chapter should demonstrate that you can work more or less independently to produce professional-quality work based on the feedback given in the earlier rounds.

Those writing a "five-chapter" dissertation—a single empirical investigation stretched over five chapters—instead of the more traditional three-investigation style will have a somewhat different experience. In a five-chapter dissertation, every chapter is different. You don't get a chance to let your writing evolve over multiple attempts at analysis. You only have one analysis. In these contexts, feedback tends to be copious at all stages, primarily from the chair, until the chair decides the chapter is ready for the other committee members. That doesn't mean that you can't tap into their expertise in writing up; you're more likely to be showing up at their office hours with 2–3 pages of text for feedback rather than sending a whole chapter. Be prepared for every chapter to require at least two rounds of revision (or new drafts) with your chair before distributing it more widely. Every chapter represents a new set of skills, so cumulative feedback is less possible than with the multiple-analysis version.

Thinking Developmentally

This multi-round structure of a dissertation is a developmental process. It allows your chair to gradually grant you more independence in your research practice and writing. This is a deliberate process; it is not an abandoning because your adviser no longer finds you and your work interesting, the most promising, or anything else. Independence is the goal: it's what you're striving for. You won't have a senior faculty member's input to rely on for the rest of your research career. The dissertation defense is a formal way of confirming that you have all the skills needed to function as a researcher. You can design and conduct research, write it up, and incorporate feedback according to field norms without extensive supervision. You're being granted independence, not being abandoned. At the end of the day, the outcome of your doctoral studies is not your dissertation. It's you.

RECOMMENDATIONS FOR READERS

1. Envision the dissertation as a developmental process of becoming an independent researcher. This process may not always be clear from the student's perspective.
2. Ask if you need help organizing your dissertation process. The more specific your questions, the more helpful your adviser can be.
3. The perceived "lack of structure" in the dissertation process is part of the hidden curriculum, and it is meant to encourage students to develop confidence in their own skills.
4. Dissertations generally progress from heavy input and editing from the adviser and/or committee to a more hands-off, consultative relationship. See feedback as a ladder, not a chute, and seek feedback from people who view it the same way.

The Job Market

8

Navigating the Affective Component of the Academic Job Search in a Precarious Market

Amy Collins and Kaity Prieto

Today's market for academic positions is best described as precarious, with uncertainties about position availability, job security, benefits, and more. During the COVID-19 pandemic, faculty job openings in the United States dropped 70 percent (Langin 2020), and faculty wages and/or benefits were frozen or reduced at a considerable number of institutions (American Association of University Professors 2021). Decreases such as these continue to disproportionately impact faculty job applicants who identify as women, LGBTQ+, and/or scholars of color (Kelliher 2021), as evidenced by other chapters in this book. The authors of this chapter recently navigated searches for academic positions. As job applicants, we were aware of these statistics, which contributed to feelings of fear and pressure.

We encountered opposing messaging about these uncertainties. Well-meaning advisers, colleagues, and friends assured us to stay positive; everything would turn out fine. This perspective is part of a "cultural logic of precariousness" or a hidden curriculum that leads individuals to focus on their personal responsibility for their circumstances, when their situations are in large part dictated by systems beyond their control (McLean and Dixit 2018, 291). In other words, the job search process is a giant chute with very few ladders, and these well-meaning comments obscure this fact. McLean and Dixit described the logic of precariousness in their analysis of self-help books for adult learners, which promoted individual positive thinking while ignoring systemic contexts and influences. The messaging to stay positive and the pressure to maintain a hopeful outlook are at odds with the reality of perilous circumstances (McLean and Dixit 2018), such as the academic job market.

When a candidate struggles or encounters setbacks during the job search, they may blame themselves or others in their sphere of influence, rather than the job market itself and the system of hiring policies and conventions that sustain it (McLean and Dixit 2018). This messaging is part of a hidden curriculum that creates and reinforces feelings of self-doubt (Calarco 2020). Feelings of self-doubt and defeat can impact how candidates perform in the search process (White-Lewis 2020). It is essential to strike a balance between a realistic understanding of job prospects while also maintaining healthy confidence.

Our recent searches brought us face-to-face with this precariousness. Beginning with our own narratives, we now address the common feelings and emotions that may arise during the job search process.

> Amy: I'm a white, cisgender woman, and a first-generation student/academic. I searched for faculty roles in late 2021. I'm from a working-class community where folks encountered layoffs and concerns about livable wages, which were always on my mind during the job search. Not understanding the search process or the scarcity of postings, my family put well-meaning pressure on me to "finally attain the dream." They expected I would receive offers for multiple positions in my home state and were initially upset to learn I was applying more broadly. Further, I needed two attempts to finish my PhD, and I wondered how search committees would perceive this. So, when friends texted me, "Stop worrying, it will all work out," I felt dismissed. Overall, I struggled with emotional regulation while wrestling with the fear that if I didn't secure an interview or land a position, I would be letting many people down.
>
> Kaity: I am a white, cisgender, bisexual/queer woman and a continuing generation student from a middle-class background. I completed my PhD in spring 2020 and entered the job market at the start of the COVID-19 pandemic—a truly precarious time. I interviewed for one tenure-track position before opting for the security of an administrative role at my doctoral institution. I embraced the opportunity to strengthen my CV, teaching and researching during my "free time." The experience underscored how deeply I desired a faculty position; I was terrified that my PhD would have "all been for nothing" if I couldn't realize my dream. I also worried that my CV would mark me as a queer scholar engaged in queer research and wondered how biphobia might negatively shape my job prospects. Lastly, I was concerned about navigating the job search alongside close friends turned competitors. Well-meaning family assured me things would work out; I was "too smart" to not get hired. What, then, would it mean if I didn't?

Our narratives reveal several themes: questioning one's self-worth, understanding the role of identity in the job search, managing relationships, and navigating toxic positivity. With these dynamics in mind, we offer several suggestions for applicants, colleagues, friends, and other supporters, and for institutions.

RECOMMENDATIONS FOR READERS

1. **For applicants, understand that your employability does not equal your self-worth.** Securing a position is a delicate balance between your professional

background and departmental needs (e.g., topic knowledge, methodological expertise), many of which will remain hidden to you. Much of the process is beyond your control. Although that is scary, it also means that you can separate the outcome from your sense of self. Instead of agonizing over what you cannot control, perfect what you can and otherwise attend to your well-being. Create ladders for yourself by asking for help and being clear about the support you need the most. This might mean commiserating with friends who are also on the market. Decide up front how transparent you would like to be about one another's processes and then lean into that honesty. Jealousy will inevitably rear its head, but we found that celebrating with one another while more privately grieving our own losses can help.

2. **For family and friends unfamiliar with the process, and for advisers who may be removed from the current market landscape, you will likely stumble as you try to help.** Insisting that everything will work out sounds dismissive and divorced from the realities of a precarious job market. Help create ladders instead by listening to the candidate, validating their emotions, and encouraging them to take care of themselves. The uncertainty they are feeling is grounded in reality.
3. **Finally, for departments or offices that lead training (e.g., an academic job market series), center this in an ethic of care.** Placing all emphasis on statistics such as "only X percent of positions are tenure-eligible," without a counterbalance of support, reinforces feelings that the job search chute is insurmountable. Focus on both technical skills, such as preparing a CV or writing a cover letter, and on affective skills. For instance, you might encourage attendees to draft a support plan, attending to internal work such as self-care and attention to well-being, as well as external resources. Who do they feel comfortable turning to for emotional support? Where might they seek technical expertise for help with navigating the process? (These support networks may not overlap.) Finally, offer workshops on non-tenure track and industry opportunities, being mindful not to frame these pathways in deficit language.

If you're on the job market right now, we hope our chapter validates your feelings, and we encourage you not to fall for the cultural logic of precariousness.

9

Navigating the "Hidden Curriculum" as an International Scholar

Irmak Yazici

Introduction

International scholars face several specific challenges within academia; many arise from the limitations pertaining to their nonimmigrant status. This chapter is a "heads-up" for international scholars—it outlines the "chutes" they should be wary of and discusses the few "ladders" available for them to overcome the challenges of pursuing a career in academia outside their home countries, only to a certain extent. It is also a "call for action" for institutions—the number of international scholars in the United States has fallen by 9.6 percent since 2019 according to a report by the Institute of International Education (IIE) and plummeted by 31 percent post-pandemic in 2020–2021 (Institute of International Education n.d.).

Being an "Alien" in Academia

According to the Immigration and Nationality Act (INA), an alien is an individual who does not have US citizenship and is not a US national; aliens can be resident and nonresident, immigrant and nonimmigrant, asylee and refugee, documented and undocumented. For example, if you came to the United States as an international graduate student, likely with an F-1 (student) visa, you would be a nonimmigrant alien. If you have plans to remain in the United States as an international scholar, that is not a straightforward, linear path.

International graduate students who would wish to continue working in US academia have a few options. The first and most common way is to start your Optional Practical Training (OPT) right after your graduate program comes to an end, which provides you with work authorization for a year; it can be extended for another year in some cases. With an OPT, you can hold a temporary research/teaching position. If you still have not found a permanent or tenure-track position, once your OPT expires, you can hold another temporary position with a J-1 (exchange visitor) visa for a maximum duration of five years. This option comes with two important caveats: depending on a few criteria regarding sources of funding and skills or field of work, you may be required to return home for two years and will be ineligible to work in the United States before fulfilling that requirement; and whenever your appointment under the J-1 visa expires, within those five years or earlier, you will be ineligible to begin a new J-1 research scholar or professor program at any US institution for twenty-four months. Importantly, international scholars are not eligible to receive visa sponsorship for administrative positions, such as those that involve curriculum development, program management, or student advising, regardless of the skills and expertise they may possess in these areas. The one and only ideal option seems to be finding a permanent, tenure-track position, for which the institution can offer sponsorship that will allow you to work under a specific type of visa as a nonimmigrant alien, known as the H1-B visa. *However, many institutions signal that they prefer hiring a permanent resident or a citizen over an international scholar.*

"Will You Now or in the Future Require Sponsorship?"

This question is one of the many daunting parts of a job application for an international scholar. Regardless of how well you may think your work fits into a particular academic position, your answer to this one question can determine whether you will even make it to the interview shortlist. This is disheartening information to face in addition to already harsh realities of the academic job market.

Ironically, the general statement in almost all job application forms assures candidates that X is "an equal opportunity institution" and it "prohibits discrimination and harassment of any kind based on race, color, sex, religion, sexual orientation, national origin, disability, genetic information, pregnancy, or any other protected characteristic as outlined by **federal, state, or local laws**." As much as this seems to value diversity by committing to prevent discriminatory hiring practices, international scholars are, in practice, excluded from this assurance for diversity and nondiscrimination. There is no clear answer why the sponsorship question finds its way into academic job application forms, given that universities do not have a cap on the number of H-1B work visas they can sponsor to employ international scholars, and employers should not inquire into any candidate's citizenship status (see US Citizenship and Immigration Services; US Equal Employment Opportunity Commission).

One potential reason can be the cost of H-1B sponsorship: it is about $4,000 for the candidate, and each dependent (spouse and children) would add about $400 to the cost. Receiving an approval can take 6–8 weeks unless the university is willing to pay an additional $2,500 for expedited processing that will shorten the process to fifteen days. If this is a primarily a cost-related issue, this "education-for-profit" approach should be concerning for the future of academia in terms of diversity and inclusion (Nussbaum 2017). Universities risk losing talented scholars who will contribute to the prestige of the institution because of the technical requirements for legal work.

Border Politics and the Value of a Transnational Academic Community

Although universities are among the institutions with no cap on the number of H-1B work visas they can sponsor for nonimmigrant aliens, other concerns seem to prevent universities from providing equal opportunities for international scholars to pursue careers in academia. Mobility that transcends borders is an essential merit that promotes diversity in academic research, teaching, and outreach. Given the salience of anti-immigrant nationalist discourses within and outside of the United States, this is a crucial yet largely overlooked matter in academia.

A holistic, comprehensive assessment of these problems points to the need for systemic changes to fulfill institutional missions of diversity, inclusion, and equity in a way that does not presume factors such as citizenship and residency or discount the value of human dignity. These restrictions suggest that, as an international scholar, you are not considered to have settled where you had been living and working as an "alien" for the past decade or so, including the time of your graduate and postgraduate research and/or teaching. Scholars build social capital in their programs that enables and fosters academic success, and the legal constraints of the current visa and immigration system undermine and disrupt these important networks. Removing these barriers for international students should be a top priority for academic institutions to sustain diversity and accessibility for all, especially given that academic institutions are not bound by the visa sponsorship restrictions that apply to other industries.

RECOMMENDATIONS FOR READERS

1. Institutions should remove questions concerning work eligibility based on residency and/or citizenship from job application forms.
2. Institutions should provide a user-friendly guide for international graduate students to clarify their options and constraints after graduation.
3. Institutions should initiate/innovate international peer networks to facilitate communication among/between international students and faculty.
4. Disciplinary support networks can advocate for scholars who cannot conduct research in their home country due to threats to their life and/or well-being based on their identity (e.g., LGBTQIA+ scholars) and/or due to their field of study (e.g., religion, gender, free speech).

10

Scaling the Chute: Academic Job Hunting while Mothering

Christine I. Kugelmann

Introduction

If you visit any playground, you'll see children happily climbing the ladders to get to the top of the playground equipment. What happens when a child is forced to scale the slide because the ladders are blocked by other kids? What happens when the child is told that she can't use the ladder?

Conversely, you will also see parents tell children to climb the ladders and go down the slides, not vice versa: the unwritten rule of the playground. This unwritten rule is explicit in the directions for the game Chutes and Ladders, which attempts to mirror what happens on the playground.

Children learn both the unwritten and explicit rules of games and play, but how does this translate to academia?

Similar to the playground and Chutes and Ladders, most academics strive to get to the top (full professorship), but disproportionately, women—and more specifically, mothers—are forced to either stay at start (contingent, nontenure-track positions) or scale the chutes (seek alternate positions in hopes of achieving a tenure-track position in the future) to get to the top themselves. Nontenure-track positions generally prevent advancement in the academic game, and scaling the chute is often difficult or even impossible.

How can academic mothers play the game and succeed when the rules are institutionally biased against them (blocked ladders)? What are the unwritten rules of academia? How can we change, disrupt, or work around those rules so more of us can win the game?

A Major Problem in Academia

According to the American Association of University Professors, although the majority of PhD-holding lecturers and instructors (contingent, non-tenure track faculty) are women, fewer than 43 percent of women are tenured or on the tenure track, and an appalling 32.5 percent are full professors. The numbers for women of color are even more grotesque, and all women are paid less than men with "women faculty earn[ing] 85 cents to men's dollar" across all ranks (Colby and Fowler 2020; "NEA Higher Education: Faculty Salary Analysis: 2022–2023" 2024). This disparity is even more problematic for contingent faculty, and lecturers specifically, because they earn approximately $10,000 less a year than assistant professors who may have significantly less experience ("COE—Characteristics of Postsecondary Faculty" 2025). This means that women are less likely to be hired into a tenure-track position or be promoted while also earning less than men.

These statistics clearly show that women, and mothers even more so, are disproportionately affected by the expectations (stated and unstated rules) of academic institutions.

Higher Education and Expectations

As we all know, academia's rules are much different than those in other industries because tenure-track faculty are expected to be hired at an assistant professor level with teaching experience, published peer-reviewed papers, and successful conference presentations, all of which takes time and effort, and generally occurs during the rigors of graduate school. Because of this expectation, women tend to put off having children during graduate school because "they fear that they will not be taken seriously and that their professors and future employers will disapprove" (Mason, Wolfinger, and Goulden 2013).

These fears are well founded as women with small children are 21 percent less likely to get hired in a tenure-track position than childless women, although women with older children are far more likely to get hired (Mason and Goulden 2002). PhD-holding graduates generally apply for assistant professor positions "between 27 and 40 years old," which is also the time most women start having children (Gallardo 2020).

Academia's expectations create hard (and incredibly unfair) choices for women, especially when women finally have children, because 75 percent of childcare and housework, unpaid care work, falls to mothers, which means that they simply can't research, write, publish, and present at conferences due to time, mental, emotional, and physical bandwidth constraints (Perez 2019).

The Hiring Process

The academic hiring process is also problematic for women, and mothers specifically. Hiring requirements depend on the type of academic institution. Teaching institutions focus on "teaching experience, teaching philosophy, commitment to diversity, fit, and collegiality" while teaching and research institutions may require "collegiality, teaching experience and teaching philosophy, mentoring and research with undergraduates, and scientific communication … feasibility, fit, and scholarship." Research institutions prefer "scientific vision, scientific independence, fundability, scholarship, and fit for the position" (Clement, Dorman, and McGee 2020).

This study is based on the scientific field, but these requirements cross over to other disciplines as well, and it's important to notice that "fit" is a requirement at each type of institution, but what does "fit" actually mean? How can we "fit" when our paths have been different due to our womanness and motherhood?

Research explains the "fit" issues that mothers face in academia. There is a clear bias against mothers in "screening recommendations" and "fit perceptions" in the hiring process, which means that hiring committees often look for candidates who are like themselves or are representations of what they believe a "good academic" looks like, but for women who took time off to have or raise children and postpone their own research, writing, or conference presenting, they already experience ladder blockage due to the perceived lack of "fit" (Heilman and Okimoto 2008).

For example, if a university is hiring an assistant professor who "fits" with the cultural or current makeup of the department, a woman, and a mother more so, will not be their choice.

Because a major unwritten expectation for potential faculty is that they should follow the traditional, linear trajectory from undergraduate school through graduate school into a tenure-track line, mothers often don't "fit" this perception; they have had to take a different road to academia than men.

My Story

This issue has directly impacted my own life as I am part of the thousands of women who interrupted traditional academic expectations by giving birth to and raising four children after earning my master's degree. I was relegated to adjunct work, happy to have some kind of teaching job, and for 16½ years while I raised children, I watched others climb the ladder to win the game.

When I finally earned my PhD at the age of fifty-two, I discovered that I was perceived to be too old to climb the ladder and play the game at all. In fact, one colleague specifically told me that I was too old to be hired into a tenure-track position, which I found devastating. In short, I didn't "fit."

I realize that I will spend the rest of my career as contingent faculty, but luckily, I have been full-time for eight years now. Don't get me wrong: I love my job, my institution, and my students, but I wanted more. I deserve more. Mothers deserve more, especially single mothers who are juggling everything including all financial concerns for their family.

RECOMMENDATIONS FOR READERS

Recommendations for Hiring Change

Does this mean the game is not winnable for mothers or women who want to be mothers?

Calls for changes to academia are not new, but simply equalizing the number of women in academia does nothing to solve the underlying problem, which is the systemic meritocracy of the hiring process (Powell 2018).

If this is the case, the only option is to demand a rewrite of the rules, changing the expectations, and "reimagining of academic career pathways: diverse, flexible, and individually responsive to the health and family needs of academic workers." How can we "reimagine" academic pathways to dismantle the biased meritocratic system? (Dwyer and Flynn 2018).

1. **Hiring committee members should be required to take unconscious bias recognition training before evaluating applicants.** In this training, they would do more than just recognize their own bias; instead, they would learn "to manage their biases, change their behavior, and track their progress" (Gino and Coffman 2021). It's vital that training is not a one-time meeting but occurs over time to become ingrained in academic culture, ultimately changing the fabric of academic expectations and rules.
2. **Hiring expectations should be changed to ensure that "fit" is not a primary criterion for candidates.** Having and raising children directly cause gaps in résumés, years between degrees, and fewer publications and conference presentations, and these issues may prevent the hiring and academic progression of brilliant, capable researchers, writers, and teachers.
3. **The current meritocratic system of higher education, including extreme expectations of publishing and conferences which prevent mothers from gaining experience, should be abolished.** Women should not be negatively impacted by their desire to have children.

Unblocking Ladders

One major "rule" of academia is that faculty are hired as contingent or tenure/tenure track with no crossover in these lines. Contingent faculty are teaching faculty, those who teach more classes to more students, while tenure/tenure-track faculty teach fewer courses and have research and service requirements.

Although the workloads may be similar, the tasks and "game expectations" are very different as are the perceptions of the value of those tasks. Even though higher education is about student learning, more value is often placed on research, which justifies higher salary levels for tenure/tenure-track faculty.

Despite this, higher education needs to prioritize and place higher value on teaching, including during graduate school, to give women, and specifically mothers, a chance to advance their careers even though they often have less time, mental, emotional, and physical bandwidth than their male counterparts.

In addition, providing resources on campus for faculty could prove invaluable to increasing equity for mothers, such as child care and mentorship.

Chutes and Ladders is a fun game with winners and losers, but higher education is not a game, so the "rules" need to change.

Section Two

Ascending the Ladders and Rising through the Ranks

Non-Tenure Track Faculty, Junior Tenure-track Faculty, Tenure and Promotion, Service/Teaching/Research Balance, and Senior Faculty

The Why

This section focuses on the pathway through the profession. Each contributing author addresses a phase in the academic career, providing practical insights and illuminating the challenges and opportunities that faculty encounter. This section is for the graduate students who hope to build a traditional career in higher education—one where they enter into a tenure-track position, spend six years in a probationary period, sail through the tenure and promotion process, and retire decades later as a full professor. It's for the pragmatists who are looking at the reality of the academic job market in a time of immense uncertainty for higher education. It's for new junior faculty who are weighing choices about the prospect of starting a family while starting a career, who are considering the demands of balancing service, teaching, and research and meeting mid-tenure review expectations. And it's for the campus decision makers (department heads, upper-level administration, and senior faculty) who play key roles in shaping hiring, tenure, and promotion processes.

Getting a tenure-track job and then earning tenure is heralded as the highest priority and greatest achievement in an academic's career. The reality stands in stark contrast to the expectations graduate program directors set for their students: the tenure-track job is elusive or at least harder to come by than it once was. According to a March 2023 report by the American Association of University Professors (AAUP), the academic workforce in the United States has changed dramatically in the past 30+ years. The academe of today is dominated by mostly contingent faculty in both full-time and part-time positions; in 1987 about 47 percent of faculty lines were non-tenure track as compared to about 68 percent in 2021, and women and underrepresented minorities (URM) hold most of these positions ("Tenure and Contingency in US Higher Education" 2023). Fewer tenure-track lines and more contingent positions presents an increasingly risky job environment for all scholars, especially for those who are not well-versed in the hidden curriculum and the rules of academic chutes and ladders. The vulnerability of contingent academic work is compounded by the multifront assault on higher education in the United States. Prospective students and their families have shown increasing skepticism about the value proposition of higher education (Kelderman 2023). In early 2025, threats to dismantle the Department of Education added uncertainty about federal funding for colleges and universities, student financial aid, and policies designed to ensure equitable access to higher education for historically excluded scholars (Wood and Claybourn 2025). At the state level in the United States, legislatures have considered and adopted policies constraining or outright banning efforts to promote diversity, equity, and inclusion, limiting academic freedom, and curtailing curricula (Bryant and Appleby 2025; Quinn 2025).

Now more than ever, it is important to support emerging scholars from a variety of backgrounds and perspectives, give them the best opportunity to discover important new findings through their research, and engage with students to prepare them for all the challenges they will face in a rapidly changing world. Scholars who struggle with the hidden curriculum also contribute to a stronger academy by bringing a diversity of theoretical perspectives and methodologies to solve puzzles in innovative ways. Mentorship is a reliable way to retain talented scholars in the profession, including how to balance service, research, and teaching obligations, how to negotiate, how to navigate the institutional landscape, and how to weather the ups and downs of career stages.

Yet many mentorship efforts focus only on the early phases of academia, especially for women+ and historically excluded scholars, and those from non-elite institutions to increase support that should help them progress through the ranks. The hidden curriculum is not exclusive to junior faculty, and many scholars need support to redefine their professional goals and survive mid-career malaise. Senior scholars can find themselves in a new post-tenure game for which there are few rules, few benchmarks, and even fewer players who can serve as role models and mentors. We wrongly assume that mid-career and senior scholars have "got it all figured out" when really they may find themselves having survived to "academic adulthood" only to learn that there are few—if any—codified rules of the game for senior scholars.

Along the way, the rules of the game change regarding expectations for service, teaching, and research productivity that may differentially affect faculty's prospects for satisfying the requirements for progressing from one professional stage to the next. For example, service assignments are inequitably assigned to women+ other historically excluded faculty who are disproportionately given internal departmental and low-profile service responsibilities as compared to their men colleagues (Guarino and Borden 2017; Murdie 2017). These activities are often time and labor intensive and fail to contribute to the metrics that help faculty achieve their annual and probationary metrics toward tenure and/or promotion.

Women and historically excluded faculty are also solicited for their identity-based representational value on committees to increase the perception of diversity. Students count on them for guidance, eager to appeal to a shared identity. These realities increase the burden on scholars who already are at a disadvantage in the academy, who may be apprehensive about saying no to these types of requests for service. Simply put, the emotional labor and invisible workload for women—particularly, women of color—on campus creates additional strain. Mentors, department heads, and senior colleagues can serve as advocates for scholars in tenuous positions and help them navigate the departmental and university-wide politics by providing cover and advice for how to effectively curate their service profiles. The following chapters discuss themes of "rising through the ranks" in varying capacities and situations, including special challenges facing non-tenure track colleagues, and the junior-to-senior scholar pipeline through the gauntlet of tenure and promotion.

Succeeding in the Academic Path from Early Career to Senior Scholar

Non-tenure Track Faculty

Someone graduating with a PhD today is more likely to land a non-tenure track (NTT) job than a tenure-track one, significantly more likely if they are from a non-elite institution or are from a historically excluded scholar identity group. Scholars who land in a non-tenure track position post-PhD are often met with either judgment or pity—or both. Landing in a nontenured position is viewed as an individual failure rather than a consequence of systemic changes that have dramatically altered the composition of higher education.

Amy Cooter's chapter, "The Perpetual Impostor," describes the culture shock of the author's undergraduate experience as a quasi-first-generation student from a rural community attending an elite private institution. In both her undergraduate and graduate programs, Cooter observed the noticeable differences in responsibilities and coping mechanisms between low-income and more financially comfortable peers. Wealth and privilege can make surviving in the academy an easier ordeal—akin to "drawing from the Community Chest" in "higher-ed monopoly." Her most important contribution, perhaps, is recognizing the connection between undergraduate students from similar socioeconomic and geographic backgrounds as hers who also are overrepresented in the ranks of contingent faculty. Social capital stratifications that help high-school students from affluent districts succeed at the undergraduate level (while peers from underfunded rural areas struggle to integrate new vocabulary like *syllabus*) tend to persist at the graduate level. Some knowledge is just not intuitive, and work-study funds may not cover the cost of "hidden curriculum" lessons. Knowledge and wealth accumulation accrue over time, as do gaps and deficits in these areas.

Landing a non-tenure track position, however, does not have to mark the end of one's research trajectory. Indeed, as Holley Hansen discusses, getting involved with undergraduate researchers is one way to stay research-active in a contingent position. In her chapter, "Overcoming the Research Funding Barrier: Undergraduate Research as an Opportunity for Non-Tenure Track Faculty," Hansen describes how outdated policies can prevent NTT faculty from accessing grant funding. Her chapter is particularly useful for NTT faculty, for administrators in offices of sponsored projects, and unit heads or department chairs. Despite the rise in long-term academic positions, such as research, teaching, and clinical faculty, some granting agencies still require principal investigators (PIs) to be in tenure-track lines. External funding is often used to support research projects, and contingent faculty generally have high teaching loads. Although many internal opportunities through research support offices have followed these same research-focused funding priorities, many institutions are offering support for faculty who engage students in research projects.

In "On the Outside, Looking In: Pathways to Success for Non-Tenure Track Faculty," Karen Huxtable-Jester and Paul Diehl write for both NTT faculty and their supervisors and provide rich insight into the dynamics of contingency in terms of both chutes and ladders. They offer the perspective that contingent faculty are often excluded from departmental and disciplinary networks that help to provide not only valuable professional opportunities but also an integral sense of belonging and identity in their academic community.

Whereas tenure-track colleagues may complain about interminable faculty meetings, contingent faculty are often not even invited and therefore miss crucial updates about the department and institution. The lack of inclusion creates cultural and informational divides and gaps in shared governance when NTT are unable to contribute to decision-making processes related to the department. NTT faculty are also often excluded from professional development opportunities such as funding for conference participation.

For contingent faculty, we want to highlight the pervasive myth that their position may someday convert to a tenure-track faculty line. This may be one of the biggest lies we tell contingent faculty: hold on, hang in there, we may be able eventually to turn your line into a tenure-track position. Departments do not necessarily disingenuously string along their contingent faculty, and they may offer this hopeful path with only good intentions. However, it rarely happens. Your departmental colleagues will view you through the lens of the position in which you entered the institution. If you start as an instructor or visiting assistant professor, you are defined as an instructor; no amount of exemplary service roles, publications, grants, or outstanding teaching evaluations will likely alter this initial perception of you as a scholar. In the climate of scarce resources, tight budgets, and limited new tenure-track faculty lines, departments are disinclined or simply unable to convert contingent faculty they already employ to a tenure-track line. This generally feels like a very personal slight to the scholar in a contingent position, but in reality, it's a function of cognitive dissonance first described by Tversky and Kahneman (1981). Beyond the effects of perception, institutional barriers may make internal hires more difficult.

PhDs are also unlikely to be hired in the same department where they earned their degree because it is difficult to step into an egalitarian, collegial role after having been in a hierarchical-subordinate student-adviser role during the doctoral phase. Unfortunately, the job market is increasingly unforgiving, and external offers are inefficient, costly signals for the job candidate, the hiring department, and the home department and university. Huxtable-Jester and Diehl encourage NTT faculty to become more engaged with the campus community, to connect with a supportive community as well as raise their institutional profiles and visibility.

Even so, many research support or sponsored projects offices do not readily think of NTT faculty when making decisions about funding allocations. Hansen suggests that NTT faculty reach out and get to know personnel in these offices, especially scholars in the humanities and social sciences who are often less obvious grant-getters than peers in the physical sciences, engineering, and medicine/health care. NTT faculty often do not have access to research assistants, and by recruiting—and funding—students to engage in research-oriented projects, contingent faculty win in several ways simultaneously. NTT faculty teach students the important skills of how to do meaningful research, they diversify their portfolio and CV by obtaining funding (which may also include travel and conference support), and they also make progress in their own research agendas.

Junior Tenure-Track Faculty

Kelly Bauer's description of her pre-tenure probationary period conjures images of stacks upon stacks of reams of printer paper and the endless bureaucratic demands that necessitate this environmentally unfriendly pipeline. Getting an academic job, according to Bauer in "Struggling to Find Purpose in the Paperwork: USCIS Petitions, Job Applications, and Tenure Files," is as much about being organized and disciplined in the application process as it is about knowledge and skill and connections. She details the mountains of paperwork involved not only in completing her dissertation and graduate degree, including filing for graduation, but in compiling her mid-tenure review during her third year in a tenure-track position and submitting her tenure file at the end of her probationary period. This is compounded by the labyrinth of paperwork involved in a multinational marriage, supporting her spouse in filing for US citizenship, and taking on the role of department chair and the administrative details that entails.

Paperwork is paperwork, and it is almost always a slog. However, it bears underscoring how complicated and nonlinear the green card and citizenship processes can be, especially when undertaken as individuals and without institutional support from an employer or office of international affairs (or equivalent). Many academics have nontraditional relationships, in the sense that they do not look like 1950s-era television shows with a stay-at-home support spouse and a sole outside-the-home income earner. Academics often meet their partners while in graduate school and start their family formation at the same time as they start their first academic careers. They may hold separate bank accounts and credit cards and may never have met each other's families. They may not share a last name, breaking with customary traditions that make their legitimate relationship less believable and convincing to immigration policies.

Zora Wolfe shows how "Developing an Intentional Mentor Network" would benefit people in Kelly Bauer's position. Mentors can make things easier on us by showing us shortcuts, cheerleading our achievements, and helping us avoid potholes in our careers. A mentor is not a one-size-fits-all job description, and Wolfe suggests that scholars benefit when they have options in their mentoring relationships. Mentors can fill different gaps and serve in varying capacities; some will help with departmental or university politics, some will help with work-life boundaries, some will be coauthors or provide feedback on manuscripts or methods, some will evaluate your teaching, and some will write letters of recommendation for jobs or in support of tenure and/or promotion.

Broadly speaking, mentorship across ranks is essential. Some departments, for varying reasons, have no viable mentors; this is not a deal-breaker, as mentors can come from other departments or disciplines or different institutions altogether. The goal of a good mentor should be to make your life easier than it would be without one, and to make it easier now than it has been in the past. As Shane Gleason, Diana Ivy, and Kelly Miller point out in "From the Top: Chairs' Role in Developing Faculty Success," department chairs play an integral role in supporting faculty. They implore chairs to spend time getting to know faculty as human beings, especially in light of the recent COVID-19 pandemic that disrupted the normal functioning of higher education for several years. Faculty often internalize the decisions made by upper administration to keep the institution solvent and keep faculty delivering content knowledge in classes during difficult times, such as the great pivot from in-person to virtual education in March 2020.

Tenure and Promotion

Getting through the tenure and promotion process is a mix of elements—some that an individual can control and many beyond their control. Managing the research pipeline is paramount to success and something that individuals can develop (Lebo 2016). Unlike many industries with set schedules and billable hours, academics have nobody to tell them to quit working at midnight, or not to work on the weekends. The "absent-minded professor" mentality still dominates academics' workflow schedules in a time when working idiosyncratically is a luxury. The diversification of academia has also coincided with calls for more professionalization, including defining better work-life boundaries. The humblebrag of "I haven't had a day off in months" is not an ode to productivity but, rather, a misplaced flex that demonstrates working inefficiently. We do not need to work all the time to be productive or successful.

Having a rigorous work ethic can help move projects efficiently through from concept to publication and lead to improved emotional and psychological health and overall job satisfaction. Part of this rigorous work ethic is adopting a "no one-off" rule. There should be no single-use activities, and scholars should maximize the effort they expend by getting multiple products out of a single project. For example, Windsor and Kronsted (2022) found that most people never resubmit a grant proposal that doesn't get funded the first time (Windsor and Kronsted 2022). Many people also don't know that the body of a grant proposal and any new research or pilot study data can be reused—copied and pasted—into an article for publication. And although public-facing work often doesn't "count" toward tenure and promotion, alt-metrics such as citation counts and uptake into the public sphere can raise individual scholars' profiles in the discipline and beyond. It can be worthwhile to write a short blog post, social media thread, or a piece for The Conversation about new findings and perspectives from your research.

Academics do not earn tenure on research alone, of course, and service occupies a significant amount of time. Patrick Homan writes about how service assignments can lock faculty into a "service trap" that also can lead to burnout and decreased productivity and well-being. His chapter, titled "The Chutes and Ladders of Service at a Small Liberal Arts College," identifies the ways that excelling in service assignments leads to more service assignments, which can intrude on time spent delivering high-quality teaching and engaging in research. Small Liberal Arts Colleges (or SLACs) do not have the sheer size and volume of personnel available to larger public and private institutions. Thus, SLACs rely on faculty to undertake the service that keeps the university functioning.

In "Doing Away with 'The Way We Do Things around Here': Clarity and Equity in Tenure and Promotion," Rashna Richards provides evidence of tangible ways that informal and haphazardly applied norms disproportionately harm faculty from underrepresented groups. The faculty handbook is the grand arbiter of what counts toward tenure and promotion, and it provides the governance structure for evaluating whether faculty have met the requirements to progress to the next stage of their career. Too often, the spirit—rather than the letter—of the law makes or breaks this decision, as in the cases where senior faculty may enlighten only some of the junior faculty about the informal rules of the game in their department.

Historically excluded scholars often don't have access to this private information because all too often they don't have senior faculty or mentors who look like them in their department. The "in-group" is often defined by outwardly visible identity characteristics, such as sex or race. Although mentorship through the tenure and promotion process should be identity-agnostic, in practice, the informal social networks within the department and institution create information gap disparities about the subtle cues that faculty voting on tenure and promotion pay attention to.

Richards's perspective highlights the importance of the trio of recommendations that we made in *The PhD Parenthood Trap*: policies should be clearly communicated, transparent, and equitably applied. Codifying and clarifying the informal, invisible standards that can make or break a tenure case and sharing this information with all faculty is only part of the solution, though. As Richards discusses, it is critical to ensure that the invisible judgments—also known as implicit biases—are addressed among faculty members who are deciding their colleagues' career fates. Implicit bias training improves the thoroughness and thoughtfulness of portfolio evaluation and provides the opportunity for what Richards calls "strategic reorientation in thinking about equity." The original conceptualization of tenure provides career security to "men of high gift and character"—indicative of a time when women and other historically excluded scholars were rare occurrences in the academy.

The core concern is that the context for evaluating scholarly productivity is rooted in a historical version of academia where few scholars were women, BIPOC, LGBTQIA+ (openly), or from the Global South. The tenure and promotion yardstick is enclosed in a time capsule from an era that scarcely matches the reality and diversity of contemporary academia. The core concerns, research themes and methodologies, and siloed disciplinary agendas of fifty years ago still provide the architecture for evaluating scholarly output from colleagues whose lives, lived experiences, and careers look vastly different. This is because many of the senior faculty on gatekeeping committees were hired, tenured, and promoted under this outdated system and have not been required to update their priors (in Bayesian terms) about fair and equitable promotion practices.

Service, Teaching, and Research

In tenure-stream positions, faculty are expected to engage in teaching, research, and service throughout their career. In contingent positions, teaching and service generally constitute the bulk of the workload, with minimal or no research expectation. Teaching and service can be both chutes and ladders: when curated with care, courses and service roles are meaningful exercises, can contribute to and stem from exciting research agendas, and make the academic career a rewarding one. The contributors in this section highlight considerations related to service and teaching, offering readers a clear view into opportunities and obstacles for contingent, pre-tenure, and post-tenure faculty alike.

Gretchen Peterson takes the chair's perspective in her chapter titled "Tackling the Role of Department Chair while Living with an Invisible Chronic Illness." Similar to many of the contributions to this book, Peterson's experience intersects with many themes, including service and administrative roles and invisible workloads such as caregiving and illness that may not have outward presentations. The overarching thread from this chapter is to build deep leadership within your department, not only for providing support during times of health challenges but also because faculty also become more invested in the department and develop experience with many roles and responsibilities.

The other theme in this chapter is that there are very few academic emergencies. The administrative workload has its ebbs and flows, with more activities and responsibilities during the hiring season and at various predictable times during the semester, perhaps fewer during the summer. Peterson offers implicit advice to communicate expectations with deans and other administrators and to set reasonable, individualized goals for yourself in the chair role. Taking on a new administrative role presents many chances to learn and grow, and sometimes growth takes uncomfortable forms. Stress may manifest as illness, and those with chronic health conditions should take extra care to maintain physical well-being—and psychological and emotional well-being. Being a chair may also invite new health problems; dealing with contentious departmental politics can take its toll. Use sick leave as you need it, and prioritize your health.

In a small academic community, it is hard to say no because everyone knows everyone, and the system relies on the logic of collective action (Olson 1971). In other words, smaller groups are more cohesive; there is more accountability and visibility of effort. It's easier to hide in a 250-person lecture hall than it is in a ten-person seminar. SLACs may use moral authority arguments not only to prevent free riding but also to coax faculty into taking on more than they ought to for the good of the department (or college). In systems with small memberships, shirking is noticeable, and small changes make big differences. Some departments have two faculty members; losing one means losing 50 percent of the department. This is a very different scenario than losing one faculty member in a department of thirty people. Larger departments can more easily absorb challenges and distribute (or redistribute) service assignments among members.

The accountability and visibility of efforts in small groups should encourage members to do a good job—only this has its drawbacks as well. Faculty members who excel at their service assignments get more and bigger assignments. In departments of all sizes, a perverse dynamic is at play: faculty who do a poor job of service (or teaching, for that matter) assignments tend to get fewer requests to serve. In one department, course evaluations of one faculty member were so consistently low that they were "rewarded" with a 0-0 teaching load. The better you do in service roles, the more roles you get, and the less time you have to spend on other activities that are core to the profession, such as research.

Carrie Liu Currier uses a familiar metaphor to describe this service trap in "Musical Chairs: Service, the Curse of Competence, and Delayed Promotion." She writes that service assignments are like a game of musical chairs, only the goal is to get eliminated early. The implication, of course, is that the last person seated in the chair bears a disproportionate service load as everyone else has been relieved of their role in the game. Faculty doing a great job get rewarded with more service, while doing a lackluster or even decent job gets rewarded with less service. This perverse incentive structure does not emphasize equitable distribution of labor or accountability.

Moreover, service assignments tend to fall disproportionately to scholars from historically excluded communities. Academic units with less diversity are more inclined to lean on their "diverse" scholars for essentialist representational characteristics. This also leads to burnout and at least temporarily absolves the institution or department from making meaningful changes toward diversity so long as they have a faculty member or two from underrepresented groups to serve on all the committees. This situation places the burden of diversity on the individual faculty member; they likely understand that absent their role on the committee, it would be largely homogenous and lacking a diversity of perspectives and lived experiences. It's a difficult position to put a junior faculty member in—weighing the options of not contributing a valuable perspective to an important decision or process or protecting research and personal time. It's not always easy to say no.

Service is not necessarily a burden, however, and it is important to understand that you can learn something from every service assignment. You can learn who holds the power and ability to make decisions. You can make allies in other departments and with staff and administrators. You can make yourself indispensable in some way. And you can parlay your service roles into other tangible products, such as reports, blog posts, or even journal articles. Academic journals are increasingly inclined to publish thought pieces and research articles about emerging trends and solutions to problems in the profession.

Service assignments and teaching loads may be outside the bounds of what individual scholars can control. Saying "no" to new preps or demanding service assignments is not always easy or feasible, especially during the probationary period when new faculty, or faculty in contingent positions, are eager to demonstrate collegiality and contributing to the goodwill. In "Who's Going to Teach It? Equitable Distribution of Course Development Demands," Tara Parsons describes many inequalities related to teaching assignments, including how women and historically excluded scholars are disproportionately overburdened by the task of preparing and teaching many new courses. Departments must offer the requisite coursework for students to progress through their degree programs, and tenured faculty generally have first right of refusal in selecting their courses. This means that contingent and junior faculty often bear the brunt of the intellectual labor required to do a good job preparing new courses.

Students increasingly behave like—and are treated like—customers and coursework as a transactional activity. Students assign disproportionately harsher evaluations to women and historically excluded scholars, and rigorous analysis has demonstrated that these evaluations exhibit hallmark biases (Gelber et al. 2022; Mengel, Sauermann, and Zölitz 2019; Peterson et al. 2019). Moreover, teaching evaluations are one of the core metrics used in annual faculty evaluations, criteria in decisions about merit raises, and constitute a sizable proportion of the tenure and promotion portfolio. Faculty in precarious positions—junior and contingent lines—are asked to teach a wider array of courses and deliver them flawlessly and with an eye toward student-centered "edutainment." This situation is unsustainable, not conducive to health and well-being, and can quickly lead to burnout—especially for scholars with intersectional identities who are disproportionately burdened by new course preps and service assignments.

Senior Faculty

The post-tenure slump is real. When faculty successfully move from pre- to post-tenure roles, they may experience an untethered feeling of "now what" that defines the first part of their life as a tenured professor. This "now what" feeling is a product of having been on a singular, goal-oriented track, with expectations and deliverables to meet at an unsustainable pace. Their careers had been defined by the pursuit of tenure and achieving the departmental and disciplinary benchmarks required to keep their jobs. They now face the opportunity to broaden their research (and service) horizons and entertain ideas about a range of options not available to them as pre-tenure, early career scholars.

In "Burnout, Compassion Fatigue, and Secondary Trauma: Self-Care in Higher Education," Tami Micsky writes for all faculty and academic leaders with the capacity to make organizational change about the need for prioritizing mental and physical health, especially during stressful times. The combined effects of isolation, stress, and having other caregiving responsibilities can create burnout, compassion fatigue, or secondary trauma. Burnout can happen from a mismatch between work responsibilities and self-efficacy and when work-life boundaries are blurred. In academia, virtually nobody will tell you to go home or stop working. In fact, humblebrags about time spent working are quite common. Rather than acknowledging that working all the time is quite inefficient, the tendency is to emulate this unhealthy pattern rather than find ways to keep work and life in their respective places. Compassion fatigue is an empathetic response that happens when faculty absorb the stresses and challenges that students and other colleagues share with them. It is intimately linked to secondary trauma, a phenomenon that describes the emotional and behavioral responses that arise from knowing that a traumatic event or stressor has happened to someone else.

This chapter is an important read for everyone: although it is geared toward faculty and institutional leaders, it is widely applicable even beyond academia. Micsky provides tangible steps and suggestions for identifying—and addressing—the mental and physical well-being needs of those experiencing burnout, compassion fatigue, or secondary trauma. Our students and colleagues are living real lives, with real traumas and tragedies, and they share these things with us for many reasons. But most faculty are not trained therapists or mental health clinicians, and taking on these roles without the requisite training can not only be harmful to the other person but harmful to you—and perhaps even create situations of legal liability. It is so important to have compassionate boundaries and help connect people in crisis with professional resources on campus or in the community that can best help them. And connect with them so you can best help yourself.

One of the tempting options for mid-to-later career scholars is moving from faculty to administration. In "So You're Thinking about Moving into Academic Administration (aka, the Dark Side)?," Mark Boyer provides some decision-making heuristics for faculty members considering administrative positions. Graduate training does not prepare us for administrative roles; some universities provide funding for professional development and leadership training, so take advantage of these or ask for them. He suggests having close, trusted confidants with impeccable judgment and discretion that you can turn to for advice and commiseration, and cautions that your previously friendly relationships can become more distant and perhaps even adversarial as the power dynamics change in the department.

Still, faculty have no control over many things in academia, and being an administrator offers the opportunity to help shape policy, make decisions, and help students and colleagues resolve problems and overcome challenges. In her essay "From Faculty to Administrator," Shannon Blanton writes for post-tenure scholars about the benefits and trade-offs of becoming an administrator. Post-tenure faculty know the parameters, dynamics, and expectations of their jobs, including the balance between teaching, research, and service. Stepping into an administrative role can be overwhelming, and it's not uncommon for new administrators to feel out of their depth, especially if they are appointed into their role rather than through a competitive search. Administrators' curriculum vitae take a different format than do non-admin faculty's, with leadership achievements and skills foregrounded, and research downplayed. At some levels, search firms may coordinate the hiring process on behalf of the university;

one way to gain insight into this process is to serve on a hiring committee where a search firm is retained.

One of the enticing aspects of faculty life is scheduling flexibility and having control over your time commitments. As Blanton notes, in administrative roles, your calendar is controlled by others, and you lose the ability to determine your own schedule. This may be more difficult for faculty in the family formation "season of life," where illnesses or incompatible school-university calendars require juggling childcare if children are home from school when you're expected to work. There may also be few road maps or dedicated mentors to shepherd you through the process, but as Blanton notes, administrative positions can be tremendously rewarding and can have far-reaching, tangible impacts on students and faculty and the overall direction of the university.

These authors note that the challenges that some scholars face may be less visible to chairs, including those from historically excluded groups such as first-generation, BIPOC, and LGBTQIA+ scholars, and contingent "faculty on the fringes" such as adjuncts, visiting assistant professors, and instructors. They implore chairs to be accessible and provide individualized mentoring experiences for faculty—but chairs cannot do this alone. Chairs can facilitate a culture of mentorship in their departments by instituting mentorship pairs, which can benefit the mentor as well as the mentee. It can also encourage mentorship across ranks, reaching mid-career and senior scholars as well. A decentralized, paired mentorship program can empower other faculty and potentially reach even more faculty than if the chair alone is responsible for mentorship.

Takeaway Points and Best Practices

Non-Tenure Track Faculty

Unless you are 100 percent satisfied in a contingent faculty role, keep one foot in the academic job market. If you hope to have leverage to convert your position to a tenure-track line, you will likely need to have an outside option.

Apply for every bit of funding you can, whether for research, teaching, conferences, or travel. Ask for funding support from your department or college. Make friends with people in the research support office. Make the case for why you also deserve funding.

Collaborate with other colleagues. Coauthorship is one of the best ways to accomplish research projects when your primary role is in teaching, especially if you have a heavy teaching load. Choose your coauthors wisely.

Junior Tenure-Track Faculty

Cultivate a roster of mentors that can serve different roles and functions. Make sure to thank them and pay it forward when you can.

Keep a list of potential letter writers, people who are familiar with you and your work, and who you could ask for a letter of recommendation for jobs. If someone at a conference says they like your paper presentation, make a note and send them an email thanking them.

Do not take on too much service work early in your career. There are no academic emergencies that someone in your position should fix.

Turn off email push notifications on your phone.

Set clear work-life boundaries and keep track of your research productivity by using a GANTT chart or spreadsheet.

Do not take rejections personally. If the reviews are ugly, find any kernel of truth that would make the paper better, address it, fix it, and resubmit it somewhere else. Persistence is rewarded with success. Adopt the mindset of the Japanese proverb "*Nana korobi, ya oki*," which means to fall down seven times and get up eight.

There are competing perspectives on whether junior faculty should apply for external funding. One is that any funding anytime is great for your career. However, you cannot underestimate the amount of time that administrative and managerial tasks will consume. Grants also may produce delays in your publication pipeline. For example, one scholar found herself eighteen months behind on a project because of an additional layer of IRB through the granting agency. In a six-year probationary period, this can represent a significant setback.

Chairs, Deans, and Other Administrators

Protect junior faculty from excessive teaching loads that include many new course preparations and from time and labor-intensive service assignments.

Reduce the amount of paperwork when necessary. One example of this is requiring a list of references from job candidates in the initial screening process rather than a full letter of recommendation for every applicant. This saves the applicant, the letter writer, and the committee time (and paper). Only ask for letters of recommendation from candidates the hiring committee is seriously considering interviewing, provided this complies with HR and OIE regulations.

Department chairs play integral roles in supporting faculty and should provide an empathetic, supportive environment, especially during times of crisis. At the same time, chairs should take care to ensure that their support is clearly communicated, transparent, and equitably applied. Everyone should feel equally welcome and supported by their chair (or unit head).

Communicate the unspoken rules of success for tenure and promotion to all faculty, apply these metrics equitably, and make the process more transparent so that all junior faculty have the opportunity to reach them.

Literally give contingent faculty the tools to succeed. This includes office space essential for meeting with students and conducting research, access to the photocopier, and material support such as funding for conferences as available.

Create a culture of recognizing and rewarding talent and promoting from within. Do not overlook the skills and qualifications of productive NTT faculty just because they're already on the departmental payroll. NTT scholars generally take great care to demonstrate commitment to the department and the institution, and if they are doing great work, treat them as viable job candidates when tenure-track lines become available.

Support NTT faculty in seeking and applying for funding opportunities, as contingent faculty may be less obvious candidates for PI roles to research support offices. Use grant funding to support activities with multiplicative effects, such as undergraduate research that produces students with research training and capacity building and faculty with a cadre of research assistants to advance their own research projects.

Senior Faculty

You might feel a bit lost post-tenure; as it turns out, this is normal. An academic career often is compared to a marathon, but the pre-tenure probationary time is a sprint. Running the first leg of a marathon as a sprint is unsustainable.

Coauthor with junior faculty and serve as PI on grants where they are co-PI. You should take on the administrative tasks so they can focus on the research and deliverables that will get them through the tenure pipeline successfully.

All Faculty of All Types and Ranks

Take care of your mental and physical health. Be knowledgeable about—and use—the resources available to members of your academic community.

Conclusion and Transition

The chapters in this section examine the challenges and opportunities that arise in a range of faculty roles, from non-tenure track faculty to tenured senior faculty. The lessons learned from the lived experience and research the contributing authors share resonate not only with scholars in these specific roles but also with aspiring academics still in undergraduate and graduate programs who wish to begin academic chutes and ladders with a keen awareness of the profession and its hidden curriculum.

Guiding Questions

1. What motivates you to enter or stay in the academic profession? How can you focus your efforts on these core interests or motivating factors?
2. How can you link your research, teaching, and service efforts so each inspires the other?
3. If you are a contingent faculty member, is there a long-term path for you on your current campus? If not, how can you leverage teaching and research opportunities to best position yourself to continue your job search?
4. Are there aspects of academic leadership that interest you? If you are an early career scholar, how can you explore potential opportunities for leadership on your campus? If you have already earned tenure, how might you take on a leadership role in your department or elsewhere on campus?

Non-Tenure Track Faculty

11

The Perpetual Impostor

Amy Cooter

"I think that's everyone. I'll start handing out the syllabus." *Syllabus*. It was easy to decode as I sat for my first class as an undergraduate, but I had never heard that word before. Vanderbilt University, a small, private research university in Nashville, Tennessee, had been my dream university in high school. It was just over four hours from my family and had an excellent (and climbing) academic reputation with a beautiful campus that felt much more comfortable to my rural raising than any campus embedded in a cityscape.

That vocabulary lesson was among my first exposures to a new cultural framework. I was the first in my direct family to have a traditional college experience. My dad attended technical school, and though my mother obtained a degree, it was after marrying at age eighteen. She never lived on campus nor had many of the other typical college experiences, so she felt unable to help me select a college. My small-town guidance counselor was worse, telling me that Vanderbilt would never accept me despite my outstanding credentials. I was indeed accepted and received an enormous amount of need-based financial aid that, alongside some parental support and work study, allowed me to attend.

Vanderbilt was almost everything I could have asked for academically: rigorous, engaging, and flexible enough to allow me to explore a variety of subjects before choosing my majors. Socially, the environment was something for which I could have never adequately prepared. My father did not have running water in his house growing up, and although circumstances were substantially better in my childhood home, we rarely had money for anything beyond necessities. Meanwhile, some of my fellow students' parents transported their favorite horses cross-country and boarded them near campus so their children could continue equestrian lessons.

Today, more first-generation and other low-income students attend Vanderbilt than was true twenty years ago, though precise numbers are not reported. This increase has been facilitated by implementing a need-blind admissions process and a program called Opportunity Vanderbilt that is intended to fully cover demonstrated financial need without loans. Vanderbilt says this program has played a large role in its increasingly selective application process and high national ranking ("Ten Years of

Opportunity at Vanderbilt" n.d.). And yet, data the university released in 2018, the tenth year of the program, said the average family income of program recipients was "nearly $110,000," or 174 percent of the US median household income for that year ("Ten Years of Opportunity at Vanderbilt" n.d.; Rothbaum and Edwards 2019).

When I chose a top-three PhD program, there were similar contrasts between my trajectory and the more typical academic experience. But it was easier to hide behind my work even when, for example, some members of my cohort regularly relied on their parents to fly them home for impromptu mental health vacations.

The effects of Vanderbilt's economic skew came back into sharp relief when I returned as a nontenure- track (NTT) faculty member from 2013 to 2022. I continued to be acutely aware of my first-gen identity, which helped me connect with students of similar backgrounds. Many students confided in me about their struggles having to work even with a full scholarship so they could help pay bills at home, or having faculty members not provide extensions when they had to miss class to assist a family member with a medical appointment, or having challenges trying to determine their career trajectory.

But my biggest personal lessons this time concerned my NTT status. Only about 24 percent of faculty jobs nationally are tenure-track positions (Besas 2021), and yet enormous stigmas exist about those whose primary responsibility is to teach, stigmas that can alone be a "chute" to some remaining in the academy. NTT faculty are often barred from chairing undergraduate honors theses or participating on graduate student thesis committees in any capacity. The claim is often that NTT faculty are immature scholars who are insufficiently aware of ongoing research to serve in these functions. This assumption is false, but it is facilitated by how universities may discourage NTT faculty from research engagement. Vanderbilt funding for NTT research remains limited and can only be used for certain direct expenses, not for salary supplements or course releases. The 2021–2022 school year was the first year that university-level funds supported NTT faculty's conference travel, and NTT research time is more typically done on a volunteer basis, often with fully out-of-pocket expenses.

Funding is not the only barrier to NTT inclusion. My colleagues and I were repeatedly told not to discuss our research and were noticeably omitted from both official and casual faculty gatherings, replicating the sense of status-based exclusion I experienced as a first-gen student and acting as another possible "chute" for some experiencing this ostracization.

Barriers to NTT inclusion are also harmful to students who often cannot work as research assistants on unique but unfunded NTT research efforts. Students also cannot expect NTT faculty who have perpetual uncertainty about job security and a lack of resources for course building and grading to be fully invested in their classroom experiences. Many NTT faculty nonetheless prioritize their students despite these hurdles. Although national data is lacking, during unionization efforts to improve our circumstances, Vanderbilt NTT faculty discovered that a great many of us had been first-gen college students and discussed how such first-gen NTT faculty likely stay in underpaid and underappreciated positions partially because we want to be a resource for students that we ourselves needed as undergraduates.

RECOMMENDATIONS FOR READERS

Based on my experiences, here are some suggestions for what colleges and universities like Vanderbilt can do to be more inclusive and avoid some "chutes" away from academic careers. Some schools are already doing these things. Some suggestions may not apply to every circumstance while others may apply to faculty with other identities beyond first-generation or NTT status. These suggestions collectively work to decrease the social distance and manufactured power differentials between NTT and other faculty to ensure that campuses are a productive and welcoming environment. Some suggestions address the underresourcing that NTT faculty experience and that serves as an enormous barrier to novel and meaningful research.

1. Do not assume NTT equates to temporary or unengaged; do assume it means under-supported.
2. Increase salaries and stability.
3. Provide more and easily accessible funding for research.
4. Establish sabbatical semesters for NTT research or other activities after satisfactory service.
5. Include NTT faculty in active (and compensated) engagement in curriculum creation.
6. Prioritize retention of faculty who have long served the university mission instead of implementing costly initiatives to bring in newcomers ("$100 Million 'Destination Vanderbilt' Initiative Launched to Recruit Top Faculty, Address Essential Challenges" 2020).
7. Reward service in retention assessments.
8. Do not rely exclusively on student teaching evaluations that can be biased against women faculty and faculty of color (Flaherty 2021).
9. Do not rely on tenure-track faculty who may not be strong teachers to evaluate NTT teaching.
10. Support unionization efforts across the board, not only for NTT faculty but also for postdocs, grad students, and staff.

12

Overcoming the Research Funding Barrier:

Undergraduate Research as an Opportunity for Non-Tenure Track Faculty

Holley E. Hansen

Climbing the academic ladder requires research. Publications shape hiring and career advancement decisions. For contingent faculty—adjuncts, visiting professors, lecturers, or other non-tenure track (NTT) positions—producing research is key to securing a tenure-track job or continuing in long-term contingent positions.[1] Although a lack of research time is one hurdle NTT faculty must overcome in developing a strong research agenda,[2] they also face challenges in securing funding and other forms of research support.

To avoid the research "chutes" that can derail a career, all faculty benefit from greater access to research resources (e.g., course release time, research assistants, discretionary and travel funding, summer salary). Those with more resources publish more articles—a pattern that holds even when accounting for gender, race, subfield, position (full- versus part-time), or teaching load (Hesli and Lee 2011). The rise of "Open Access" journals, which can require authors to pay several thousand dollars to have their work published, further reinforces this resource-publication gap. Well-funded researchers can publish more and, therefore, receive better jobs at universities and research centers.

NTT faculty (even those in full-time, long-term positions) often face barriers in securing resources—barriers enacted by a hidden curriculum reinforcing a two-tier academic system. Internal and external funding is frequently limited to tenured or tenure-track faculty only. In fact, many notices of funding availability list "tenured or tenure-track" as an eligibility requirement for principal investigators (PIs). Due to this funding exclusion, NTT faculty have a difficult time accessing the same resources tenure-track faculty take for granted. Lack of discretionary and research assistant funding prevents faculty from carrying out resource-intensive projects. Inadequate travel funding makes it difficult to maintain coauthorship relationships, informal networks, and professionalization—all of which provide the social and mental support critical to success in the field. Finally, reinforcing the time hurdle, lack of access to sizable grants means that NTT faculty have less funding for course buyouts. The overall result is that NTT faculty are at a severe disadvantage in producing research, building professional reputations, or securing permanent/tenure-track appointments.

This systemic exclusion rests on a few outdated norms. First, "tenure or tenure-track" is seen as a proxy for "long-term employment," reflecting a belief that NTT faculty are temporary only. Because research costs (e.g., salary, equipment, facilities, and administration) vary by institution, some funding agencies prefer to support faculty who they assume are less likely to switch institutions midway through a grant rather than adjust budgets. Second is the belief that NTT faculty are an "academic underclass where one lands due to individual—rather than systemic—failure" (Windsor, Crawford, and Breuning 2021, 510).

Both these norms are outdated. In 2018, NTT faculty comprised more than 30 percent of full-time faculty at higher education institutions.[3] And this percentage has grown: more than half of these institutions have replaced tenure-track lines with contingent appointments in the past five years (Tiede 2022). Given these trends, many new academic hires will spend some time in an NTT position. The replacement of tenure-track with contingent positions also means that these lines increasingly will be long-term. As the ratio of NTT faculty grows, the current system reinforces existing patriarchal hierarchies in academia (Rennane et al. 2022) *and* undermines institutional funding, given that an increasingly smaller (and aging) pool of faculty are the only ones eligible for external grants.

However, supporting the research agenda of NTT faculty can yield several benefits to their home institutions. It improves the overall quality of instruction, as faculty who are more engaged in research are better teachers (García-Gallego et al. 2015). It promotes institutional diversity and equity by ensuring the professional development of underrepresented groups who are significantly more likely to hold NTT positions (Flaherty 2016). It also, as I argue below, offers an opportunity to improve undergraduate research.

Personal Reflection

My own transition into NTT faculty was shaped by two challenges: entering the job market during a major recession (a time of tenure-track hiring freezes) and the infamous "two-body problem." We were ultimately able to secure employment at the same institution, but like many spousal accommodations, my position was NTT. It provided stability and travel funding, but access to other research resources proved more challenging. I had been highly successful at securing research funding as a graduate student, but it quickly became apparent that my NTT status made me ineligible for many of the grants advertised in our college's funding opportunities emails. I continued to apply, though this meant coauthoring with tenure-track faculty—and always listing them as lead PI regardless of who the lead author was.

I had long valued undergraduate research, but I only began to view research mentorship as a potential ladder out of the research resource dilemma when I was approached by a student who wanted to work as a researcher—even though I did not have money to pay her. She valued the training and pointed out that our college considered unpaid research work community service. Community service, in turn, made her eligible for other awards and scholarships. Mentoring her allowed me to explore university resources intended to support undergraduate researchers—and few required tenure-track status. Working with her and other students allowed me to wrap up old projects, get them published, and start new ones coauthored with students. Further, my NTT appointment with its higher teaching load emphasizing introductory coursework meant I was ideally positioned to recruit promising new undergraduate researchers from our department.

Undergraduate research mentoring requires a considerable time commitment. NTT faculty also should avoid reinforcing existing inequalities: low-income students often must prioritize a paying job over volunteer RA work. Universities can play a major role in striking this balance. For instance, our college reallocated work-study funds toward undergraduate research assistantships, with these positions awarded based on the quality of the project and potential benefits to students rather than faculty status. Programs like this can "feed two birds with one hand" by connecting students to professional networks and giving NTT faculty the resources necessary to advance their research, ensuring that both groups continue to climb their academic or career ladders.

The Road Not Traveled

Although being an undergraduate mentor has assisted me in producing research, it also has helped me avoid one of the under-discussed challenges facing NTT faculty—the issue of social isolation. NTT faculty report significantly higher levels of job dissatisfaction compared to their tenure-track peers (Crick, Larson, and Seipel 2020); and although job insecurity, low wages, and heavy teaching loads are frequent concerns, many NTT faculty also feel excluded from the social and intellectual fabric of their departments. In fact, research suggests that issues of equity, collegiality, and a sense of belonging are perhaps the most significant predictors of job satisfaction across faculty types regardless of tenure status (Ott and Cisneros 2015). Yet the main NTT contributions that they make to their departments—such as developing new courses or advising students—often go unrecognized.

Serving as an undergraduate research mentor has helped me avoid the social isolation that many NTT faculty experience. By building strong, ongoing relationships with students beyond the classroom, I've created a sense of continuity and purpose in my teaching. My work has also led to recognition by some within my department, and I have offered advice to other faculty interested in engaging undergraduates in their own research. Working with different university programs has also allowed me to connect with colleagues across the university who are committed to advancing undergraduate research. In addition, it has allowed me to create ties to others in my broader field of research who similarly value such mentorship. This community has helped me continue up the professional ladder, even when other factors make progress difficult.

RECOMMENDATIONS FOR READERS

Best Practices for Promoting Research Collaborations:

What NTT faculty can do:

- Pursue external grants that fund undergraduate research experiences (and seldom require tenure-track PIs).
- Get to know your institution's office of sponsored programs or grants support office.

What sponsored programs and other campus offices can do:

- Engage with NTT faculty to help them become aware of and apply for these external opportunities.
- Develop or expand internal funding lines supporting undergraduate researchers.

What department and unit heads can do:

- Educate their NTT faculty about university resources that support undergraduate research mentorship.
- Build undergraduate research mentorship into the NTT faculty course load.
- Publicly recognize the value provided by NTT research mentors as they promote institutional missions and excellence in teaching/service.

13

A Placeholder for Paused Progress

The Editors

This book originally included a chapter on pathways to academic success for both civilians and service members through professional military education institutions. The authors applauded the United States Department of Defense for its promising commitments to diversity, equity, and inclusion. The contributing authors had written the draft chapter in 2024 under very different circumstances.

In late January 2025, changes in the US government, including within the Department of Defense, forced the authors to withdraw their chapter. This placeholder stands as a recognition of the stark changes occurring within the United States and the swiftness with which new chutes can open in the profession as a result of changes in national policies and practices.

14

On the Outside, Looking In: Pathways to Success for Non-Tenure Track Faculty

Karen Huxtable-Jester and Paul F. Diehl

Non-tenure track (NTT) faculty are a heterogeneous set of university faculty: adjuncts who might teach only one course, visiting and postdoctoral scholars, part-time instructors, and full-time instructors hired on a one-year or recurring basis. They are contingent employees, hired according to fluctuating institutional needs and with much lower compensation than tenure-system faculty receive. The lack of tenure or the guarantee of continuing employment is the common element. Thus, they are defined by what they *are not*. The hurdles ("chutes") they face are a combination of rules and processes hidden from NTT faculty and/or to which they are denied access (Haviland et al. 2023).

Chutes[1]

Lack of Inclusion and Communication

To administrators, and sometimes students, NTTs are largely invisible. Many have no campus office or share one, making it difficult to meet privately with students. They might have little or no exposure to colleagues, who might not even know that they teach in the same unit. NTTs might not be included in email lists or invited to faculty meetings where decisions are made that affect their positions. Their anonymity is reinforced by not being listed on the unit's web page or faculty directory. The consequences of this isolation not only impair NTT well-being and sense of belonging, but they also make NTTs less effective in their teaching.

Sustained connections with others on campus and the sense of engaging in shared practice play a critical role in professional development. NTTs risk being less informed about what is needed and why regarding many aspects of their roles. NTTs often hope to have their contingent status converted to a permanent position—a transformation that rarely comes to fruition.

Lack of Guidance and Mentoring

NTTs are rarely included in new faculty orientations. They may be hired shortly before or even after the term begins and left to figure out requirements or expectations for office hours, grade distributions, course policies, and more. Finding information on routine procedures such as how to order textbooks, use the library, or park can be difficult and time-consuming. In addition, NTTs might be unaware of expected course learning outcomes or how their course(s) fits within larger program-level objectives.

NTTs may teach for years without receiving feedback on their performance. They may regard asking for feedback as risky and shy away from bringing possible problems to the attention of those in authority. This may result in teaching that attempts to minimize student complaints rather than to maximize learning. Yet feedback is essential for improvement and arguably, for job satisfaction. When guidance is not offered, NTTs must consult with peers or administrators to seek it out.

Lack of Practical Support

Many NTTs do not get the resources they need, such as office supplies or photocopies. They may not have support staff or teaching assistants. NTTs might not have lab equipment or supplies for class demonstrations, or institution-supplied computers for instruction or preparation. These are barriers to effective instruction when NTTs are responsible for large numbers of students, all of whom need attention outside of class for advising, letters of recommendation, and more.

Lack of Respect

The relatively low pay for NTTs is symptomatic of lack of respect (Bradner 2022). Many assume that NTTs are not in tenure-track positions because of some deficiency or failure to perform adequately in research, when 50 percent of the tenure-track positions are offered to scholars from only the top ten institutions (e.g., in the field of political science). The lack of respect for NTTs is especially strong when they are paid less for equivalent work, not acknowledged in institutional policies, and have no voice in faculty governance. When faculty are evaluated using traditional, largely research-focused measures, NTTs appear to fall short. Because administrators are experienced in evaluating research but far less well-trained in assessing teaching, they may fail to recognize the outstanding teaching of faculty whose primary role is instruction. If administrators rely on student ratings of the learning experience rather than a holistic evaluation of teaching effectiveness, NTTs may be disproportionately affected by gender, race, and ethnicity bias.

Ladders[2]

Most NTT faculty cannot depend on their institutions to change the conditions that keep them marginalized. Accordingly, to counter these chutes, we present proactive strategies ("ladders") that NTT faculty can take both to mitigate the deleterious effects of how they are treated and to realize the unique strengths of NTT roles. It is difficult to combat systemic obstacles at an individual level (Cipriano and Buller 2021), but understanding the system will help NTT faculty identify or create opportunities to overcome barriers.

Information Seeking and Self-Advocacy

Self-advocacy and creating one's own professional path are strategies for accessing the necessary rules. Engaging in self-advocacy can be harmful to women as their requests are denied, and they are penalized for speaking up. Nevertheless, NTTs might find it worthwhile to request guidance from their department chair or equivalent, from experienced faculty peers, and from a center for teaching and learning unit on campus. Administrators will likely welcome requests for guidance regarding expectations, routine procedures, and better understanding of the role of their courses in the overall curriculum.

Lack of support is more likely the result of benign neglect rather than reluctance or hostility to provide it. Requests for office space (even if shared), technology tools, photocopies, and office supplies are reasonable and should be granted. An important ladder to success is to be vocal and visible while also being agreeable and accommodating. Self-advocate.

Getting Involved with the Campus Community

NTTs also can seek opportunities and experiences that shape the job to what they want it to be, in effect writing their own rules. Serving on students' undergraduate thesis and other committees, participating in shared governance (where allowed to do so), and attending departmental colloquia and other events offer ways to demonstrate commitment to the common good, time permitting. Committee service provides connections to others and a chance to prove one's value publicly. The danger, however, is exploitation, with NTTs performing unpaid labor without recognition or support. By engaging in some service, NTTs can become known, develop a reputation, and consequently have a voice in the program or even across the campus. The key is to choose roles that they find personally fulfilling and can practically manage to avoid being exploited.

Developing and Documenting Teaching Effectiveness

Another way to rewrite the rules and make others aware is to document and demonstrate evidence of teaching effectiveness. Evidence of effective teaching should go beyond student ratings of their learning experience to developing a teaching portfolio. Portfolios should include evidence of course and curriculum design and development, course materials, products of student work, and indicators of student learning. Whether requested or not, these can be provided to administrators in charge of evaluation.

Perhaps the most effective way to demonstrate teaching effectiveness and evidence of continuous improvement is to engage in the scholarship of teaching and learning (SoTL). Far from an extra burden on already busy instructors, SoTL can be integrated into the design of a course to generate evidence of which teaching strategies, assignments, or policies achieve their intended outcomes.

RECOMMENDATIONS FOR READERS

1. Provide office space and essential equipment and supplies; provide ways for NTTs to be involved in campus life and be included in shared governance.
2. Provide feedback and resources for improvement; initiate a transparent process for promotion and retention of NTTs with appropriate benchmarks.
3. Develop an inclusive climate of respect for NTTs. Provide support for NTTs to develop and document their teaching effectiveness; and provide funding for SoTL and other professional development (e.g., conference travel).

Junior Tenure Track Faculty

15

Struggling to Find Purpose in the Paperwork:

USCIS Petitions, Job Applications, and Tenure Files

Kelly Bauer

Stacks of paperwork define my journey as a junior faculty: United States Citizenship and Immigration Services (USCIS) petitions, job applications, and tenure files. Certainly, there were stacks of paperwork before, notably my fully printed out dissertation—a stressful, but personally meaningful exercise that represented a sense of hope and potential. But the excessive paperwork that continued through my personal and professional trajectory as a junior faculty member at a small liberal arts university in the Midwest represented something different: institutional standards and expectations of success that did not match my own and were not accompanied by institutional support or care. Academia frequently comments on how faculty question their purpose after tenure (aka the "post-tenure slump"), assuming that the structures, support, and metrics of the tenure-track offer junior faculty a sense of purpose and direction. But what realities do these paper trails obscure? Paperwork offers institutions a facade of certainty, documentation, and transparency but often leaves those producing that paperwork without meaningful outcomes, certainty, or purpose.

May–July 2016

I skipped my PhD graduation and first graduation in my first faculty position to get married. My husband and I scrambled to assemble a 123-page petition to adjust his immigration status in the United States, documenting evidence of our relationship—marriage certificates, utility bills, signed affidavits, medical exams, photographs, and so forth. I also compiled my second-year faculty review file, sorting through hundreds of physical pages of student evaluations in attempts to narrate my teaching effectiveness. I felt all but effective that first year on the tenure track: I made no progress on my book or other research, taught six new-to-me classes, received lukewarm student evaluations, and got stuck with too much service. From my point of view, I had more than sufficient evidence of my marriage and much less evidence of an effective first year on the tenure track.

November 2016

The immigration officer said we had not provided sufficient evidence of our relationship to substantiate our petition. Apparently, I could have put anyone on my university health and life insurance policy (although they required marriage documentation), or on car insurance, utility bills, and financial documents. Apparently, my father would say anything to support me (although his signed affidavit about our relationship was submitted under penalty of perjury). The officer left our case pending, sending us away with a formal request for more evidence of our relationship. How could they ask two PhDs for more evidence?! I canceled my afternoon research methodology class on the drive home, unable to imagine talking about evidence-based causal inference. I also couldn't help but think about how this was playing out weeks after one of the most consequential elections for US immigration policy. The next day, we sent off a 200+ page packet of every acceptable document on their Request for Evidence and an itemized cover sheet. That same semester, I served as department chair, submitted my second-year review, and sent out more job applications; our immigration paperwork eventually was approved, my second-year review was supportive, and my job applications received no responses.

October 2018

My husband's two-year green card neared its expiration date, and we sent off a new pack of more than three hundred pages of evidence. By that point, my husband had accepted a research position at a university across the country, so we included years of our twice-a-month cross-country flight records. USCIS was averaging an 18+ month processing time, meaning the only evidence we had of his legal status in the country was a piece of paper saying the petition was received and processing. I submitted more rounds of job applications with a glimmer of hope that we could end up meaningfully employed in the same city.

December 2019

We received another request for more information. What more could we possibly document? Could we highlight or underline important parts of documents? Could we send the papers in a box rather than their letter-sized return envelope? We sent another 300+ pages of information. The request was approved nearly immediately early in 2020, as was his eventual citizenship application. But this paperwork battle shook us to our personal and professional cores. We spent late nights fighting over how to format evidence and talked regularly about what to do if our petitions were denied. I sent more articles and my book manuscript, which felt meaningful and fueled optimism about job options.

October 2021

I submitted my 248-page tenure file, and the muscle memory from submitting USCIS paperwork created doubt and frustration. Certainly, I was proud of the work that my tenure file represented: thought-provoking lesson plans and classes, meaningful relationships with students and alumni, and a book based on more than ten years of work. But a lot of that tenure paperwork was evidence of pain and resentment from entirely too much work that made me feel like I was being pushed into a chute out of academia while being told I was doing great. And unlike the USCIS paperwork, I didn't have a lawyer to shepherd me through the tenure process; I was the most senior member of the department and the chair, so I tried to build my own ladder with supportive mentors in and outside my institution.

These stacks of paperwork represented the struggle and lack of fulfillment over 8+ years, attempting to play multiple games at once to generate the right paperwork for my institution, the range of institutions I was applying to, and USCIS. What was this paperwork really evidence of? How could it be sufficient for this range of purposes? It was enough for my institution and USCIS but insufficient for the more than one hundred faculty positions I applied to while on the tenure track. Life was both spinning and on hold as we waited to figure out our next steps while bound to the structure and constraints of these paperwork requirements.

How might we find purpose while wading through others' bureaucracy? The presumed meritocracy and transparency of paperwork obscures uglier processes that unevenly impact those of us navigating those processes. A gap is inevitable between institutional bureaucratic evidentiary requirements and the metrics and outcomes that are personally and professionally rewarding and meaningful; seeing, internalizing, and acting in these gaps took me too long, and many others chose more fulfilling careers elsewhere. Do tenure standards translate to career fulfillment? Do higher education institutions ask or care about career fulfillment? Hopefully, we can shift evaluation metrics and processes to align with fulfilling academic work, but in the meantime, we need to acknowledge that this facade of certainty, documentation, and transparency benefits and shields institutions while leaving those producing paperwork in the lurch.

RECOMMENDATIONS FOR READERS

1. Hiring committees should ensure that job advertisements clearly convey the desired qualifications so applicants can direct their efforts toward the jobs with the best potential fit and streamline paperwork and processes to reduce paperwork for candidates. If a committee feels that they need specialized materials (e.g., the job that asked for an annotated four-page syllabus), consider only asking a short list of candidates to submit that.
2. Faculty groups, department heads, and campus administrators should ensure that necessary elements of university bureaucracy are not burdensome. This includes

first, limiting paperwork required to, among other things, apply for promotion, propose a new class, or request conference travel funding; and second, investing in technology that facilitates rather than burdens institutional processes for, among other things, registration, advising, or promotion.

3. Evaluation processes can contribute to faculty frustration and burnout; campus decision makers should ensure that course evaluations, annual evaluations, pre-tenure evaluations, and tenure and promotion processes have clear guidelines tied to specific, meaningful objectives and work to reduce the paperwork burden on faculty navigating these.
4. Universities should train search committees to ensure that gendered assumptions about family status do not impact hiring practices and create meaningful programs and support for faculty navigating two-body problems.

16

Developing an Intentional Mentor Network

Zora M. Wolfe

To navigate a complicated, often opaque academic landscape, new tenure-track faculty must develop an intentional mentor network to reveal the chutes and ladders of academia and guide them through their transition to successful tenure and promotion. Fortunately, more and more institutions are recognizing the need for mentorship. However, even if a campus has an official mentoring system in place, the mentoring provided may not fully meet the needs of all new faculty. Therefore, new faculty should not rely merely on what is provided but, rather, intentionally be proactive and develop a network of mentors to support them in specific ways.

What Is a Mentor?

Often, when one thinks of a mentor, we envision an older, more experienced faculty member who will take us under their wing and provide sage advice to navigate the challenges and struggles of a new position, helping us avoid the chutes that could derail our career. This notion reflects a traditional understanding of the mentor as "a father figure who sponsors, guides, and develops a younger person" (Ehrich, Hansford, and Tennent 2004, 519). Although mentoring is used in many different fields, such as medicine, law, education, and business, the specific definition of a mentor can take on a number of different meanings, particularly based on the profession (Ghosh 2013). For example, within the field of education, the definition expands to the idea of a "cooperating/mentor teacher" who provides practical advice, problem-solving ideas, and moral support (e.g., for a student teacher), to one who is an educative mentor who also helps to illuminate the *how* and *why* of an educator's practice (Stanulis et al. 2019). This implies that a mentor can serve many different roles, including providing support specific to research, teaching, or service, as well as being a cheerleader or someone who can provide growth experiences and space for inquiry and reflection to propel us up the ladder.

Why Do You Need Multiple Mentors?

One person should not be tasked with fulfilling all the different roles a mentor can serve. A mentor can provide shortcuts and institutional road maps for procedural questions, from how to submit conference reimbursements to more substantive support such as making interdisciplinary introductions across campus. Particularly in the realm of academia, a new tenure-track faculty member is responsible for juggling the different streams of teaching, research, and service. Thus, finding mentors with varying areas of expertise is helpful. A faculty member who demonstrates success in the classroom can be a useful mentor in the area of teaching, offering insights into what supports and scaffolds you can provide to ensure student success. Another faculty member may provide guidance into what committees to join that would align with your interests and protect your time. All these spaces have different chutes and ladders, so having multiple mentors can provide a broader scope of how to navigate the various landscapes.

Who Can Be Your Mentor?

A mentor can be a peer or a more senior faculty member. For example, as a new faculty member trained in a practitioner-oriented EdD program, it was helpful for me to seek a mentor who could guide me through the research and publication process. I was fortunate to find someone through a writing group who was at a research university with a successful publication record to show me how this specific ladder works. This demonstrated that a mentor could be someone at a similar rank external to your institution. Although initially I sought this person as a research mentor, our relationship has grown to one where we mutually support each other in different areas through our academic journey, from submitting our tenure files, to applying for grants and navigating sabbaticals. In a way, we became mentors to each other in different aspects of our academic life. Although we often tend to seek mentors who we think we would relate to (e.g., women seeking female mentors), I would suggest broadening your circle of possible mentors, for example, by challenging the gendered mentoring trend, to gather multiple perspectives and gain different insights, to disrupt existing biases in academia (Windsor and Thies 2021).

When Do You Connect with a Mentor?

Mentorship can happen both formally and informally. Many conferences and associations have innovated formal mentorship pairing or professional development. However, developing informal relationships throughout your journey allows you multiple opportunities to reach out whenever you need extra guidance or support without necessarily formalizing the mentor-mentee relationship. Your mentoring needs—and the mentors who meet them—will change, particularly as you move through different stages of your career (pre-tenure, tenure, administration). Proactively building your mentorship network will help prepare you for career progressions, especially because the chutes and ladders may present very differently in these different stages. For me, it was especially helpful to reach out to various people as I was contemplating my next steps after tenure, to inquire into their experiences in different paths, and for them to make introductions and present new ladders and opportunities.

Where Do You Find Your Mentors?

For some people, you may have a mentor assigned to you through your university or department. Although this may be helpful in some cases, at other times the relationship is at best not a good fit, and at worst, is toxic to your career. Consequently, you need to create your own opportunities to connect with others, even if it may be beyond your comfort zone, disciplinary specialization, department, or institution. Volunteering to serve on committees (maybe as recommended by another mentor?) or attending events such as faculty talks or coffee meet-and-greets with the university board of trustees increases your visibility as well as introduces you to others beyond your department. Joining external mentoring programs and even social media networks has been useful in expanding my mentor network. For example, Facebook groups have offered opportunities such as shared syllabi resources, leading to an invite as a guest lecturer; calls for chapter manuscripts, leading to a writing circle for contributing authors; and study participant recruitments, leading to an interview that developed into a friendship around similar research interests and family dynamics.

How Do You Use Mentors?

Finally, as you develop your network of mentors, you need to use them in a manner that respects their time. Depending on your relationship with a specific mentor, you may set up regular times to meet or you may only connect on an "as needed" basis. Knowing what you seek from each mentor relationship can help you ask specific direct questions that use your mentor's resources and expertise. In addition, by asking for referrals to other people to talk to, mentors can help extend your network even further.

RECOMMENDATIONS FOR READERS

1. You need many mentors in your academic universe to help navigate the chutes and ladders.
2. Mentors can be formal or informal because chutes and ladders may also be formal or informal.

3. Mentoring needs and relationships change and evolve over time because the chutes and ladders in front of you may also change and evolve over time.
4. Broaden your idea of who can be your mentor because chutes and ladders are present in many different spaces.
5. Consider becoming a mentor to help others avoid the chutes and discover the ladders.

17

From the Top: Chairs' Role in Developing Faculty Success

Diana K. Ivy, Shane A. Gleason, and Kelly M. Miller

You finished graduate school and landed your first academic job. You cleared some major hurdles. But your development as a teacher-scholar isn't complete. Indeed, you'll never really be finished developing. Whereas faculty advisers are critical to graduate student development and success, an oft-overlooked aspect in higher education is the role of administrators and seasoned colleagues, who are pivotal to faculty development and success. This book creatively uses the metaphor of a "chute" to refer to obstacles that create setbacks for faculty or that may make them feel forced out of the profession. In contrast, "ladders" are actions, opportunities, and communication that administrators and seasoned colleagues can provide to propel teacher-scholars forward and encourage continued participation in the profession.

"Administrators" is a broad term inclusive of everyone from department chairs to assistant deans, deans, provosts, vice presidents, and even presidents. But for junior faculty in particular, the department chair is often the most consequential administrator, playing a key role in faculty development by both tailoring feedback to specific needs and creating/fostering collaborative spaces. Of course, some chairs do not accomplish these important activities. Even if a chair does act in ways to reduce obstacles and provide opportunities, it's wise to seek collaborative support and mentoring from seasoned colleagues as well.

At the most basic level, like everyone else, faculty members want to be understood. Not feeling understood by one's supervisors and colleagues contributes to burnout. Particularly since the onset of the COVID-19 pandemic, faculty burnout is rampant (Dewey, Pautz, and Diede 2024; Gewin 2021; Mahali, Sevigny, and Beshai 2024; Taylor and Frechette 2022; Xu and Wong 2023). Certainly, a critical obstacle or "chute" is burnout, meaning a shift or deterioration of motivation. Burnout is associated with the intense emotional labor that goes into the professorial role and is more likely when working with a student body that is primarily first-generation. Emotional labor can easily seep into a faculty member's research time, instructional preparation, service motivation, mental health, and work-life balance. Although burnout is a common concern, it's particularly applicable to junior and first-generation faculty, Black, Indigenous, and persons of color (BIPOC). Members of these groups disproportionately perform the emotional labor of supporting students and colleagues, but are often the least heard in faculty meetings (Berheide, Carpenter, and Cotter 2022). Moreover, they tend to be the least visible to chairs (Mena and Vaccaro 2017). Such a situation can create a negative context in which faculty members performing a lion's share of the invisible labor in the institution may be the least supported.

Within hierarchies, gatekeeping is common. When faculty cannot communicate with administrators and typically only deal with administrators' gatekeepers, such as administrative associates, the distance between the two factions increases and can lead to a chasm that erodes morale and damages the institution over time. Although it's easy to view administration as a distant, detached entity seen only a few times a year, it's important to remember that department chairs (with critical administrative roles) are the most consequential persons for junior faculty members. If chairs engage faculty as individuals, not just as items to contend with on a "to-do" list, faculty will be more motivated in their work, and burnout may be thwarted or at least slowed. Powerful contributions or "ladders" chairs can offer are to see faculty as individuals, help foster collaborative relationships, work to address specific challenges, and support faculty as they develop.

Although typically chairs evaluate faculty on a set of standardized metrics such as student evaluations, publication impact factors, and number of committee assignments (perhaps at the behest of upper administration), effective chairs go beyond a "one-size-fits-all" approach toward a holistic view of fostering faculty success. Chairs should tailor their mentoring to meet each faculty member's situation. To this end, assessment and mentoring should take the form of an open door and unstructured conversations. Chairs should take the time to get to know faculty and their concerns *prior* to a major personnel decision. What's of no matter to one faculty member may be of great consequence to the next. Based on their concerns, chairs should route faculty to resources that will be most beneficial for them. For instance, a junior faculty member struggling with teaching controversial topics might be referred to a more seasoned colleague, perhaps in a related field, for mentoring.

Seasoned colleagues and chairs alike can offer unstructured conversation and tailored advice, but chairs can play a unique role in creating collaborative environments in which all faculty members—especially junior, first-generation, and BIPOC—have a seat at the table and feel involved in charting a course for the institution's future. This can include everything from faculty brown bag sessions to professional development opportunities. Creating this environment also leads to increased informal collaboration. For example, a collegial department culture may give junior faculty space to process the challenges of the tenure track with contemporaries. Such a culture may also create an environment in which informal chats turn into mentorships and possibly friendships. Strategies a chair exerts can build a sense of culture and belonging between faculty and the institution.

Thus far, our advice assumes chairs will see faculty as individuals and will actively strive to create and foster collaborative spaces. This represents an ideal climate that, sadly, is not present in all departments. Department culture may wax and wane over time, particularly as academia changes rapidly, and student needs evolve constantly. In these instances, it's incumbent on faculty members to advocate for themselves. They should seek "ladders" with regard for mentors with whom they "click," as well as spaces in which they can feel seen and heard by colleagues. Such spaces may cross disciplinary and departmental boundaries. This can be done in many ways. Attend mixers, be friendly with your colleagues (a simple "hello" walking down the hallway), and initiate or invite conversation. More important, don't be afraid to ask for advice from seasoned faculty. In some instances, these connections evolve naturally into mentorship relationships. Mentoring comes in many forms; some connections remain strictly professional whereas others are coupled with friendship. Even if you have a supportive chair who follows our advice, multiple mentors is a key ingredient for success. Of course, building mentorship networks is easier said than done, especially for junior, first-generation, and BIPOC faculty who are particularly prone to being "invisible" in academia.

Although taking time for tailored mentoring and seeking mentors is often difficult with packed schedules, demands from the community and officials, student issues, and campus emergencies, working collaboratively keeps chairs and faculty alike academically sharp and enhances empathy toward faculty members. The "hidden curriculum"—the unwritten rules or norms that develop at an institution—can be unearthed and challenged by faculty members and administrators alike, working together for the common good, providing more "ladders" than "chutes." It's particularly incumbent on department chairs to view faculty as individuals and to create collaborative spaces, and for faculty to avail themselves of these opportunities and efforts.

RECOMMENDATIONS FOR READERS

1. Successful chairs make frequent and consistent efforts to get to know their faculty individually, to the extent that each faculty member is comfortable.
2. Wise chairs become aware of the "chutes" in their departments and institutions, making an honest inventory of those structures and practices that may represent obstacles to faculty development, success, and persistence.
3. Effective chairs and other administrators develop communication strategies for addressing the "chutes" and creating the "ladders" to faculty success.
4. Faculty should seek a community within the institution, being open to looking beyond disciplinary or departmental boundaries. Mentoring can happen in unexpected places. Activities that develop community and foster a sense of belonging should be encouraged and supported by chairs.
5. Although an individual approach to mentoring from chairs and seasoned faculty colleagues may take longer in the short run, it will pay long-term dividends for the institution as a whole and faculty members as individuals.

Tenure and Promotion

18

The Chutes and Ladders of Service at a Small Liberal Arts College

Patrick Homan

In the game of Chutes and Ladders, the chute is not a trap per se—as you can see it coming. So, in this sense, what I am calling a "service trap" fits more into the *hidden* curriculum of higher education as an unwritten dynamic or obstacle that might hinder faculty success. Following in the footsteps of previous work on imbalances in academia (e.g., Crawford and Windsor 2021), the term service trap is something I developed in an effort to describe a phenomenon I have observed over my years of experience at a small liberal arts college (SLAC). I believe that a service trap is particularly troublesome at SLACs because of their increased emphasis on internal service compared to other institution types (Tierney and Bensimon 1996; Porter 2007). The size of SLACs not only provides greater expectations and more opportunities for faculty service, but these institutions are dependent on faculty engagement across all aspects on campus (Baker, Lunsford, and Pifer 2017), possibly to survive, and thus are more likely to employ an "all hands on deck" mentality. Consequently, faculty feel obligated to step forward in a range of service areas outside the normal expectations (Jafar, Feldman, and Chrisler 2017), leading to "uncounted time."

A service trap is a paradox, in that faculty efforts to get more involved service-wise can prove detrimental to their teaching and research (Hughes 2014). In the end, the situation that the faculty find themselves in, overwhelmed and overstretched, hinders instead of helps them on the path to earning tenure (or being put on the tenure track) and promotion. Some of this can be attributed to the fact that, frequently, service roles at SLACs can be incredibly time-intensive or snowball beyond what was originally expected. For example, leading the model United Nations team or a study abroad trip, both of which I love to do, are substantial investments of time with recruiting, fund-raising, and meetings outside normal class times. This has led many in higher education today to urge faculty to "say no" to new projects (e.g., Rockquemore 2010)—a challenge for early career academics who need to fill out their CVs. In this vein, the examples and descriptions below are to help serve as a warning so faculty are not caught unaware in the future and can avoid the pitfalls of a service trap, a specific type of chute that many of us could face.

At my university, a faculty member can provide service in three general areas—the department level, the college and/or school, and university-wide. For example, my current department only has two full-time faculty; therefore, the responsibilities that my colleague and I have are unique compared to a larger department with more faculty and resources. This increased burden of various service tasks, such as advising and mentoring (although enjoyable), can have an adverse effect on faculty as they try to keep the department afloat. For instance, taking a course release to focus on research could be difficult for a full-time faculty member in a small department. Personally, I had reservations about taking parental leave because I was worried about the impact it would have on my department and students. When departments are small, the role of chair can also be thrust upon junior faculty due to a lack of other options—not to mention other department roles such as internship coordinator, club adviser, or independent research mentor. With survival on the line, many small departments have no choice but to rely increasingly on their junior faculty for service, and these commitments come at an opportunity cost for those still trying to find their footing in the classroom and with their research agenda. And with a loose footing underneath us, we are much more likely to slide down a chute or experience setbacks both professionally and personally.

My university recently realigned its academic units, and with this has come its own new layer of service expectations or opportunities. Not only does my college have its own regular meetings but also its own committees. Moreover, our resulting faculty governance structure asks that faculty represent their college on the Faculty Senate. In fact, I served on our Faculty Senate for three years while still untenured and often found myself worrying about how my votes might lead me down a chute, such as impacting my future tenure application. Faculty responsibilities at the college level also include serving as the director of a school (a subunit of our colleges) or overseeing interdisciplinary majors or minors. As our new colleges have gotten off the ground, numerous faculty (even untenured ones) have taken on administrative roles, many times on an interim basis, due to leadership turnover. Consequently, the blurring of the line between faculty and administrator has been a challenge for issues of faculty governance as well as tenure and promotion files. For example, if someone is teaching less because they have had to fill the role of an administrator, what does that mean for them as they go up for tenure at a teaching-focused institution? Thus, these demands within the college have created not just more service but also sticky situations or more chutes on our path toward faculty success.

Lastly, the university as a whole can offer a wide range of opportunities that might sink a faculty member into a service trap. For instance, my university is increasingly tuition-dependent; therefore, faculty have been asked to do much more to help directly recruit students such as create new programs or "prioritize"—an incredibly burdensome task that involves reimagining our curriculum (Dutt-Ballerstadt 2019). Other university-wide initiatives, such as work on diversity, equity, and inclusion (DEI), can be incredibly demanding sources of extra service for faculty despite their worthiness. Moreover, DEI work (as well as service in general) can often fall on the shoulders of underrepresented faculty, especially women (Mayo 2023), who already face barriers to tenure and promotion outside these types of service traps (Hanasono et al. 2018). With demographic trends shrinking university enrollments, faculty at SLACs often feel obligated to step up and help meet the pressures of today's competitive higher education environment, but this only contributes to the juggling of increased responsibilities that faculty face—not to mention the chutes we must jump over while carrying these undue burdens.

Service is not inherently a negative experience, as it can come with important opportunities for growth and learning for junior faculty. At the same time, the service trap does not take hold in some "aha moment" like Admiral Ackbar realized in *Return of the Jedi*; instead, it consumes a faculty member more like a frog in boiling water. Therefore, I would offer the following advice for faculty at SLACs. First, while saying no to more service is a good motto, it does not work for everyone. So, I would urge faculty to be more organized or intentional with their time commitments. Find strategic service opportunities that overlap with your research or teaching so as not to create new learning curves. Second, reach out to others for help or guidance and develop a support system that might be able to tell you when you are overwhelmed. Talk with your dean or senior faculty on campus about service requirements so it is clear how your institution counts service—some are more inclusive than others. Connect and lean on faculty at other institutions through your professional associations and networks. For example, the International Studies Association just created a new "Teaching Centric Institutions Caucus" where resources might be helpful. Lastly, do not be afraid to give yourself a break for a while and regroup. We are all juggling many things, and doing "more with less" is never a bad idea; it can help us see more clearly where the chutes and ladders lay ahead.

RECOMMENDATIONS FOR READERS

1. Take on specific service roles that provide ladders or opportunities for your professional growth and learning.
2. Be mindful of the "service trap" and its related chutes—keep track of how much you are already doing and be intentional with your time.
3. Cultivate a supportive network of colleagues that can help you navigate both the chutes and ladders.

19

Doing Away with "The Way We Do Things around Here":

Clarity and Equity in Tenure and Promotion

Rashna Wadia Richards

In an incisive preface to her edited collection on the tenure review experiences of minoritized faculty, Patricia A. Matthew recalls her own battle at Montclair State University. Matthew had the support of her department committee, the department chair, an interim dean, and external reviewers, but her provost recommended against tenure because her scholarly outputs were not yet in print. In all the reviews leading up to that one, she had never been informed that forthcoming publications might be deemed insufficient. Though her appeal was successful, her case highlights the need to "unpack the unwritten codes that underscore various personnel processes (formal and informal) that make it difficult for faculty of color to succeed" (Matthew 2016, xv). These unwritten codes form the hidden curriculum of faculty review processes, and this chapter offers recommendations for making reviews more transparent and thereby more equitable.

Tenure and promotion processes are supposed to be firmly guided by the faculty handbook, which outlines key elements such as requirements and submission guidelines. Institutions devote plenty of space to describing expectations of excellence, typically in the areas of teaching, scholarship, and service. Still, junior faculty like Matthew regularly run up against unwritten rules of the game. Within the context of corporate cultures, Marvin Bower called such taken-for-granted aspects of an institution "the way we do things around here" (Deal and Kennedy 1982, 60). This is a useful way of thinking about higher education, which also relies on expectations that remain embedded yet unspoken within institutional cultures. Unspoken rules are generally conveyed informally, as when senior faculty with institutional memory guide junior faculty unofficially. Such a tacit culture is especially damaging for women and historically marginalized faculty, who may not have access to informal mentoring networks. These unspoken rules, often deployed capriciously, are among the many chutes that disrupt and sometimes destroy academic careers. To counter this inequity within the review process, this chapter recommends three specific interventions—

structural, strategic, and cultural—with examples of how specific institutions have implemented changes to make tenure and promotion procedures more equitable.

Structural interventions emphasize clarifying policies governing advancement processes. Most tenure and promotion guidelines rely on notions of excellence in teaching, scholarship, and service. But excellence is not an objective term of evaluation, as it is "more subject to cultural forces than many in the academy will allow" (Matthew 2016, 9). It is no wonder then that so many junior faculty members, especially those who aren't brought in on "the way we do things around here," receive conflicting messages or hazy tenure and promotion criteria. Therefore, institutions must clarify what excellence means and how it will be evaluated. Purdue University's Office of Faculty Affairs offers a comprehensive overview of criteria and procedures for tenure and promotion. In addition, it outlines the responsibilities of all individuals involved in the review process, from the candidate to the review committees to the provost to the president. Kenyon College's handbook defines precisely what is meant by "teaching excellence," "scholarly engagement," and "collegiate citizenship." Kenyon outlines what faculty are expected to achieve and what is considered essential in each area. This level of detail makes review processes more transparent, and it compels an institution to clearly label what it values and rewards.

Clarity on policies is only a first step in getting around old ways of handling tenure and promotion. Structural interventions should be coupled with strategic reorientations in thinking about equity. For if equity is a strategic priority, then it should be embedded within review guidelines. At Bowdoin College, faculty voted to add "demonstrate inclusive excellence in teaching" to their expectations for teaching excellence in their Faculty Handbook in 2021. The University of Oregon requires candidates for tenure and promotion to include their contributions to campus-wide equity and inclusion in their personal statements for review. Their division of equity and inclusion also provides support for faculty preparing these statements as well as guidelines for committees reviewing these statements. But a recent AAUP survey of tenure practices found that only 21.5 percent of institutions had specific DEI criteria (Tiede 2022). What we need is an intentional effort to make all faculty members accountable for advancing equity.

Structural and strategic interventions can be enhanced by cultural shifts that require evaluators to be personally accountable for equitable reviews. Some institutions, for instance, offer implicit bias training to faculty serving on tenure and promotion committees. Such training can include an awareness of personal biases or an understanding of data on bias in student and peer evaluations. According to the AAUP survey, 40 percent of institutions have provided some form of training in the past five years (Tiede 2022). East Carolina University provides virtual training that "gives participants the opportunity to explore their personal biases and how they may affect their participation in reappointment, promotion, and tenure decisions." Montana State University did a randomized controlled experiment by offering "bias-literacy training to randomly selected departmental RPT committees" in 2017. Their research found that "committee members who received bias-literacy training reported a significantly more supportive committee atmosphere," with each trained member "personally spending a significantly longer time reviewing each dossier" and "their committee as a whole spen[ding] somewhat longer deliberating each candidate" (Smith et al. 2018). Implicit bias training should also be required for department or division chairs as well as senior faculty who review dossiers, observe teaching, or write letters of support for tenure and promotion candidates.

The tradition of tenure originates in AAUP's 1915 declaration of principles. Tenure was conceived as "the assurance of an honorable and secure position," awarded to "men of high gift and character" by, one can safely assume, other men who were already regarded as possessing "high gift and character" (Joughin 1967). It has since been reimagined to recognize distinction in teaching, research, and service for all tenure-track faculty. But we must ensure that such distinction is recognized and rewarded equitably, that candidates don't run up against unspoken rules of the evaluation game, and that tenure comes to signify what an institution truly values.

RECOMMENDATIONS FOR READERS

1. Ensure that there is no ambiguity in faculty reviews. Deans or provosts in faculty affairs should regularly offer workshops and discussion forums for candidates to ask questions and seek clarity about expectations. The absence of clarity creates chutes that keep faculty from achieving tenure and promotion.
2. Make invisible labor visible. Faculty should be acknowledged and rewarded for their contributions to diversity, equity, and inclusion, and review policies should clearly indicate how DEI work counts in faculty reviews. If DEI work is seen as an opportunity or ladder to propel teacher-scholars forward, then more folks would see the value in dedicating themselves to it.
3. Require antibias training for all evaluators. All senior faculty, chairs, deans, and tenure and promotion committee members should complete training on a regular basis, and each review committee should have a designated diversity officer who can focus on hidden biases in review decisions.

Service, Teaching, and Research

20

Tackling the Role of Department Chair while Living with an Invisible Chronic Illness

Gretchen Peterson

"You can change that doctor's appointment; that is the best time for everyone to meet."

I recall being told this as a relatively new associate professor while serving on a personnel committee. The idea that my doctor's appointment would be a reason for us not to hold a meeting at a time that was convenient for others was being called into question. The message was quite clear: my need for health care should take a backseat to the needs of others when scheduling a meeting. After all, I did not look sick. What my colleague did not know was that I suffered from a chronic illness, ulcerative colitis, that required regular doctor's appointments that had to be booked well in advance.

Every academic who suffers from an invisible chronic illness has likely faced this same pressure as they navigated their career. Chronic illness is one of the chutes that can cause setbacks in academic careers. Colleagues question the severity of an academic's invisible illness and dismiss the toll that illness takes on trying to achieve the productivity expected for advancement. The idea of taking on a significant service role with administrative responsibilities while trying to manage a chronic illness can be overwhelming. But that is precisely what I did beginning in 2013. I served as department chair for three years at my first institution and was then hired by my current university to serve as department chair; I held that job for eight years.

My goal in writing this piece is to explore the aspects of the hidden curriculum that I had to uncover that ultimately allowed me to be successful as a department chair, all while initially managing a chronic illness, later falling severely ill, then having gastrointestinal surgery, and now being considered a person with a disability. The theory underpinning my approach to being a department chair is Erving Goffman's (1959) dramaturgical approach, which argues that individuals are actors performing their roles according to the definition of the situation. Although role performances require the cooperation of others, individuals have flexibility in negotiating how they define the situation and enact the role of department chair. Thus, individuals have some flexibility that allows them to take advantage of the ladders that can promote career success.

Hidden Curriculum Lesson #1: Rely on Your Colleagues to Get the Work of the Department Done.

Although some tasks as department chair must be handled by the chair, other tasks do not always have to fall on the chair. Part of managing the administrative workload while managing a chronic illness means relying on others in your department to help get things done. I learned this lesson the hard way when I was so sick that I simply was not able to handle everything, but I have since found the value of relying on my colleagues. Colleagues provided support by covering my in-person classes when I was hospitalized or just too ill to make it to campus. This type of support from colleagues is an important ladder contributing to success. People feel more invested in the department and its initiatives when offered the opportunity to help, which allows you to take advantage of everyone's talents. Department chairs often find they can count on certain people to take on additional tasks. The problem that arises is that it is easy to continue to call on the same people to complete extra tasks resulting in workload imbalances among faculty and potentially shutting some faculty out of opportunities to develop a service profile that could ultimately lead them into administration. When you make a more concerted effort to ask for volunteers, you allow all faculty to gain experience in different areas. I have often been surprised by some of the tasks people will volunteer for, such as attending outreach events early on weekend mornings. In another example, the entire department contributed to writing our most recent program review after volunteering for working groups for each of the report sections. Tapping into the expertise and interests of everyone in the department makes a chair more effective in their role. Faculty can cultivate these types of relationships with colleagues by providing assistance when needed.

Hidden Curriculum Lesson #2: Use Options for Remote Work When Possible.

In the spring of 2018, I found my illness escalating, and I ended up hospitalized three times in just a couple of months. I had only been at the University of Memphis for a couple of years, so did not have enough sick leave banked to cover taking time off from work completely, which meant that I had to continue working as much as possible while ill. I was fortunate to have colleagues who assisted with my teaching because I could not be physically present in the classroom. I was able to stay in touch by email and phone and manage my duties as a department chair working remotely as often as possible. As my illness continued to escalate, I transitioned to teaching exclusively online to accommodate unpredictable flare-ups.

As I was preparing for major gastrointestinal surgery in summer 2020, I was faced with the decision to take leave (which would have caused financial strain for my family) or resume chair duties during my recovery. Ultimately, financial need pushed me to work as chair during my recovery. In some respects, I was lucky that I had this option. The ongoing pandemic meant that all the meetings that previously would have required my attendance in person were now being hosted virtually, so I did not need to be physically present at the university. In Peterson (2022), I used autoethnography to illustrate how the pandemic improved accessibility for people with chronic illnesses by moving to virtual attendance.

One lesson learned from the pandemic is that being physically present in an office is not necessary to be productive and effective. In the immediate aftermath of the pandemic, I had hoped that universities would take the lessons learned and continue to provide options for virtual attendance. Such options would benefit not only people with chronic illnesses but also people with care responsibilities. However, we have seen universities pushing for return to in-person work. Despite this push toward being physically present, it is still possible to create a schedule that allows for considerable remote work as a chair. So much of our contact has shifted to email that department chairs can perform their roles without always being physically present in a space and can mold this administrative role to suit their needs. Flexible work arrangements with options to work remotely can serve as a ladder supporting success.

Hidden Curriculum Lesson #3: Create Your Own Vision for What It Means to Be a Successful Department Chair.

As a newer faculty member, I believed that the department chair had to be in the office all the time to be ready to take action. That is precisely the model that I witnessed during my early career. Although we may tend to model our work as department chair after what we have known, chairs can modify the culture of what it means to be a chair in a particular department. We do not have to do things that same way as a previous chair did them.

Make the role your own. To do this successfully, you need to get direction from your supervisor about their expectations for successful department chairs. Once you know the expectations of higher administrators, you then can focus on how to enact the role in a way that meets those expectations and allows you to take care of yourself and your chronic illness. Making the role of department chair your own allows you to better take advantage of the ladders that support success and avoid the chutes that can derail success.

The main message should be that the role of the department chair can be molded to suit the needs of faculty managing chronic illnesses. Returning to Goffman's (1959) metaphor equating daily interactions to theatrical performances, the role of department chair can be managed as a performance and constructed in a way that allows faculty managing chronic illness to be successful in service roles with administrative responsibility.

The Road Not Traveled

When I first took on the role of department chair, I attended a workshop designed to prepare a group of new chairs for our new roles. One piece of advice that I still remember from that workshop was that most of what we deal with as chairs are not emergencies. The point was that we need to take time for ourselves and that immediate action is rarely required.

That advice truly shaped my performance in my role as chair. Over my eleven years of service as chair, I encountered very few actual emergencies. By not pushing myself to act immediately when it was not truly needed, I was able to maintain better work-life balance. This balance was critical to being able to manage my chronic illness for many years while serving as a department chair. Finding balance can provide a ladder promoting success, whereas a lack of balance can become a chute that derails our success.

RECOMMENDATIONS FOR READERS

1. Rely on your colleagues to get the work of the department done. Cultivate ongoing relationships of mutual support with colleagues.
2. Use options for remote work when possible. Clarify expectations from your supervisor regarding your presence in the office.
3. Create your own vision for what it means to be a successful department chair. Perform the role in a way that best suits your leadership style and allows you to be successful.

21

Musical Chairs:

Service, the Curse of Competence, and Delayed Promotion

Carrie Liu Currier

Musical chairs is a game where there is always one fewer chair than players. As music plays, individuals round a circle of empty chairs until the music stops, and players compete for an available seat. In each round, the winners are those seated, and the losers are eliminated from the competition. The goal is to stay in the game by continuing to have a seat in the circle. If we consider service roles as a game of musical chairs, where the chairs represent service positions that need to be filled, the winners are not those seated. Contrary to the goal in the childhood game (occupying the last remaining seat), in academia, the goal is to get eliminated early. An early exit from the service game allows more time to focus on individual pursuits, such as publishing, and can put one on a faster track to the ultimate academic goal of promotion to full professor. In each case the reward of time goes to those who do not take a seat in the service circle. Although many of us have focused on service as an important way to shape our departments, our institutions, and the academy at large, being successful in that game comes at a cost, which is delayed promotion.

At first glance, service appears to be part of an academic ladder that encourages continuation in the profession, by asking talented and competent faculty members to invest their time in their institution or discipline. However, in reality, service is an academic chute that creates a host of setbacks to scholars who invest too heavily in this area. This chapter focuses on the relationship between service and promotion and addresses three challenges I have experienced as a first-generation Asian-American woman attempting to ascend the academic ladder: the inability to say "no" to service involving underrepresented groups; the increasing service demands placed on women of color in general; and that service for women and other historically excluded groups essentially holds minimal value in university tenure and promotion structures. The solutions to these problems are not simple, but we can be more creative in finding ways our institutions can reimagine service as a path to promotion rather than an obstacle, which can have the added benefit of enhancing diversity, equity, and inclusion (DEI). If

DEI is to address some of the pitfalls that keep underrepresented groups from obtaining the same achievements as their peers, and to enhance the recruitment, retention, and promotion of women and minorities, then serious changes need to occur regarding how we assess the overburden of service on these scholars.

Studies have shown that women of color feel tokenized, isolated, and experience self-doubt, which can lead to racial battle fatigue, lower workplace satisfaction, and retention problems (Hsieh and Nguyen 2020; Ponjuan et al. 2011; Smith 2014). However, service is one area where underrepresented scholars can feel a sense of belonging in the academy, and especially in service related to DEI. *Nobody questions whether we are qualified to discuss how our identity is relevant to the task at hand.* Service also has a more immediate impact and acceptance compared to teaching and research. The satisfaction we receive from service differs from our majority colleagues, who are less likely to feel the need to change their institutions or the academy to "fit in" and be seen. Women already experience service at rates 1.5 times higher than men, where they are asked more often to serve and are less likely to decline (Cardel et al. 2020; Guarino and Borden 2017). Because service is seen as more than just part of our job and taps into our sense of identity, we cannot readily say "no" to these activities: we know that absent our presence, our interests will likely not be represented. Essentially, the identity component makes service one of the *most*, not least, important elements of our jobs for many women and faculty of color.

The second service-related challenge is that DEI efforts in the academy disproportionately tap women and faculty of color for all kinds of service to diversify committee composition, creating a new demand on our time (Currier 2022; Valverde and Dariotis 2019). Most institutions of higher education lack diversity among the faculty, where research has shown that 88 percent of US colleges and universities and 99 percent of R1 institutions have populations less diverse than the overall population (Ellsworth et al. 2022). This means that a small number of individuals are serving in more roles campus-wide, *increasing* the service burden on women and faculty of color rather than decreasing it. *For women of color, this demand is even higher because committee composition can be diversified in two ways with a single member.* The supply is simply not great enough to meet this new demand. Meanwhile, some of our "majority" colleagues too quickly absolve themselves of DEI-related service by claiming they do not meet the identity criteria and are unsuited to serve or are already overrepresented.

Finally, the time devoted to service has a direct impact on the time one can commit to the most important factor in most university calculations for promotion to full professor: *research*. The problem is not just that service takes time away from research but that the reward for service well done is an *increase* in service work, which compounds the impact. Meanwhile, those that do service poorly are often absolved of further responsibilities or are no longer asked for committees (they are eliminated from the musical chairs game). Even taking on prestigious service roles, as I have, by serving as department chair and on high-profile committees in my discipline, is not treated with the same relevance as producing just one publication.

The solution to these problems is quite simple: service needs to be reweighted and reevaluated in the academy as a route to obtain promotion, rather than an obstacle.

Without changes, women and faculty of color will continue to lag behind their peers in both rank and salary, which have lifetime implications on earnings and can lead to withdrawal from the academy. Institutions must recognize the disproportionate impact of service on underrepresented groups and understand that saying "no" because you don't want to do something is a privilege reserved for those in majority groups. Ensuring that for scholars service functions as an academic ladder, rather than a chute, is an important step to improving academia.

RECOMMENDATIONS FOR READERS

1. Hire more historically excluded scholars.
2. Re-weight and reevaluate the role of service in tenure and promotion to make service part of the academic ladder.
3. Give double credit to scholars serving in service roles with intersectional identities (women and scholars of color).
4. Give greater value to service on DEI committees to encourage majority faculty to share in that service load and to highlight its importance.
5. Hold deadweight faculty accountable for exiting the musical chairs of service early by penalizing those with low/poor service or assigning them to committees.
6. Implement implicit bias training for tenure and promotion committees.

22

Who's Going to Teach It?

Equitable Distribution of Course Development Demands

Tara Parsons

In my ten years as faculty, I have prepared my own versions of four existing courses and added two new courses to our major's offerings. In that same ten-year span, a colleague from graduate school has prepared twenty-nine different courses. In our profession, one's teaching load can be "ladder" that supports a successful academic career or "chute" that overwhelms potential and stagnates careers. A multitude of factors contribute to the asymmetric teaching burden between my colleague and me, and her identity as a woman is one of them. In this chapter, I highlight the role of new course preparation in program maintenance, review the research into the service obligations of marginalized faculty, reflect on the consequences of inequitable course preparation demands, and provide recommendations to address this problem.

Most universities organize their academic side into colleges and academic units or departments that host major and minor programs each with their own course catalog. Each unit must offer the programs' required courses with enough seats and frequency that all students who need a course have access. Most departments also provide courses to a general education curriculum. The logistics of meeting these obligations are difficult. Faculty are asked to teach multiple courses and larger courses while also providing flexible schedules and various modalities.

Designing and implementing a new course might be the most time-consuming responsibility of instructional faculty. The tasks of organizing a syllabus, curating readings, developing and administering assessment materials, maintaining a learning management system, and writing and delivering a semester's worth of lectures are labor intensive and inflexible. The first day of class arrives, whether or not you are ready. Failure to perform these student-centered activities results in unfavorable performance reviews and possible termination of your position.

It is understood that the burden for meeting these obligations is higher in smaller departments at primarily undergraduate institutions. You do more with less. New course design is also front-loaded in an academic career. You must *build* a course portfolio before you can *maintain* a course portfolio. But who steps up to teach the required courses when needed? Who teaches the introductory courses to lower division students with higher care needs and less academic socialization? Who teaches the less popular but essential courses? Who teaches the courses far from their research interests but core to their discipline?

The dynamics that push women and marginalized faculty into more service obligations are replicated here. Women perform more internal service, which is undervalued and often uncompensated (Guarino and Borden 2017). Hirshfield and Joseph (2012) use the term "identity taxation" to capture the labor costs demanded from faculty of historically marginalized social identities above and beyond their nonmarginalized colleagues. Historically marginalized faculty are expected to represent their identities across campus, resulting in greater service burdens while also navigating stereotypes and the resulting expectations. They are asked to *teach* colleagues about systemic injustice, which shifts the labor burden away from those responsible (Rideau 2021). If there are unmet curriculum needs, historically marginalized faculty often provide those courses due to the same pressures that raise their service burden. This was particularly true as universities increased DEI in their course catalogs.

The consequences of inequitable course preparation demands for women and marginalized faculty are significant. The less-than-stellar student evaluations from my first semester teaching (while wrapping up my dissertation work) worried me. My academic unit head waved off my concerns and advised that it takes at least three iterations of a course before it finds its groove. He was right. Faculty with numerous new course preparations miss the opportunity to reflect and revise. They are also unable to document teaching improvement data across time. Junior faculty need the opportunity to teach multiple iterations of a course before going up for tenure.

Students provide harsher teaching evaluations in courses they feel forced to take (Miles and House 2015; Uttl, White, and Morin 2013). Biases against women and marginalized faculty in teaching evaluations are well-documented (Heffernan 2022). When general education and required major courses are a greater share of one's teaching portfolio, we see historically marginalized faculty punished twice by students. These courses often fall outside faculty research interests. As a teacher, it can be difficult to exude passion and confidence on a topic outside my academic comfort zone. This, too, is reflected in student evaluations, especially for young faculty, women, and faculty of color when compared to the automatic authority granted to those who "look the part" of professor.

RECOMMENDATIONS FOR READERS

The academy must actively seek solutions, or "ladders," that address workload inequities if we wish to recruit and retain diverse faculty. Below, I provide a nonexhaustive list of recommendations concerning course portfolio building and equitable distribution of course offering demands. The responsibility for creating "ladders" should not rest on those at-risk, but I identify some proactive advice for both individual faculty members and academic units.

For Faculty Members:

- *Identify an anchor course*: Ask at interviews what course(s) you will be expected to teach every semester or year. Be clear that you expect to have 1–2 courses in your portfolio that repeat often.
- *Build a course portfolio*: Develop 5–7 courses that you regularly cycle. Remember, students graduate, and new students arrive, so demand for these courses will be stable.
- *Encourage a culture of sharing course materials*: Some of the burden of a new course preparation can be lessened if faculty share materials with one another. My department curated a shell LMS site for our required introductory course featuring video lectures, content pages, reading materials, and assessment tools. Faculty changes left the course with too few instructors to meet demand. Our hope is that the shared resources lower the preparation costs and incentivize faculty into joining the introductory course rotation so the burdens around this essential need are dispersed.

For Academic Units:

- *Identify priority courses. Ensure that every faculty member contributes*: Courses that are required of all majors (introductory, methods, theory, senior capstone) or contribute to the general education program should take priority in course selection. Review and ensure that every faculty member is contributing to these essential courses.
- *Maintain an updated course catalog*: Faculty, disciplines, and campus priorities change. Just because a course was once offered does not mean it must always be offered. When students see courses on the catalog, they expect to be able to take them. This builds pressure for faculty to meet the course catalog rather than their own expertise or the unit's core needs.
- *Give credit for invisible labor of care*: Much of the obligation of caring for students and meeting departmental needs falls on women and marginalized faculty (Reid 2021). We must find ways to recognize and reward this invisible labor in reviews. Codify internal service into your evaluation benchmarks. Provide space to document invisible labor. Decenter student evaluations in performance reviews.

Senior Faculty

23

Burnout, Compassion Fatigue, and Secondary Trauma:

Self-Care in Higher Education

Tami Micsky

Higher education faculty and staff are under increased pressure to fulfill a variety of roles and demands. Some roles may be stressful but are expected: instructor, facilitator, colleague, researcher, and tenure and promotion candidate. When working with students, some roles may be unexpected, including that of supporter, mentor, or counselor. These unique demands continue to evolve and were amplified during the COVID-19 pandemic, which increased stress and loss experiences and mental health challenges. According to data collected by Mental Health America, more than half a million people reported having signs of depression and/or anxiety between January and September of 2020, with screenings for anxiety and depression up 634 percent and 873 percent, respectively (2021). The increased incidence of anxiety and depression adds to the student-related challenges faced by faculty who must balance personal responsibilities, including relationships, parenting, and caregiving; professional responsibilities; and organizational and societal challenges. These multifaceted intersecting pressures can lead to common obstacles or "academic chutes" that create setbacks and ultimately, could force some out of higher education including burnout, compassion fatigue, or secondary trauma.

Burnout

Preceding the significant stressors and losses experienced as a result of the COVID-19 pandemic, research on occupational stress among academics indicated that stress is alarmingly widespread and on the rise (Levecque et al. 2017, 868). A 2020 *Chronicle of Higher Education* survey found that higher education faculty from tenured professors to adjuncts indicated that workloads were higher, morale was lower, and work-life balance was almost nonexistent. According to a 2020 Course Hero survey, a majority of college faculty reported signs of professional burnout with 40 percent considering leaving their current jobs (2020). More than half of faculty reported a significant increase in emotional drain (53 percent) and work-related stress or frustration (52 percent) (Course Hero, 2020). Job burnout is a special type of job stress—a state of physical, emotional, or mental exhaustion combined with doubts about competence and the value of one's work (Mayo Clinic). The experience of burnout is closely related to job role factors including overload and conflicts in the workplace. The World Health Organization (WHO) includes "burnout" in the International Classification of Diseases (ICD) as a syndrome that results from

> chronic workplace stress that has not been successfully managed. It is characterized by three dimensions: 1) feelings of energy depletion or exhaustion; 2) increased mental distance from one's job, or feelings of negativism or cynicism related to one's job; and 3) reduced professional efficacy. Burnout refers specifically to phenomena in the occupational context and should not be applied to describe experiences in other areas of life.
>
> (World Health Organization, 2019)

Those at increased risk for burnout include new, young, female employees, individuals who function as caregivers outside the workplace, individuals who feel isolated or lack support, and those with blurred personal boundaries or "overinvolvement" with individuals they serve (Simionato and Simpson 2018, 1431). Organizational risk factors include high workload demands, lack of control, poor reward structure, decreased sense of community, the perception of unfair and inequitable decisions, and the misalignment of personal and professional values and organizational values (Gabriel and Aguinis 2022, 183–90).

Compassion Fatigue and Secondary Traumatic Stress

Higher education faculty are often faced with student-related issues including mental illness, suicide, sexual assault, and personal and academic problems. The act of listening to stories and supporting students may result in an emotional toll that compromises professional performance and personal well-being. Compassion fatigue, a label proposed by Figley (1995, 2) emphasizes the "emotional residue" of the cumulative effect of caring and exposure to individuals or events that involve challenges and suffering.

Secondary traumatic stress is "the natural consequent behaviors and emotions that often result from knowing about a traumatizing event experienced by another and the stress resulting from helping, or wanting to help, a traumatized or suffering person. Its symptoms can mimic those of posttraumatic stress disorder" (OVC, n.d.). Typically, one does not associate secondary traumatic stress with the role of higher education faculty. However, anyone who works with individuals who have experienced trauma and is in a position to hear or read the stories of those experiences is at risk for secondary traumatic stress. With the increase in mental illness, suicide, significant losses during the pandemic, and trauma history, it is likely that higher education faculty could encounter a student experiencing trauma. A primary risk factor for developing secondary traumatic stress is a personal history of trauma. Signs of secondary traumatic stress are variable but cluster in three core areas: intrusion (unexpected thoughts about traumatic situations, dreams, flashbacks), avoidance (detachment, emotional numbing, low activity), and arousal (irritability, difficulty concentrating, hypervigilance) (OVC, n.d.). Individuals who are experiencing signs of compassion fatigue or secondary traumatic stress are likely to struggle with work performance, professional satisfaction, and personal wellness.

RECOMMENDATIONS FOR READERS

Organizational Change: A multilevel approach to preventing and intervening with burnout, compassion fatigue, and secondary traumatic stress that involves individual, administrative, and organizational evaluation and change would provide optimal results and create "academic ladders" to encourage persistence in the profession. Administrators can assess organizational factors that may increase the risk of faculty experiencing these challenges. Improvements can be implemented through policy change, schedule flexibility, education, mentoring, and support for self-care and wellness activities for faculty.

Individual Assessment and Planning: For individual higher education faculty, assessment is the first step toward preventing or intervening when these challenges surface. Higher education faculty can use assessment tools and wellness planning to create personal "academic ladders" for personal and professional wellness. Many tools for evaluating professional challenges and self-care practices are available online. Three examples are:

1. The Maslach Burnout Inventory (1997, 191–218) can be found online and purchased through the Maslach Burnout Toolkit.
2. The Professional Quality of Life (proQOL) measure is intended for any helper, including educators, and provides an assessment of one's level of compassion satisfaction (the pleasure derived from being able to do one's job well and the belief that one's work contributes to the organization and community), burnout, and secondary traumatic stress, which are combined into one measure of compassion fatigue.
3. Self-care assessment and planning worksheets are widely available online and provide a means to evaluate physical, emotional, cognitive, social, and spiritual wellness practices. A simple yet effective template for creating wellness goals is Maslow's Hierarchy of Needs (see Figure 23.1). The foundation consists of physiological needs, followed in turn by safety needs, belonging and relationship needs, esteem and emotional needs, and self-actualization needs (Maslow 1943). Each step in the hierarchy can guide the creation of a measurable goal for each pillar of wellness.

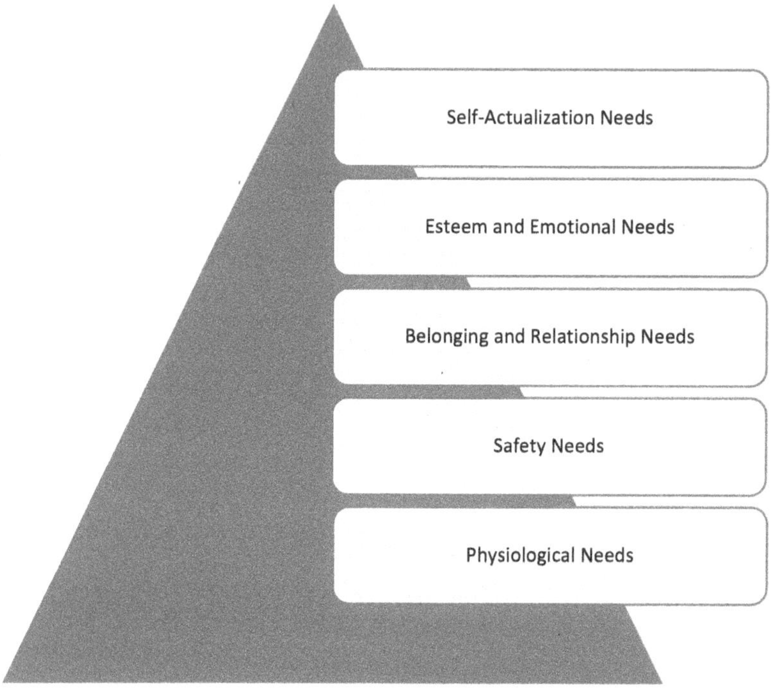

Figure 23.1 Maslow's Hierarchy of Needs. Source: Tami Micsky, based on Maslow 1943.

Compassion Satisfaction and Resilience: Faculty can examine and focus on satisfaction and resilience. To increase self-awareness, identify resources and opportunities as "academic ladders," and reflect on professional satisfaction, one can consider the following questions.

- Why did you choose your profession?
- What opportunities and resources do you have in your position or profession?
- What courses, research, students, and so forth do you find interesting and look forward to working with?
- What specific experiences with students make you feel rewarded or satisfied with your work?
- What connections with colleagues or the community make you feel rewarded or satisfied with your work (affinity group, faculty learning community, community of practice, volunteer work)?
- How do you benefit from the work you do with your students and college?

Although higher education faculty can recognize the stresses and risks inherent in the work, it is important to strive to recognize and embrace the rewards. Focusing on and building connections with colleagues can help prevent burnout and compassion fatigue. "Humans thrive in collaborative communities, where they feel a sense of belonging and meaningful contribution to shared goals and values" (Pope-Ruark 2022, 138). With proper recognition, prevention, intervention, and support from colleagues and personal relationships, faculty can avoid the "academic chutes" identified as burnout, compassion fatigue, and secondary traumatic stress and remain resilient educators who are satisfied remaining in the world of higher education.

24

So, You're Thinking about Moving into Academic Administration (aka the Dark Side)?

Mark A. Boyer

Very few academics start their careers planning to be academic administrators. Perhaps even more importantly, whether you are becoming a department head, moving into some role in the dean's office, or taking on another more specific role (e.g., leading a teaching and learning center), you most likely were provided little training during your graduate careers, and even during your earlier career path, to help you cope with the challenges that you will face in academic administration. And although both teaching and administration require a great deal of creative problem solving, they require different skill sets. And unless you are proactive, this part of the hidden curriculum will remain hidden to you.

Please note that much of what follows may sound scary and begs the question, "Why would I want to do this?" The answer that I have after twenty years in some form of administrative work is that as an administrator, you can facilitate success for your colleagues and your college or university in ways that an individual faculty member cannot. That facilitation work is quite gratifying, even if with a different reward system than you were socialized to value as regular faculty. And you can also help expose the hidden curriculum, especially to junior colleagues, in the process.

You Need Some Training

There are ways to receive various forms of training as you move into administration. Some provide formal training; some less so, but the informal is probably more important. The bottom line is to seek out—and accept—as much training as you can get.

You should work to build a network among other administrators. Finding a mentor/confidant is important for you to mine their experiences on the job, but it will also likely be important for your mental health. Being able to vent to someone or just get a gut check will be incredibly valuable as you cope with the stressors of the job. In my case, a friend, who became a department head several years before me in a very challenging department, took me on as her mentee and provided me with insights regularly about how to handle difficulties. Whether your person is internal to your university or college or someone in your field, the experience and interaction can prove invaluable.

The last point about administrative education is that you should ask lots of questions. When in doubt, ask someone who knows about things that you are working on. You may feel like you are annoying those to whom you are posing your questions. But in my experience, your superiors will be very thankful that you asked questions and didn't screw up something that they later had to clean up or that caused problems for the college or university. Err on the side of being annoying; people will thank you later.

Balancing Interpersonal Interactions

Finding the right balance between being an authority figure and having good relationships with faculty and staff is important. But it's not always easy to find the right balance. Showing some of your personal quirks and interests (e.g., music, sports, pets, etc.) helps humanize you to others and makes them realize that you may be as peculiar as they are. That helps others empathize with you, too, and to realize that you are not as cold and calculating as some of your decisions may imply. That said, you must also be comfortable with the reality that you have become the designated decision maker on many things, and you will need to tell people "no" more often than you might like.

All that said, you will almost certainly need to grapple emotionally with losing friends during your time in administration. Frankly, if you lost those "friends" while you were department head (or whatever role), they probably weren't very good friends to begin with. Your good friends will stick with you, even when you disagree on policy, approach, and more. It's also helpful to remember the quote generally attributed to Harry Truman: "if you want a friend in this life, get a dog." I have two sleeping right behind me as I write this essay.

When confronting problems, you will likely need to talk things over occasionally in a confidential setting with people under your charge or a mentor. But be very careful when you do this. Do it only with your closest staff, whom you trust completely, and a select number of faculty, whom you also trust. Otherwise, the rumor mill will be the death of you. The rumor mill will be bad enough on its own, so try your best not to feed it. This applies even when others are actively spreading rumors and disinformation. In the short run, it will be difficult and stressful. But in the longer run, being as careful as possible with your confidences (and what you put in writing to anyone) will make your longer-run life easier.

Lastly, purchase professional liability insurance. It is inexpensive for the volume of coverage you can receive and will give you some peace of mind along the way; you might need it at some point. Although it doesn't happen often, almost every administrator I know has been involved in some form of legal action during their administrative career. In most cases, AAUP or other professional organizations can point you in the right direction for a liability carrier.

(Good) Process Is Good

Good process is your friend. This pertains to everything from scheduling classes to following the stated and approved promotion and tenure process to the letter of those documents through unit-level procedures such as institutionalizing consultation in an elected advisory committee. It also means doing your best to be as transparent as you can be. You should note, though, that there are and should be limits to transparency in virtually every professional setting. That's even true in public universities with freedom of information statutes framing access to information and documents. Hence, making sure that promotion and tenure decisions stay within the bounds of confidential discussions is important. So are human resource decisions, even when people are asking lots of questions about the decisions made. At some point as an administrator, you will likely have to terminate someone's employment. And in almost all circumstances, you can't talk about the "why" involved, even though the rumor mill will run rampant.

Particularly in contractual contexts (and probably dealing with most HR issues), you should also find out the places where you have some discretion. There may not be much, but there are places where you may be able to accomplish something good. For instance, during my time as department head, the stated university policy on faculty parental leave post-birth was six weeks, and then a faculty member was supposed to return to the classroom. In this area, I found that I had a bit of discretion. To me, it made neither personal nor curricular sense to require a new parent whose child was born, for example, on September 15 in the US academic cycle to return to the classroom on November 1. Rather, I decided that such a person wouldn't be required to teach that entire semester, and no one questioned it as long as I had the resources to fill that classroom instructor role. In my mind, this discretionary decision was the right thing to do, and it also bought me some goodwill with the parents in question. It became the new standard in the department.

Get to know people in your compliance office, your diversity and equity office and others in places where you will need to interact. Cultivating these relationships informally, aside from the formal reporting aspects imposed on you, is well worth your time. During my time in administration, I could call someone and have a confidential, informal, and sometimes (sort of) hypothetical conversation, which would help me navigate a challenging situation before I (or someone under my charge) messed up something.

As with compliance, if you encounter problems with faculty or staff, it is well worth consulting your labor relations department (usually attorneys) as early in the "troubles" as possible. Particularly for those of us early in our time as administrators, the instinct often is to assume that productivity problems will improve with the right tutelage. But kicking the HR can down the road only delays working with the experts about this stuff and may make the problem bigger as time goes on. Most often, a problematic staff member in the midst of a group of competent staff will be poisonous for overall morale and productivity.

Underlying all these administrative challenges is the imperative for good recordkeeping. In our electronic world, it's pretty easy to do this with email archives. But there are a few rules to follow:

1. **Only put in an email what you would want someone to reread later.** If a dispute brews, your emails (and their tone) may become part of a formal record. The corollary here is that using the phone or in-person meetings is a valuable way to "avoid" a written record when that is a preferable alternative. Be careful hitting "reply-all"; watch for when an email to you is a bcc: versus an open cc:. Watching such detail can save you down the road.
2. **The more documentation, the better.** You may be surprised how often a single brief email will come back to be your friend. In one instance, my email archive saved my department $25,000 that had been committed to support our undergraduate program that another unit head had forgotten about committing.
3. **After a challenging interpersonal interaction, send an email to yourself documenting it.** I received this gem from the executive director of the faculty union when I took over as department head. By getting a date and time stamp from your professional account as soon after an "issue" as possible, you can't be accused of re-creating things later. Priceless.

Also priceless are the staff members you will work with in any setting. They usually are underappreciated. But in our increasingly technocratic world, **staff members are the most important people for your success**. Hence, making sure they feel comfortable working **with** (not for) you will help you immensely.

Why Would I Do This to Myself?

The not-so-simple answer to this question is that working in academic administration can be extraordinarily gratifying. It allows you to facilitate work that needs to be done by both faculty and staff. It allows you to set parts of the agenda for your unit and help faculty see and understand the broader forces at work inside and outside your institutions. This latter issue is something that our colleagues have difficulty grasping in their mostly closed research and teaching loops. Your efforts won't always be successful, but most of your colleagues will eventually get it.

RECOMMENDATIONS FOR READERS

Here are a few more brief, practical tips for managing difficult situations in an administrative role:

1. Position a clock on the wall behind where a visitor to your office usually sits. This way, you can keep track of time without having to look at your watch or your computer.

2. When needed, have your administrative assistant "interrupt" a difficult meeting with an urgent issue that has "just arisen."
3. Schedule difficult meetings with a defined time frame. One natural way to do this is to schedule a difficult meeting to end just before another meeting for which you can't be late.
4. In your most difficult interpersonal situations, ask an observer to attend. Sometimes this may not be possible (it might escalate an already tense situation), and in those cases, try to leave your door open and ask someone to sit nearby to listen.

No matter how much you prepare and how much you structure your workplace and professional life, surprises and crises will occur. The ones that happen recurrently (e.g., not enough seats in undergraduate classes) will become easier to manage with experience. But many will depend on your ability to keep your cool, to follow (good) process, and to get answers to important questions. But you must be willing to take care of the crisis in its own time frame.

In sum, academic administration will never be normal or easy, because so many of our colleagues have "narrow" life skills (sorry, but it's true, at least in my experience). That doesn't bode well for our colleagues' ability to operate within academic society (or the rest of society for that matter). But administration is indeed rewarding and can be successfully managed.

25

From Faculty to Administrator

Shannon Lindsey Blanton

As senior scholars, some people continue to focus primarily on research, teaching, and service as expected of faculty at their university. Others, however, move into roles where administrative responsibilities become their primary focus. If you are interested in the latter, one facet of the hidden curriculum is "how" you go about becoming an administrator.

Where Is the Ladder?

Some academic programs translate well into administrative positions. My background in political science and public administration has helped me in analyzing policy problems, understanding actors' decision-making, and strategic planning. Of course, by the time most faculty begin to seriously think about moving into administrative roles, their degrees have long been achieved.

One thing you can do as faculty is volunteer for service assignments that will give you the chance to develop knowledge, skills, and experience that could later make you a more qualified candidate for an administrative job. These stepping-stone leadership roles might include serving on search committees, a curriculum committee, or as director of your department's undergraduate or graduate program. By being engaged and conscientious with your service roles, you can develop a reputation as someone who is dependable and effective. You might also attend administrative conferences and workshops where you can further build your skill set, network with other faculty-administrators, and enhance your ability to "move to the next level." Hence, a key aspect of the hidden curriculum is to develop your skills and experience in areas that are relevant for administrative jobs that you might like to hold. But what then? How do you land an administrative job?

Sometimes, formal entry into an administrative position occurs in an unanticipated manner and amounts to some extent to being perceived by others as someone who has the competencies needed for the job at hand and then climbing up that ladder when you find it in front of you—even if it does not fit perfectly into your plan. That was my case when I was asked by my dean to take on the responsibilities of interim department chair. Was it part of my plan? Definitely not; I was a newly tenured associate professor and mother to young children. But I viewed it as an important service, and the experience I gained during that year and the satisfaction of others with my job performance launched me into an administrative career path that has progressed to this day. So, a lesson in the hidden curriculum is to take advantage of unexpected chances for administration when they arise, as they may turn out to be ladders that lead to further opportunities down the road.

You may have heard of instances where faculty are appointed to administrative positions within their university in the absence of a competitive selection process. Though they may have a strong record of qualifications and performance, this can lead to the perception that other qualified people are not given a fair opportunity for the same career advancement. Typically, however, searches for senior administrative positions are conducted in a formal and official manner.

Universities commonly post advertisements in outlets such as *The Chronicle of Higher Education* or *Inside Higher Ed.* Universities might also work with executive search firms to help recruit applicants for positions that are difficult to fill or highly specialized. Often, prospective candidates are contacted first by the search firm, which identifies and solicits applications from individuals who are likely a good match for the requirements of the position. Individuals may also contact them directly to express interest. Their goal is to create a strong pool of qualified prospective candidates so the university can complete a successful hire.

If you advance in the search, there typically is a conversation with the search firm, an initial interview with the search committee, and then an on-campus interview with a broader constituency for the position. In making the case for your strengths for an administrative position, it is different from a faculty search because your research and teaching accomplishments are just part of your candidacy. You need to be certain to highlight your administrative accomplishments and skills up front—initiatives you have led, outcomes you have achieved, how effective you are working with and leading other people, handling challenging situations, and so forth.

Avoid Falling down the Chutes

Almost any decision you make about your career has trade-offs. Administrative positions can give you an opportunity to make policy, shape the direction of your unit, bring about change, work with faculty and staff across the university, and have a real-world impact on the lives of students, fellow employees, and your community. As an opportunity for career advancement, there are typically financial benefits for moving into administrative leadership positions, and despite what some may think, administrative leadership involves a skill set that not everyone possesses, so you can make an important contribution to higher education.

However, it is important to realize at the outset that the "hidden curriculum" in transitioning from faculty to administrator entails change and challenge. You almost certainly will have less time to engage in teaching, research, and scholarly activity, and you will need to balance your scholarly goals as an individual against your responsibilities to others. You also will have less control and flexibility with your time, must be "on" for any urgent matters that fall under your purview, and attend considerably more meetings. If urgent matters arise, such as a student or employee crisis or a pressing request for administrative reporting, you may have to set aside other things that you had planned to do on that day. In my current position as an academic dean, I work twelve months of the year, am on campus almost all day every weekday, attend events some evenings and weekends, and formally take vacation time when I want to be "off." This is a substantial change from being a faculty member where autonomy and flexibility are highly valued, and it is a transition for you to consider.

You should also anticipate that your relationship with colleagues may change if you are in a position of authority over them. It is often quipped that faculty who become administrators "go over to the dark side," but you may find that some of your colleagues have a dark side. It requires principled discipline, wisdom, and even courage to negatively assess your colleagues, make decisions that they may view unfavorably, or be on the receiving end of angry or undeserved comments or actions. There is no easy way to manage such pressures, but it is important to keep in mind the responsibilities of your administrative position and your commitment to do a good job.

You should think about possible implications for your remaining goals as faculty. In general, I recommend earning the faculty rank of full professor prior to taking on heavy administrative responsibilities. There are so many demands on your time, attention, and energy, with added stress. It is challenging under such circumstances to remain productive in your own research and scholarship, plus there can be awkward situations if you are of less academic rank than colleagues whom you supervise.

Location may also be a consideration. Internal searches that allow you to move into an administrative position at your current university have the value of changing your job but enabling you to keep many things about your personal life intact. However, if you relocate for a position, you might need to sell and buy a home, secure a new job for a spouse/partner, move your children to a new school, and make new friends, as well as evaluate possible implications for retirement savings.

You might also give some thought to how to achieve work-life balance when in an administrative position, particularly considering the likelihood of reduced flexibility in the job. When I moved into administration as a mother of young children, I found some approaches that worked for my family. For instance, we habitually used our weekends for quality family time as well as chores and getting ready for the next week and anticipated that the weekdays would be highly focused on work and school. I also was very realistic about what extra commitments I could make during the work week. For example, I frequently contributed snacks to school events but did not volunteer to be the classroom head parent.

Navigating Your Path

It can be a huge transition to move into an administrative position, but it can also be very exciting. You will likely encounter "forks" in your path where the decisions you make will have a lasting consequence for your career and personal life. For me, I occasionally wonder "what if" I had focused more on research and less on administration? How would things be different today? "What if" I had relegated research and teaching to my past and focused exclusively on administration instead of juggling all three? Would I have less stress? Would I hold a different position today? Although I am satisfied with my choices and pleased with their outcomes, it is important to realize that you will face choices with consequences, and I encourage you to think about your long-term goals and priorities in life. With insights into this hidden curriculum, I hope you can make more informed decisions about how to find the ladders, achieve your goals, and avoid tumbling down any chutes along your path.

RECOMMENDATIONS FOR READERS

1. Seek and volunteer for administrative or leadership responsibilities.
2. Develop your skills and experience in areas that are relevant for positions you might like to hold.
3. Review advertisements for administrative jobs.
4. Make a list of pros and cons for the position and how you personally weigh them.

Section Three

Historically Excluded Groups

International Scholars, LGBTQIA+ and BIPOC Scholars, First-gen Scholars

The Why

Racial inequality, and identity bias more generally, has resurfaced as a politically salient issue since the unrest in Ferguson, Missouri, in 2014 and the death of George Floyd in 2020. The theme Black Lives Matter was met with All Lives Matter—a response seeking acknowledgment that life is hard for white-identifying people also. The All Lives Matter campaign misses the point, however: it's not that life isn't hard for white-identifying people; it's that skin color—or having lighter pigmented skin—isn't a factor making things harder. We write this chapter with full acknowledgment of our privilege as white, Western-educated scholars, and with deference and respect for our colleagues from historically excluded and underrepresented identities and groups who have faced invisible and unspeakable struggles that we have not had to confront in our lives and careers. This is not to say that we have not encountered bias and challenges for other reasons or had an easy path to this point in our careers—that's not the point. Our goal for this section is to highlight how individual and group identity-based features amplify the challenges posed by the hidden curriculum. We want to elevate the experiences of more vulnerable people in higher education such as international, BIPOC, LGBTQIA+, and first-generation scholars. In this section, the contributing authors write about their experiences so that colleagues with decision-making power, such as admissions committees, chairs, and deans, will be more aware of the challenges that scholars who identify with these groups face in their academic careers.

Being a member of one of these groups is enough to increase the potential struggles that scholars face. Being a member of more than one of these groups presents more complexity, and the effect is not cumulative but, rather, multiplicative. Having multiple identities is known as intersectionality. Individuals can hold many identities at the same time: Black *and* female; queer *and* international; first-generation *and* Indigenous. Intersectionality diverges from a binary categorization of identities where the reference point is cis-gender (your gender expression matches your sex assignment at birth) white women and men. Legal scholar Kimberle Crenshaw's path-defining work "Demarginalizing the intersection of race and sex: A black feminist critique of antidiscrimination doctrine, feminist theory and antiracist politics" identifies how the public policy space has binned identity-based issues into separate categories, such as "the women's experience" or "the Black experience" (Crenshaw 1989, 140).

In a legalistic sense, Crenshaw writes that individuals with overlapping protected classes, such as race or ethnicity and gender or sex, have faced uphill battles for remedy in courts. This is, in part, due to the complexity of accounting for multiple reference points beyond Black/white or male/female, and the lack of attention to and description of the specific challenges that individuals with intersectional identities face. In her words, "the failure to embrace the complexities of compoundedness is not simply a matter of political will but is also due to the influence of a way of thinking about discrimination which structures politics so that struggles are categorized as singular issues" (Crenshaw 1989, 166–7). In other words, we think of people as either this *or* that, not this *and* that.

This overly simplistic way of understanding human experience can be seen in the language used to describe efforts at diversifying the academy, such as the emphasis on "women in STEM." The reference category for this is, of course, men in STEM—with the implicit assumption that the men are cis-gender and white. An emphasis on encouraging women to specialize in STEM fields through targeted recruitment, mentoring, and financial support obscures the many different types of women who exist in academia, such as women of color, nonbinary women, and first-generation women scholars. It also assumes that a one-size-fits-all approach to diversifying the academy—by focusing on a singular attribute—will serve as a panacea and address all the concerns facing historically excluded scholars without surveying or accounting for the different ways that the hidden curriculum manifests across different and intersecting identities.

Let's imagine, for example, someone with two intersecting identities. What elements of the hidden curriculum might this person face in their studies or career? What chutes might ensnare them? What ladders might elevate them? What about someone with three intersecting identities from historically excluded categories—are multiple intersecting identities cumulative or multiplicative? In an earlier chapter in section two, Zora Wolfe writes about strategies to cultivate an intentional mentorship network and suggests that scholars may need more than one mentor for different aspects of the career path. This approach may also ring true for intersectional identities, where one mentor may help with the hidden curriculum—pointing out the chutes and showing the ladders—related to one aspect of someone's identity, such as being a first-generation scholar; and another mentor may help reveal the rules of the game pertinent to another identity, such as being a breastfeeding mother heading for a job interview.

To make this more concrete, consider the intersectional challenges in the following example. In *The PhD Parenthood Trap*, Sahar Shafqat writes about her journey to adopt a child as a queer woman from Pakistan with a wife from India (Crawford and Windsor 2021). Her family faced numerous obstacles in adopting their child as a same-sex couple in the United States. Adoption laws in Pakistan (Shafqat's home country) became more restrictive during this process, and India (her wife's home country) did not permit same-sex adoption. Ultimately, after many failed adoption attempts—including ones that came painfully close to fruition—the couple opted to pursue a biological family. The story ends well, but we can't forget the opportunity cost of years of doing research into the requirements for adoption in three different countries, the legal acrobatics those efforts required, and the emotional and psychological toll this took on the couple.

Scholars with intersectional identities may require many different mentors to meet their unique academic needs, answer their questions, and advocate for them in various ways. A diverse suite of mentors also offers different and complementary perspectives. One scholar mentioned asking several women whether she should take her baby to a job interview: one said absolutely not; one said it would be fine; another said definitely yes. (She ended up taking the baby.)

Finding these mentors may be more difficult than it seems. Representation matters; as the saying goes, *you can't be what you can't see.* Many scholars are the first person with the unique set of identities admitted or hired into the department. Visible allies and mentors may not be readily evident; this is not to say that scholars require a mentor with their exact set of attributes to provide effective mentorship, but if few or no colleagues look like you, it may be harder to identify allies or mentors who can support you in the identity-specific ways you need. This is perhaps why Zora Wolfe's suggestions are so important: you should cultivate many mentors to support you in the different ways that scholars need.

In reality, we likely need many mentors for different reasons—not only because people offer different skill sets, but also because burnout is real, and faculty from historically excluded groups often carry a disproportionate mentorship burden. Many departments and units still lack meaningful and substantive diversity—not only in terms of identities but also theoretical and methodological perspectives—and faculty from historically excluded backgrounds may be asked to perform additional service duties so that committees have "diversity" among their members, in addition to serving as a mentor and confidant. A committee may seek to have more representation from underrepresented minorities, such as women or people of color. If a woman of color is asked to participate on the committee, her presence may be perceived as representative of all women and all people of color as if either of these categories is homogeneous. Departments, committees, and universities may take advantage of people with intersectional identities because their intersectionality provides built-in diversity on multiple dimensions in one single member.

This is, of course, profoundly unfair to that individual. One person cannot speak on behalf of an entire population. One person does not represent the diversity within one population. One person's presence does not absolve the organization from continuing to recruit and support individuals from historically excluded backgrounds. And from the individual perspective, one person may be asked to speak authoritatively on behalf of each of their intersectional identities—for example, as a woman and as a person of color. One person may help the department or committee "achieve" the perception of diversity, and that one person may have to play many roles in that one service assignment.

Most importantly: that one person only gets credit for being one person—not the multiplicative credit they should get—for representing the various identities they assume in that service role. And if the department or organization particularly lacks diversity, the individual with intersectional identities may be recruited for many service assignments—a burden that scholars from "historically included" backgrounds are immune to. The multidimensional scholar faces implicit pressure to do an exceptional job in all their service roles and to be an exemplary representative of the many identities they represent.

The hidden curriculum of intersectional identities also implies that readily available or accessible resources may not be available to improve resilience. Many universities are turning to international student recruitment to preempt forecasted negative financial consequences resulting from the "enrollment cliff"—a reference to an impending demographic trend that will slow the pipeline of students from high school into college. International students targeted for admission to US universities likely have embedded intersectional identities, including minority backgrounds, lack of proficiency in written English, variation in academic standards and practices, and cultural knowledge gaps. Universities will need to be very intentional in their support for welcoming increasing numbers of international students onto US campuses, especially in providing wraparound services and acculturation.

Some scholars may choose to moderate certain aspects of identities, such as their gender identity, to mitigate negative career consequences (Bilimoria and Stewart 2009). First-generation scholars may struggle and mask in many of the same ways; first-gen students and faculty expend time and energy trying to learn the rules of the game while trying to appear as though they do understand them—or at least not betray that they don't. Although programs, interventions, and increased self-efficacy improve outcomes for first-generation scholars (Garriott et al. 2015), they may have additional economic, linguistic, or legal barriers such as their documentation status that complicate accessing resources designed to help them (Patler 2018).

These masking strategies are not without consequences, including the exhaustion of hypervigilance. Fake it until you make it is not intended to be a long-term strategy. From a cognitive and physiological perspective, living and working in a state of heightened awareness is mentally and physically taxing, including overall decreases in mental and emotional well-being and decline in physical health that can lead to burnout (Gewin 2021; Nagoski and Nagoski 2019). It is exhausting—and inefficient—to not know the rules of the game, especially when many of the rules are unwritten or exist as implicit norms.

It is dehumanizing—and unsustainable—not to live in your own skin and your own truth, to contort yourself to fit within the historical standard of the face of academia. Other identity characteristics are impossible to hide, such as race or ethnicity. In the classroom, international teaching assistants (ITAs) are often penalized for their accents in the student evaluation of teaching effectiveness surveys. Despite widespread evidence of implicit bias in these surveys against historically excluded and underrepresented scholars (Chisadza, Nicholls, and Yitbarek 2019; Gelber et al. 2022; Mitchell and Martin 2018; Peterson et al. 2019), they are still used in performance evaluations that determine outcomes such as tenure and promotion, and merit pay.

Identities, Intersectionality, and the Hidden Curriculum

International Scholars

Some of the biggest challenges involve the most mundane and quotidian activities, such as finding suitable housing, acclimating to new currency, getting used to American food, or getting to and from campus via public transportation. Other challenges are much bigger. Scholars from outside the United States also face the devaluation of their experiences and degrees attained at non-US institutions, as Claudio Villalobos Dintrans writes in "Implicit and Explicit Bias and the 'Rising Star' Culture." Skills and degrees do not always transfer equitably across borders, in part due to insufficient information about the curriculum and standards of compatibility for training and testing in other countries. This means that students and faculty often shed some or all their domestically acquired qualifications and certifications when they apply for school or work in the United States—as well as the pride in their achievements and the successful academic identity they shed in the process.

The audience for Villalobos's chapter is primarily international graduate students, but he also calls for changes in how university offices for graduate students provide their services. He identifies the "rising star" culture as an elitist phenomenon that preferences only certain scholars from within certain elite institutions within the United States. Elitism is endemic in academia—in some fields, 50 percent of the jobs go to people from the ten top-ranked programs. The "rising stars" tend to be those with specific academic pedigrees—whether or not their skills, aptitude, and potential are truly superior to the pool of other qualified applicants.

International students are often overlooked because they lack the institutional name recognition, they are not fluent in the US academic culture, and they may have to take a nonlinear academic path to meet the financial or educational requirements for their program, such as passing entrance or language exams. To be clear, almost everyone outside those at elite institutions is necessarily at a disadvantage on the job market because of the social capital and connections they afford. In this scenario, what international students need may not be mentorship but *sponsorship*—having a senior colleague open certain doors through active intervention: coauthoring a conference presentation or manuscript for journal submission; including the international student on grant applications (where appropriate); or leveraging personal connections and expending social capital on behalf of the student.

Lillie Padilla also offers insight into the experiences of African students in US academic institutions in her chapter, "The Academic and Social Challenges African International Students Face in the United States." Writing for US-based faculty and African students in US institutions, she describes some of the cultural knowledge gaps and gaps in wraparound services that affect students' lives. Culture in institutions of higher education in Africa tends to be more hierarchical, and students tend to be more deferential to their professors than in the United States, where students and faculty often have a more casual and informal relationship.

Part of the hidden curriculum for international students studying in the United States is having health insurance, which may be required as a condition of their enrollment in their program of study. The United States does not have universal health care, and international students may underestimate the cost of health-care coverage under normal (nonemergency) circumstances, such as preventive care, incidental illnesses, or minor injuries. Although some form of health insurance is now mandatory at some universities, many graduate students have opted to get the bare minimum coverage or decline coverage at all—at times with devastating consequences. Although life-changing or life-threatening accidents or diagnoses may be rare, they do happen, and the cost of health care without insurance coverage for anyone—let alone an international student unaccustomed to dealing with contemporary American health care—can mean crippling debt.

Navigating the American healthcare landscape is inherently difficult and opaque—few of the regulations or norms are intuitive. There may be special linguistic or cultural factors to consider for faculty or students from outside the United States as well, as one colleague learned when she went from being an adviser and member of an international graduate student's dissertation committee in the morning to being a birth doula and coach when her advisee had her first child that evening. Her graduate student was sent home less than a day later to an empty apartment far from her husband and extended family, and she struggled with postpartum depression and PTSD from a traumatic birth experience. She came from a culture where new mothers are cared for extensively by family for the first month, but she endured the isolation of new motherhood while still keeping up with coursework.

In "Replacing Chutes with Ladders: Creating Authentic Online Environments Inclusive of International Doctoral Students," Crystal Machado, Farheen Mahmood, Ronald Nyanzi, and Lizoon Nahar write for an audience of instructors and professors about how to be responsive to the needs of students taking classes virtually as a consequence of the COVID-19 pandemic. In this crisis, classes moved online overnight and without a foreseeable end in sight. Professors—with varying levels of preparation for and familiarity with online teaching—were thrust into this situation and given precious little time to transition from in-person classes. Preparation for converting seated to virtual classes usually is done over the course of several months; some faculty are even incentivized by departmental or university stipends to create web-based versions of in-person courses. Because of the pandemic, this process had to happen within a week or two.

The authors of this chapter write about how their professors' best intentions led to challenging outcomes, such as the inability to access a textbook, the choice of time zones for synchronous lectures with enrolled students spanning the globe, and curricular expectations requiring knowledge of the US educational system. Many students struggled with internet connections because of insufficient infrastructure, power outages, or other issues beyond their control. Many students chose not to show up on camera—for reasons ranging from internet bandwidth and connectivity problems to shame about the conditions of their home environments. Professors and classmates often saw a full screen of just names against black backgrounds, which contributed to feelings of isolation and disengagement. This chapter conveys both empathy and encouragement for faculty teaching to a multinational group online and offers tangible suggestions for best practices that transcend the pandemic crisis.

LGBTQIA+ Scholars

Several of the chapters in Section three complement each other as they share experiences from different historically excluded groups' perspectives. For example, the qualitative discussion that Nasir Almasri and Amirah Aly provide about identity and research from BIPOC scholars' perspectives is complemented by Austin Schutz's perspective in his chapter titled "Teaching Political Science while Queer: When Your Identity Is Political." The audience for this chapter is broad and includes students, academic peers, administrators, policy makers, and the general public. For Almasri and Aly, the question is how close is too close to one's research to be viewed as objective. For Schutz, the question is how transparent should one be about the identities that define their personhood in the classroom? When one's core identity is center stage in the political arena, such as judicial challenges to same-sex marriage and legislation about gender nonbinary individuals and groups, is it safe or wise to present oneself as congruently in the classroom as in nonacademic settings? In other words, can professors be themselves inside and outside the classroom?

This question goes to the heart of the philosophy of classroom instruction. Schutz writes about the inherent power differential between professors and students, with careful attention to the influence professors could have over students' beliefs and grades. Only data do not support the idea that professors exert influence over students' beliefs. One study found that over the course of a semester, students "drifted" toward the Democratic party, but that this ideological movement was not a result of the professor's actual or (student) perceived political beliefs (Woessner and Kelly-Woessner 2009). Another study showed that engagement in classroom academic activity had a moderating effect on both liberal and conservative students—each side became less dogmatic; on the other hand, engagement in student activities tended to push both liberals and conservatives farther to the poles (Simmons and Gross 2014). The main takeaway from this research is that although professors may be an easy target or convenient group to blame for students' shifting political beliefs, the practice of engaging with their own peers is what tends to moderate or intensify students' political beliefs.

The advice Schutz offers is well-placed: classrooms should not be a platform for anyone's personal partisan beliefs or for penalizing students who don't believe as the professor does. But note that important contextualizing factors already regulate political expression in the classroom. First, many institutions prohibit faculty or staff from openly endorsing any specific candidate running for office. Second, we do not universally consider all professors' identities to be inherently political; rather, we make assumptions about partisan leanings based on our judgments and assessments of how people present themselves and what they say. Some outward presentations and words are uncontroversial; some are not. Third, some professors prefer to conceal—to the best of their ability—their political views, whereas others are more transparent, and there seems to be very little consensus across academia about which way is ideal. Finally, not all professors are required to justify or defend their political neutrality based on their perceived political leanings or outward appearance.

The widespread concern about politics in the classroom is that professors are using their authority to indoctrinate young minds, which connects to broader, more widespread public suspicion of, misperceptions about, and disdain for what takes place inside college classrooms. Schutz writes that pedagogically sound instruction involves creating mutual expectations, making content relevant, and maintaining high standards of inquiry for the students. Students may encounter information in college that runs contrary to what they have been taught and what they believe. Research shows that it is their peers—not professors—who ultimately exert the most influence over changing or reinforcing their beliefs (Flaherty 2020).

Writing also about stepping into a political identity in academic spaces, Kelly Williams describes her experience defining her intersectional identities. "Breaking the Glass Closet: Being a Black Queer Woman in Academia" is written for scholars with multiple intersecting identities, which they may keep under wraps or may consider fully embracing. It is also for all academics a reminder that we can embrace all aspects of our colleagues' identities, not just those that are most familiar, safe, or comfortable for us. In this chapter, Williams describes the concentric identities that define her and how each aspect of her identity became clearer over time. Similar to Schutz's perspective, Williams is identified first as Black and second as a woman. Her profession—a librarian—and her identity as a queer person are invisible identities.

This chapter, although about the development and revelation of intersectional identities of one person, is also a reminder that many scholars suppress aspects of their identity and mask social behaviors for many reasons. For example, higher education has a strong heteronormative and neurotypical bias, even as the academy professes its celebration of diversity. The academic experience of gender nonbinary or nonconforming scholars is characterized by a state of hypervigilance, self-monitoring (and self-censoring), and attentiveness to their surroundings. Beagan et al. write about how the microaggressions that LGBTQIA+ scholars face amount to "death by a thousand papercuts" (Beagan et al. 2021). Their study can be described as "micro-aggressions meet fit," where "fit" is an ill-defined category used to loosely define an in-group and out-group and provide justifications not always grounded in empirical evidence for excluding some individuals from merit-based successes.

Masking, suppressing, monitoring, and attenuating aspects of one's identity take energy that could be better allocated to other healthy, productive activities. But more than this, effectively living a double life can take a psychological toll as well. Historically excluded groups also bear the burden of being the "exemplars" of their groups—speaking on behalf of all people from some aspect of their identity. People in historically excluded groups are expected to educate those around them about proper attribution of their identity—such as religious practices and historical overviews—and expected to do this with grace, understanding, patience, and professionalism. In other words, they can't show "too much" of their identity, but they must be the prototypical embodiment of their identity group as well. Scholars in this situation walk a continual tightrope, flexing the desirable qualities of their identity when it suits the larger group, and minimizing them to cater to the group's collective comfort level.

Powerful academic norms also perpetuate canonical approaches to teaching, learning, and research. In the book *Whatever It Is, I'm Against It*, president emeritus of Macalester College Brian Rosenberg writes about resistance to change in higher education. Path dependence is a powerful motivating force; and doing things the way they've always been done may be a safe, politically expedient option but not the best option to get the ideal results—especially given the seismic changes that higher education has undergone because of the COVID-19 pandemic. If we do what we've always done, we will get more of what we've always gotten. University leadership ecosystems should embrace these cohorts of diverse students and faculty for entirely pragmatic reasons because these students are the economic engines of higher education—the tuition-paying, future knowledge economy workers who will rescue risk-exposed institutions of higher education from the enrollment cliff. Revealing the hidden curriculum forces us all to examine the power of patterns and traditions. People who aren't privy to the hidden curriculum often pose insightful questions about why we do the things we do, and why things are the way they are. When we unveil the hidden curriculum, we expose the fundamental aspects of how higher education "works."

BIPOC Scholars

In "When Work Is Personal: Closeness to Research and Its Effect on Well-Being and Productivity," Nasir Almasri and Amirah Aly write about subjectivity and objectivity in research for scholars for whom a marginalized identity is not theoretical. They are writing for all scholars here, from undergraduates to senior scholars. Scholars from historically excluded backgrounds can provide layers of insight—being participant-observers in their communities—that scholars from out-groups may overlook. For Almasri and Aly, closeness to research provides opportunities for insights via cultural capital from being an in-group member that others may overlook or lack. For example, the US military's female engagement teams were instrumental in gathering intelligence and building bridges in Afghanistan by engaging with women in the community because societal norms govern limited interactions between men and women. Women US soldiers could associate and communicate with Afghani women; their sex and gender were currency that bought them entrance into a group closed to men US soldiers. Being close to the research as an in-group member provides access to privileged information.

But is there a downside to being too close to the research? Can closeness introduce bias if scholars inadvertently (or willingly) overlook important aspects of the research? These are questions in an ongoing debate between qualitative (quals) and quantitative (quants) researchers. Quants accuse quals of selectively choosing their cases and samples. Quals accuse quants of putting too much faith in big data and numbers and being too far removed from the story. Data is not *unbiased* merely because it's numerical or empirical, and it is not necessarily *biased* because it is gathered firsthand through intimate observation and interaction.

Almasri and Aly address these perspectives directly; they say that everyone has biases, and it is the responsibility of both qualitative and quantitative researchers to interrogate and examine the biases they bring personally to their research as well as within the research design, data collection, analysis, and importantly—the discussion and implications of the findings of the research. Moreover, they task all researchers to deliberately reflect on their biases and their motivations for conducting the research that interests them.

In "'What's the 411?': The Beauties and Burdens BIPOC Women Scholars Have Gleaned through Unveiling the Hidden Curricula within the Ivory Tower," Crystal White, LaSheba Hilliard, Gina Tillis, and Tera Warfield write an open letter to Ebonyé, a composite figure who represents the collective experience of the authors who identify as first-generation Black and Indigenous women scholars (FGBIWS). Their target audience includes scholars—especially women—from historically excluded categories who are working in predominantly white spaces in academia. They draw upon the experiences of both historical and ancestral figures and their own lived experiences to empower current and future generations to succeed in academia.

The authors do this in several ways: they encourage historically excluded scholars to create their own supportive communities because, in many cases, those resources are not provided by the institution. They encourage young women scholars to lift each other up and not engage in a tug of war or gatekeeping (Williams 2014) but, instead, support each other and provide public goods for each other that the institution or discipline doesn't provide.

We offer an important note of caution here. Susan Sell provided one of the most important lessons from her vignette in *The PhD Parenthood Trap*: other women are not automatically allies based on sex. It is unsafe and unwise to assume that other women in the discipline will fundamentally have your best interests at heart, because women compete for a limited number of spots—not only with men but with each other as well. The gendered stereotypes of women "lifting while they climb" is certainly true in many cases, but not universally. Women of color continue to report that their ideas are appropriated, uncredited, not only by men but by white-identifying women. White, Hilliard, Tillis, and Warfield encourage young scholars to demand equity and accountability from professors and advisers and withdraw consent from being made invisible through uncompensated labor or practices that maintain the status quo of subordination within the academy. Authorship should be attributed. Ideas should be credited. Initiative should be rewarded.

First-Generation Scholars

First-generation scholars are students or faculty who identify as the first in their family to attend or graduate from college or graduate school. Although "first-generation scholar" as a concept and identity can be used in many ways, colleges and universities consider students to be first-generation students if their biological parents did not attend college. (Choy 2002; *The Chronicle of Higher Education* n.d.; Gable 2021; LaGesse 2023) A first-generation graduate student, then, is someone who identifies as the first in their family to attend or graduate from an advanced-degree program.

First-generation student status is often used as a criterion for financial aid, including federal aid programs such as the Pell Grant (in the United States) (LaGesse 2023). Importantly, first-generation students do not enjoy the same economic benefits of higher education as their peers with college-educated parents. A study by Pew Research found that first-generation, college-educated heads of household earn substantially less and have less wealth than college-educated heads of household with college-educated parents (Fry 2021). This finding underscores the reality and broad influence of generational wealth and highlights the constraints that first-generation students face.

Students whose parents graduated from college are more likely to earn a degree from a four-year institution, a finding that holds up across racial and ethnic groups in the United States (Fry 2021). If your parents successfully navigated the hidden curriculum of undergraduate education, you are more likely to enjoy the benefits of at least some awareness of academia's norms, structures, processes, and unwritten rules. The reverse, of course, is also true: if you do not have parental or familial guidance in the process of preparing for college applications, choosing a college or university that fits your interests and provides the support systems that will help you thrive, or completing coursework and making the most of your four years on campus, starting and finishing your undergraduate degree will be more difficult. This is moderated by family culture—is a college education aspirational and valued, or does this pursuit make them an outlier? Being a first-gen student can sometimes make students feel ill-at-ease both at home and at school, not quite fitting in either place.

Being the first in your family to finish college and graduate school and to pursue an academic career can be a source of pride while also creating a sense of isolation. Daniel Mallinson writes for fellow first-generation scholars in his chapter, "Being in Limbo as a Working-Class Academic." He observes that first-generation identity often creates a sense of in-between, one that can drive you to feel out of place both at work and among family but can empower you with unique strengths. The "blue-collar academic," as Mallinson considers himself, possesses "grit and grind" and down-to-earth relatability. One's working-class upbringing can instill a sense that if there is work to be done, it needs to be done; the blue-collar academic can "grit" through rejection (manuscript submissions, grant proposals, job applications) and "grind" from one pressing task to the next. The challenge for first-generation students who persevere is to ensure that they persist in the right ways and don't expend their energy going down unfruitful paths. Part of the hidden curriculum is knowing where and how, and how much energy to expend on academic activities.

We all face rejection at some point in our careers, and the ability to keep going, to refocus on the task at hand, and to improve the work in response to criticism is a valuable skill. Relatability stems from the tendency to "code switch" across classes, to change the way you speak or interact with different groups, particularly to switch in and out of accents, dialogues, or use of particular terms, particularly to avoid alienation or prejudice (Cuddy 2022). Someone can betray their socioeconomic background by using context inappropriate (or appropriate) vocabulary or turns of phrase. One colleague mentioned they picked up the phrase "as well" and began using that instead of "also"; that was met with ridicule from friends back home who said that since going away to a large, urban university, they had begun to talk differently.

Blue-collar academics' ability to code switch helps them interact more easily with students and staff than their colleagues who grew up in white-collar households. Relatability among faculty, staff, and students helps foster a stronger sense of community in a classroom or department and is a skill that first-generation academics shouldn't discount. Code switching is also laborious—it's about being deliberately bilingual across cultural contexts—knowing which vocabulary to use when and where. Some languages have this baked into the grammar—such as the informal you "tu" or "tú" versus the formal you "vous" or "usted" in French and Spanish, respectively. English—the language of instruction in the United States—does not have this feature, making vocabulary and style cognitively demanding in and out of the classroom.

T. Mark Montoya's chapter, "Academic Border-Crossings: Ladders for First-Generation Student Success," discusses the borderlands first generation students and scholars navigate, often working twice as hard with little to no recognition from the academy or understanding from family. Montoya suggests that academia and its hidden curriculum construct citizens and noncitizens—those who gain access and those who remain outside and apart. Much like geopolitical borders and notions of citizenship, the borders around the academy are social constructs; they can be challenged and changed. Recognizing that first-generation faculty are border crossers who have successfully navigated the hidden curriculum and become academic citizens, Montoya calls on them to help first-generation students find and scale the ladders. Like Mallinson, Montoya identifies the unique contributions of first-generation academics, including strength rooted in difference, the ability to ask new questions and challenge outdated notions of academic citizenship, and the capacity to identify and translate the hidden curriculum more broadly.

Takeaway Points and Best Practices

For Students

Learn from everyone you can and make use of all the resources available to you. As you confront challenges and failures, keep going. Mentors can help ensure that your struggle is purposeful and sending you in the right direction.

Cultivate and use a supportive network of mentors and peers, including those who share a facet of your identity and those who are reliable allies. Ask for their help and their presence throughout your journey and lean on them when necessary. Recruit others to the network who may face similar challenges—you learn by teaching.

For Faculty

Be mindful of the privileges and hidden advantages of living in a place with reliable internet and adequate infrastructural resources. Offer options such as flexible deadlines and recorded lectures for students struggling with synchronous courses. This applies both to international students and students from rural or underserved areas within the United States dealing with the digital divide.

If you identify as a member of a historically excluded group, you undoubtedly will be asked to serve on committees, speak about your experiences, and mentor students or colleagues because of one or more of your identities. Say "yes" to the roles that bring you joy and give you energy. Don't feel compelled to say "yes" to every request, particularly if the time commitment is heavy and the contribution to your education or career is minimal.

If you do not identify as a member of a historically excluded group, be a good ally. Pay close attention and seek out students or colleagues who may need extra support and be proactive about offering to be a resource. Amplify the voices of students and colleagues who identify as members of historically excluded groups; don't speak about their experiences without their input and consent.

For Unit Heads or Department Chairs

Recognize the unique contributions your colleagues from historically excluded groups bring to the table (or the classroom or department). Empower them to use these strengths and help protect them from disproportionate service assignments and tokenism.

Advocate for more support for historically excluded students, faculty, and staff from your campus administrators.

For Administrators

Ensure that wraparound services are sufficient for international students, including clearly communicated expectations for health care, adequate support for off-campus living, and perhaps even workshops or seminars geared toward making the hidden curriculum of being an international student in the United States more transparent.

International students may need additional support with writing and/or speaking. Writing standards vary widely, and the emergence of generative AI has complicated the landscape of academic dishonesty as schools scramble to adopt standards and practices.

Guiding Questions

For Students:

1. What kind of additional cognitive and emotional labor do you engage in due to your identity in academia?
2. What meaningful support have you been offered—or wish you had been offered—that would improve your experience in higher education?

For Job Seekers:

1. In what ways does your identity shape the types of jobs you apply for—and would take—to further your career?

2. What conditions or situations are "deal-breakers" for you on the job market?
3. What additional concerns do scholars with intersectional identities face on the job market, and what support is needed for them to succeed?

For Faculty, Mentors, and Campus Leaders:

1. When writing letters of recommendation for students or colleagues from historically excluded groups, in what ways are you mindful that your narrative adequately and equitably reflects their skills?
2. Job ads often note that "women and minorities are especially encouraged to apply"—in what ways does your department's or institution's hiring record substantively reflect this language?

Conclusion and Transition

Faculty and students from historically excluded groups bring diverse perspectives and lived experiences to the academy. Supporting international scholars, BIPOC scholars, LGBTQIA+ scholars, and first-generation scholars requires a willingness to listen and learn from the challenges they face as they navigate academic chutes and ladders. By understanding where students and colleagues encounter chutes (and how they avoid or fall down them), scale ladders, and even how they start the game in the first place, each of us can play a role in making the academy more diverse, equitable, inclusive, and accessible.

International Scholars

26

Implicit and Explicit Bias and the "Rising Star" Culture

Claudio A. Villalobos Dintrans

The myth of meritocracy—work hard and you will achieve your goals—persists in academia regardless of background, race, and age. However, despite the increase in the number of students and researchers involved in STEM (science, technology, engineering, mathematics), the field broadly lacks substantive diversity at the faculty and senior levels. The lack of diversity has created, among other effects, a massive exodus of postdoctoral fellows from academia (Langin 2022), alongside a "rising star" culture within faculty search committees. Despite recruitment and retention efforts aimed at diversifying the undergraduate-to-doctorate pipeline, scholars from diverse racial, ethnic, nationality, and/or non-elite academic backgrounds are being excluded despite their outstanding credentials, aptitude, experience, and credentials (Matias, Lewis, and Hope 2022).

In theory, faculty search committees aim to find candidates who complement or fulfill the needs of their respective departments and can provide evidence of their potential as successful independent researchers. However, lately, search committees may be influenced by implicit bias in deciding who to interview and hire (i.e., ads may even explicitly state that the department is looking for "rising stars"). What determines the rising stars' status in academia? Theoretically speaking, a rising star is an academic, usually young, with a substantial productivity record and one or multiple awards or grants in their portfolio. These "features" should provide evidence to search committees with enough information to determine the ideal candidate; however, it is easy to see how these credentials can be absorbed by implicit biases. During a departmental talk, I once heard a faculty member introduce the speaker as having a "perfect academic career," quickly realizing it was not referring to the productivity or work ethic of the speaker but to having obtained all his degrees from Ivy League schools. A recent study found that only 20 percent of academic institutions produce about 80 percent of faculty hires (Flaherty 2022).This problem extends beyond STEM to the social sciences; 50 percent of tenure-track faculty positions in political science are offered to candidates from the top ten institutions (Oprisko 2012). These data do not diminish the aptitudes or skills of those labeled as "rising stars" but challenge us to look beyond this limited set of parameters when searching for successful faculty candidates.

As I entered the faculty job market, aiming for research-focused positions, I began to question whether my nontraditional academic pathway and experiences would be an advantage or disadvantage. At twenty years old, I obtained my undergraduate degree in Chile in biological sciences. The lack of opportunities in my research area led me to immigrate to the United States to pursue a doctoral degree in neuroscience. I worked for a few years in a research laboratory, learning the steps and procedures for applying to graduate school in the United States, which can be dramatically different from other countries. I enrolled and earned my long-sought PhD degree after only three and a half years, working with an excellent mentor, albeit not one from a "top-tier" institution. I thought I was quickly escalating the academic "ladder." Personal and immigration issues led me to return to Chile for my first postdoctoral experience, experiencing the first of many setbacks or "chutes" in my career. Visa timelines and academic job opportunities are not always optimally aligned.

Though I faced a steep learning curve to familiarize myself with the new project and scientific environment, I earned a government grant to support my research; gained a new set of laboratory, management, and communication skills; and got my career back on track. While in Chile, I met and married a US citizen (also an academic), and we decided to move back to the United States; returning paused the progression of my academic career and put another chute in my path. Despite my familiarity with the immigration process, it took much longer than expected. I forwent several job opportunities because of the delay in processing my work permit. Restarting the journey toward obtaining a faculty position was not the ideal, seamless, research-oriented, "perfect" academic career I had hoped for.

I had hoped that my diverse experience, resilience, publications, and my ability to develop new lines of research would make me a competitive candidate in the academic job market. For three unsuccessful cycles of applications, interviews, and rejections, I learned that my academic path was not aligned with the search committees' priorities, and I was definitely not a "rising star." My experience had independent validation: studies showed that school pedigree, CNS (collectively the publications from *Cell*, *Science*, and *Nature*), and a K99/R00 grant (NIH, National Institute of Health—path to independence award) weighted considerably more than other factors during the recruiting process (Sheltzer 2020). These metrics limit applicants' academic opportunities, especially those with nonlinear career paths or from non-US institutions.

It is hard to overlook that many "rising stars" seem to come from a relatively limited set of universities. Although a recent study attempted to demystify this assumption (Hsu et al. 2021), the authors limited their scope to successful applicants with job offers, ignoring the big pool of applicants who did not successfully land an academic position, showing that these factors were not necessary to obtain a tenure-track faculty position. This study suffers from selection bias because it looks only at successful applicants rather than the entire pool (Fernandes et al. 2020). Another study showed that a small minority of universities supply a large majority of faculty across fields, exacerbating top schools' hierarchies of prestige (Wapman et al. 2022). Further, K99/R00 grants have an eligibility limitation of five years after PhD completion and showed significant racial inequity (Taffe and Gilpin 2021), highlighting how applicants following a straightforward academic pathway are more likely to obtain these grants, therefore securing faculty positions. Few "rising stars" coming from alternative career paths can meet the specific benchmarks associated with that designation, leading search committees to overlook—even disqualify—candidates with nonlinear backgrounds and academic paths.

Academia has an elitism problem that contributes to and exacerbates not only the lack of faculty personnel diversity but also a paucity of ideological and methodological diversity. Historically excluded scholars, including those from underrepresented racial, ethnic, economic, and national backgrounds, are not counted as "rising stars" because they often follow nontraditional, nonlinear paths—phenomena viewed by search and hiring committees as weaknesses rather than strengths. The problem is not with the "rising stars" themselves, but with the narrow framework used to identify, hire, and promote them in academia.

The Road Not Traveled

The ultimate academic goal in my field seems to be a tenure-track position. Perhaps if I had attended a more prestigious graduate or postdoctoral program, stayed in the United States, and continued in the same line of research throughout my career, I would have been a more competitive candidate in the eyes of search committees. As hard as it is to predict academic success, my nonlinear career pathway has provided me with multiple life experiences and skills that have allowed me to build a life and contribute to the advancement of science in a way I did not envision at the early stages of my career.

RECOMMENDATIONS FOR READERS

1. Identity-based and ideological homogeneity is a bad practice embedded in the academic system; diversity enriches and strengthens scientific inquiry. Homogeneity can come not only from race and ethnicity but also from experiences and even institutions. Expanding the spectrum of diversity for academic recruitment will contribute to the enrichment and development of research and learning programs.
2. Search/hiring committees should be aware of their internal biases for a "perfect" career and make conscious efforts to interview, hire, and support scholars with nontraditional or nonlinear academic backgrounds.
3. Search/hiring committees should reweight and reevaluate the metrics by which they assess candidates, steering away from implicit biases (CNS publications, grants, programmatic prestige) and leaning toward metrics that recognize the value of diverse life and career experiences.
4. University offices supporting international students should make policies and processes as streamlined, clear, and efficient as possible for scholars who face additional obstacles with visa and immigration deadlines and varying cultural expectations.

27

The Academic and Social Challenges African International Students Face in the United States

Lillie Padilla

Introduction

Every year, the number of African international students who come to study in the United States increases. According to the Institute of International Education (2019), from 2018 to 2019 the number of African international students in the United States increased 20 percent. Most of these students come from sub-Saharan Africa, with Kenya, Nigeria, Ghana, and South Africa having the most students. For many African students, the United States offers a higher quality of education compared to what they would have received in their homeland.

Yet the processes involved in coming to study in the United States can be overwhelming, from choosing a school and an academic career to navigating where to live and getting a student visa, among others. When one finally arrives in the United States, the excitement slowly begins to fade when the realities of life here set in. One faces language barriers due to differences in accents and intonation, culture shock, adapting to the American diet, finding an apartment, making friends, and even transportation to and from the university to one's residence. This adjustment becomes even more difficult for Africans who are well-to-do individuals in their home countries because they need to adapt from ostentatious lives in their home countries to very modest ways of living in the United States. These difficulties align with the "chutes" in the academic chutes and ladders metaphor, demonstrating how setbacks such as culture shock, financial hardships, and limited support systems can disrupt progress and make individuals question their choice to pursue education abroad. At this moment, one begins to question the decision to come to the United States to study and whether leaving all family and support groups behind is worth it.

The Academic Challenges

African international students face many hurdles in academic programs in the United States (Banda 2018). The academic requirements and expectations back home differ from what one faces here. In the United States, there are multiple classes to choose from, several weekly assignments, several class presentations, numerous readings, and differences in student-faculty relationships. Many African students have never done class presentations, attended office hours, or had to speak in class because student-professor relationships in African countries are more formal and more hierarchical than those in the United States. Moreover, because of the vast number of university students, coupled with the lack of technology (computers, PowerPoint materials, auto-graded tests, etc.) and the frequency of power outages, college students generally do not receive weekly assignments.

I wish I had known about the differences in the academic requirements before I came to the United States. In my first month, I had completed more assignments than I had ever completed in my four years of undergraduate school. I was tired and stressed, and I realized that my academic background had not prepared me for the American-style education. Thus, in consultation with my professors, I sat in a few undergraduate classes to get the basics needed to understand my graduate program. In addition, I made sure I attended all the office hours of the professors whose classes I took. Sometimes, I only went to office hours to verify that I understood the terminology being used in class. Looking back, I am grateful that my professors were patient with me. The one-on-one office hours not only helped with my confidence in the classroom but also my academic performance. Moreover, as I observed the day-to-day interactions between professors and students, I began to appreciate the informal environment and the fact that I had a voice and an opinion concerning my program of choice.

In addition to my professors, I sought out colleagues who could act as informal mentors. With these colleagues, I could bounce ideas for research papers, speak about grant applications, and learn how to give classroom presentations. This mentorship complemented the formal mentorship channels and helped me overcome the academic challenges I faced in the program.

The Social Challenges

Like the academic, the social challenges I faced made adjustment to life in the United States very difficult: the lack of a support system, low self-esteem, adjusting to the climate, difficulty in making friendships, discrimination, stereotypes, financial struggles, cultural differences, the perception of time, among many others (Boafo-Arthur 2014; Mwangi et al. 2018).

Overcoming cultural differences as an African international student is an important part of being successful in the United States. One must adapt to several cultural differences: the orientation to time, the meaning of friendships, personal space, tipping, do-it-yourself, and assertiveness, among others. Adapting to these cultural differences while maintaining one's unique identity is a struggle. I learned that having an open mind and embracing diversity is important. However, in the process of this adaptation, I maintained my own identity by surrounding myself with others who shared similar beliefs.

In addition to the cultural differences, African international students often lack a support system (Baba and Hosoda 2014; Mwangi et al. 2018). Before arriving in the United States, I did not realize how much I needed the support of friends and family back home. It was in the United States that calling home became a part of my daily routine. Moreover, in addition to relying on my support system back home, I created support groups here: friends from the African International Student Association, classmates, and professors. I also got involved in many school events, leadership, and volunteer activities outside the classroom. Through these activities, I not only became familiar with the social expectations but I also expanded my circle of friends. I realized that spending time with friends, professors, mentors, and colleagues reduced the social isolation I was feeling.

I also learned the importance of taking care of my mental health while studying in the United States. Back home, mental health issues were rarely spoken about, and mental health struggles were seen as a sign of weakness. To ensure that the academic pressures did not affect my mental health, I learned to add leisure activities as a part of my routine. I also acknowledged my emotions as valid and not as a sign of weakness.

RECOMMENDATIONS FOR READERS

1. The hidden curriculum exists across all domains, not just academia (accents and intonation, culture shock, adapting to the American diet, finding an apartment, making friends, and even transportation to and from the university to one's residence, tipping, personal space).
2. Be prepared for more academic expectations (more assignments) and adopt time-budgeting skills.
3. The nature of professor-student relationships is more egalitarian and less hierarchical.
4. Mental health is health; caring for your well-being is important and legitimate.
5. You can join existing communities and build your own while staying connected to your home country and family.

28

Replacing Chutes with Ladders: Creating Authentic Online Environments Inclusive of International Doctoral Students

Crystal Machado, Farheen Mahmood, Ronald Nyanzi, and Lizoon Nahar

When Life Gives You Lemons

Due to COVID travel restrictions, we could not start our curriculum and instruction doctoral journey together in the United States. Instead, we attended six-hour-long Saturday synchronous classes from our home countries. Lizoon, who began the DEd program in Fall 2020, taught science in Bangladesh (forty hours per week) and raised her ten-year-old daughter with help from her mother and husband. Farheen and Ron joined the program in Spring 2021 while managing their respective jobs and parenting responsibilities in UAE and Uganda, respectively. As learners holding multiple minority identities, we realized the need for increased awareness among US administrators, faculty, and students about the challenges international students face due to language, cultural differences, time zone differences, and unfamiliarity with the US education system.

Using Herrington's Framework to Reflect on Our Online Experience

After the worst pandemic was over, we documented the experience of taking doctoral courses online from our respective countries in the form of personal narratives. Following this, we used Herrington et al.'s (2009) Authentic E-learning Model which includes three basic components: Learning Resources, Learning Tasks, and Learning Support, to analyze these narratives and name patterns across our shared experience.

Cognitive Dissonance while Adapting to Online Pedagogy

Doctoral students need access to learning resources, a strong internet connection, and some experience with online instruction. Our professors uploaded syllabi, rubrics, samples, and other instructional material to the Learning Management System, Desire to Learn (D2L), well ahead of time and kept the lines of communication open with us. However, their best-laid plans related to textbook choice and course delivery methods presented some challenges. Neither were the textbooks available in our country nor could we use debit cards to buy them online because our banks did not allow international transactions. In addition, our access to a strong internet connection varied. Ron had to travel a long distance for reliable internet access when the costly plan ($40 per week) he had bought needed to be better. It disconnected during class due to load shedding or internet connectivity failure. This affected his conceptual grasp and contribution to discussions.

Our prior experience with distance education and time zones challenged us initially and affected our performance. Although Ron had taken three-hour-long synchronous classes, this was a new experience for Farheen and Lizoon. Unlike our counterparts in the United States who attended our synchronous class meetings on Saturdays from 8 a.m. to 3 p.m., different time zones challenged us. For Ron and Farheen, the class was from 4 p.m. to midnight; for Lizoon, 6 p.m. to 2 a.m. Staying seated for six hours at a stretch after a busy morning compromised our health and well-being; we developed body aches and other health issues.

Our professors provided us with technology-rich instruction, including opportunities for virtual involvement, collaboration, and communication with cohort members through synchronous Zoom sessions, the course management system—D2L, and cloud-based technologies such as Google Docs and OneDrive. We experienced varying levels of cognitive dissonance with these technologies, course navigation on D2L, and the storm of email communication we received. We did not know anyone except through virtual interaction; we hesitated to ask for help, relying silently on our cohort's private WhatsApp group. Fortunately, we bridged the digital divide when we moved to the United States by taking advantage of university-provided health, well-being, and resources workshops.

Ethical, racial, and cultural differences affect individual instructional design and learning. It became clear to us that faculty were more accustomed to offering curricula tailored to a US audience. We found the assignments difficult, time-consuming, and draining. Again, our US counterparts had a competitive edge because the textbooks were written and discussed from a US perspective. Lizoon noted that it took twenty hours to complete reading that others may have completed in five hours; this was partly due to their lack of familiarity with the K–20 US education system. For example, Lizoon and Farheen found it challenging to interpret the context and relevance of examples in the textbook that included games they knew little about. In addition, our lack of awareness of the context in the United States and our peers' and professors' limited knowledge of our respective countries made synchronous group discussions challenging at times. Being more accustomed to conventional lecture methods, we felt less prepared to share our viewpoints. Lizoon often wondered whether her peers and professors could understand her pronunciation. At times, we resorted to passive listening, partial learning, and feeling completely lost.

Replacing Chutes with Ladders

Faculty can combat the challenges that arise from weaker internet connection and time zone fatigue students experience in a variety of ways. They can be proactive and send out a pre-session survey to elicit information about students' location, time zone, bandwidth—and plan accordingly. Students should also communicate this information and request accommodation where necessary. Faculty can support learning by offering synchronous and asynchronous elements to ensure that all students have opportunities to engage with course materials, peers, and the instructor. In addition, faculty should also offer a wider range of consultation times in the morning, afternoon, and evening. They should follow up with students who may have had connectivity issues, which will help them feel more connected with the class.

The academy is not immune to implicit bias and stereotypes. Faculty can internationalize the curriculum and make it more inclusive in terms of content and pedagogy to help international students feel a sense of belonging, ensure access to course materials, and support the achievement of learning goals. Faculty should research the countries where students come from and integrate relevant course materials and examples that resonate with them, which could foster a culture of empathy among peers. Instead of traditional textbooks, faculty can prescribe Open Educational Resources (OER)—students can access these via the internet at little or no cost. If books are unavailable, students should not hesitate to request an OER alternative. Faculty can make discussion prompts and assignments more meaningful by allowing students to tailor them to their home countries' context and needs.

Faculty need to adopt a more proactive approach with students who are less comfortable with technology. Faculty can foster empathy and resilience from the beginning of the semester by encouraging students to share unique challenges through email or chat so that they can make necessary accommodations throughout the semester. Faculty should include a variety of learning tasks so that all students can take part in at least some activities. Faculty can shorten synchronous meetings by including more asynchronous meetings, giving international students ample time to engage with and process materials at a time that is convenient to them. They can also record synchronous sessions and make them available for students. Flexibility on deadlines and workload is essential because the different time zones limit opportunities to have students' questions answered and not enough time to complete the assignments. Finally, faculty should ask students for feedback on their learning experiences and use this feedback to inform course design and instruction.

RECOMMENDATIONS FOR READERS

1. Administrators and faculty must survey students to identify logistic hurdles (time zones, internet connections, access to books) and adjust the syllabus accordingly.
2. Faculty should consider using OER and pedagogy that allow for the exchange of a wide range of perspectives.
3. Faculty should record synchronous sessions and make asynchronous more available.
4. Faculty should set flexible deadlines to accommodate students with unique challenges.

LGBTQIA+ Scholars

29

Teaching Political Science while Queer:

When Your Identity Is Political

Austin Schutz

As an educator, navigating an identity that is understood as "political" is challenging both because of how it intersects with expectations for pedagogical practices that many departments and schools have and because many people map assumptions about bias and competency onto others based on perceived or actual identity. These academic chutes cumulatively compose the challenge I will call "teaching from the closet": to maintain standards of neutrality, instructors must be neutral about matters of justice, especially those that concern them directly. This may even include hiding aspects of their identity that might be perceived as political. The impacts of teaching from the closet differ depending on the intersections of peoples' identities, including how their appearance or mannerisms are interpreted.

I arrived at the University of Alabama during the 2016 US presidential election. This was a particularly challenging time; I and other marginalized students, faculty, and staff experienced harassment because of our identity—in my case, as an openly gay man (but importantly, white and cis). One of the least extreme examples was "fuck your safe spaces" written in sidewalk chalk outside of the LGBTQ+ student lounge and the department of gender and race studies. Around this time, a professor teaching graduate students how to teach advised us that "students should not know your partisan orientation by the end of the semester." Maintaining ideological neutrality in the classroom—generally referring to some element of nondisclosure of policy or political preferences—is common advice in the discipline I call home, political science (Weaver 1998; Gardner 1998; Freuh et al. 2008) because of fears that a combination of instructor power and beliefs will affect student behavior and learning outcomes (Rom 2021, 588). However, we were living in a world where the 2016 Republican Party platform still argued that marriage equality was a result of an "activist judiciary," stating that "we do not accept the Supreme Court's redefinition of marriage" (RNC 2016, 31). Even now, several states (e.g., Alabama, Florida, Idaho, etc.) have passed or are passing laws that criminalize queer and trans life that place my friends and loved ones at risk. Should I be silent about laws and opinions that result in my own oppression or more importantly, the oppression of others?

The 2016 and 2020 elections caused many political scientists, including the professor leading our seminar, to change their perspectives on ideological neutrality in the classroom in part because of the obvious threat to US democracy (Masket 2018). However, the dynamic between ideological neutrality and issues of identity has always been fraught for scholars from marginalized backgrounds. When students encounter instructors with marginalized identities, they form beliefs about these instructors' expertise and politics (Agathangelou and Ling 2002; Sampaio 2006; Novkov and Barclay 2010). Teaching evaluations are also affected by student perceptions of identity (Martin 2016), and students form assumptions about partisan affiliation whether or not instructors disclose them (Kelly-Woessner and Woessner 2006). So, how efficacious is "neutrality"?

My belief is that this kind of neutrality does not benefit students in their civic *or* professional life. Classes should *not* become a bully pulpit for instructors, but instructors *should* model respectful engagement while, at the same time, *upholding* values of mutual respect when they are violated (including combating transphobia, sexism, racism, homophobia, and other forms of hate). This is particularly important in disciplines that prepare students for public service but is of general importance in that students do not encounter a depoliticized world outside the classroom. This model of teaching places more demands on instructors and may raise fears of "indoctrination," but I want to describe three practices I use to ensure that classes remain respectful and intellectually challenging.

Create *Mutual* Expectations

The best time to address a problem is before it can happen. Mutual expectations of class conduct can be developed in many ways, but it is important that students and professors understand the needs of all parties in the classroom. I develop mutual expectations in two ways. First, I include accountability mechanisms for myself and students in our syllabus (e.g., reporting mechanisms and ways to talk to me about classroom issues). Second, I reserve part of the first day of class for a discussion on respectful dialogue. These discussions might result in changed classroom policies, but at minimum, they allow students to come to an initial understanding of what respectful discussion looks like.

Make Content Relevant

Another practice I have found helpful is to make course content relevant by selecting case studies that have geographical and topical proximity to what students experience. In my classes, this has elevated discussions for two reasons. The first is that this helps students relate complex concepts to proximate issues in a more straightforward manner. For example, learning about convict leasing and petty larceny laws in

Alabama (Holloway 2009) makes reading *The Racial Contract* (Mills 1999) in my unit on social contract theory more accessible. Second, realizations about the historical and social fabric of place often lead students to be *more philosophically open*. This does not mean that they are more apt to be indoctrinated but they are willing and excited to engage with complex material and treat their own conclusions as contingent rather than fixed, *especially when their prior assumptions have been disrupted.*

Maintain High Standards of Inquiry

Higher education should allow students to develop methods of inquiry and critical thinking that help them as concerned citizens and in their occupations. This means that instructors should develop standards for what quality contributions look like. These standards may be minimal—"do the reading"—but they may also include introducing students to methods of inquiry that involve interpreting or analyzing evidence to support a position or hypothesis. When these standards are not met, incomplete, initial, or mistaken arguments can be addressed with rigor, kindness, and fairness.

But … What if I Taught from the Closet?

Although these practices are broad, cumulatively they represent an affective orientation to teaching that I hope you will consider whether or not you have a marginal identity. In fact, it is this professional ethos that has allowed me to continue in the academy, and I believe the wider adoption of policies that dispense with neutrality is a ladder from the abyss for many.

But let's imagine for a moment that I did take advice about remaining "neutral." How would my students encounter me? Some of them would no doubt be more comfortable; perhaps they would express their dislike of people based on who they are. This would, in turn, make other students feel *unsafe*, not just *uncomfortable.*

College is also a time of moral development as much as intellectual development. As an instructor, am I helping students live an "examined life" if they are not challenged to think about these issues? Although institutions of higher education serve an important function in conveying content area knowledge and career skills, they should not cede their role in facilitating moral introspection and socializing public servants—though this does not mean that they should or can impose a particular ideological orientation on students.

As a person, I would certainly have left academia if I felt hiding aspects of myself was a prerequisite for this profession, *and I would be right to do so.* Neutrality is not an option for me, nor is it for many others. Beyond this, it is not helpful for students who will encounter ideological and moral difference in their lives and places of work. Instead, well-considered policies that allow students to explore ideas different from their own, that make marginalized students feel safe, and that draw clear boundaries for respectful dialogue model the very qualities students will need in civic life and in their careers—whether in public service or otherwise.

Conclusion

I hope that I have argued convincingly that it is possible to have a democratic, rigorous classroom where instructors with marginalized identities do not have to "teach from the closet." I hope that I have also convinced people who are differently (or not) marginalized, that instructors *better prepare students* to engage in civic life by dispensing with certain kinds of neutrality in the classroom. Further, I hope that this is a contribution to a discussion in higher education about how instructors can be supportive of students with marginalized identities while also creating classes that stimulate intellectual and ethical development.

RECOMMENDATIONS FOR READERS

1. Recognize that members of the academy with marginalized identities are not perceived as "politically neutral," and are often directly affected by laws and movements that stigmatize groups (e.g., Florida's recent move to prevent accurate teaching about Black history). Missing this nuance is an academic chute that forces many to exit the academy.
2. Uphold basic standards of respect that recognize the validity of marginalized identities. For example, trans students should not have to defend their identities to peers when discussions center on issues affecting them. Not doing so prevents students who might otherwise serve their communities to forgo additional training for specialized careers (e.g., counseling, social work, etc.) or who would continue as public servants in higher education—it is one of the "first" academic chutes.
3. Create mutual expectations of classroom conduct centered around respecting differences, but which do not compromise on the first two recommendations. This will be a ladder for colleagues and students that reinforces the expertise, authority, and worth of people in higher education who experience the effects of other people's biases.
4. Recognize that barriers to inclusion do not just come from students but also from faculty. Holding ourselves accountable for these changes will address many "leaks" that result in a less diverse, less accommodating profession.

30

Breaking the Glass Closet:

Being a Black Queer Woman in Academia

Kelly Williams

Allow me to introduce myself. I am Kelly, a Black woman librarian.

Our identities are tied or connected to many different intersecting factors. Sadly, our identities are sometimes decided for us by others based on appearance or proximity. When I walk into a room, I am automatically identified as a Black woman. Black will always be the leading identifier that others use, no matter what. Being a woman always comes second. In academia, particularly academic libraries, I am a Black woman who happens to be a librarian. At the beginning of my academic library career, I quickly learned that even though identifying as a Black woman in academia came with its hurdles, heartache, microaggressions, and battles, it seemed a lot safer to stick with those labels than to label or identify myself fully and authentically. I came to the realization that I would have to deal with the academic chutes and ladders that oftentimes plague my profession. The "chutes" are the obstacles that create setbacks or force scholars out of the profession (e.g., lack of parental leave, discriminatory hiring practices, or toxic tenure and promotion committees). The "ladders" are the opportunities that propel scholars forward and encourage their continuation in the profession (e.g., earning a large grant, landing a tenure-track job, and having a supportive mentorship network). It was time to see how my journey would go.

As time passed, and I continued to not be myself holistically in several areas of my life, I began to suffer because of the damage to my overall well-being and happiness. Eventually, I realized it was time to add another label or identifier. I am ready to add another identifier to my original label dichotomy: queer.

Let me offer a little background so things can be in perspective. I was raised in a religious family in a very small, conservative town. Growing up, I never saw a Black librarian of any gender, let alone librarians who did not conform to the expectation of heteronormality. I did not meet a self-identified Black librarian until I was well into adulthood. That day was life changing. She was regal, elegant, brilliant, and everything I hoped to be. I wanted to encompass or embody those characteristics. I wanted to inspire other Black or even BIPOC librarians as she did for me. Once in the rigmarole of my career, I quickly realized that these things would lead to ostracization, impostor syndrome, hostility, and almost burning out.

The library employee demographics do not include a lot of individuals who look like me. I was determined to prove that I belonged and that I was just as capable as my peers. I felt like I had to choose between being a representation of a Black woman librarian or a queer librarian. I was unprepared to deal with what this meant. I decided to choose my race/ethnicity over my sexual orientation. I could hide my sexual orientation; I could not hide my race/ethnicity or gender. Dealing with the fallout of being queer was a battle for another day. At the beginning of my career, I was trying so hard to fight the negative stereotypes attributed to Black women in academia that I forgot to be my authentic self.

After some self-reflection and feeling like I had proved myself and my abilities, I decided that if I wanted to inspire other librarians, it was time for me to embrace my own identity. Little did I know what doing this would mean. I slowly tested the waters by dressing in a more gender-neutral way. I even cut off my hair. These two simple basic forms of self-expression led to people I had worked with for years bullying me relentlessly. It was almost as though my need for self-expression led them to feel comfortable expressing their homophobia. Keep in mind that my sexual orientation was never "outed." My coworkers assumed or had a suspicion. Just the simple fact that my appearance changed caused my coworkers to behave in this way. I received underhanded comments and awkward inquiries into my personal life. At first, I naively believed they wanted to get to know me, but I realized they just wanted to know how they could or should treat me.

One of the most unique and frightening aspects of the world of academia, particularly academic libraries, is that it is small and intertwined. The fear of even more doors closing in my face or being denied a chance just because of someone's misguided opinion led me to realize that I had to choose to conform and step back into my glass closet or risk being labeled as a difficult or angry Black woman. As a Black woman, I already feared that I must present a different version of myself to be accepted (Brown et al. 2018). This reality is one of the many academic chutes that I knew I would face. So, I decided to hide that part of myself again for my career and to have any semblance of peace at work. I chose career over self.

After conforming again, I successfully moved up the academic ladder at a steady pace at various academic libraries. I was the token, safe Black woman. I was upbeat, a team player, and did not cause trouble, all by staying in the glass closet I was entombed in, both by choice and circumstance. Please do not misunderstand. These traits are a part of my character, but I understood the need to overexaggerate them to make others feel safe in their ignorance. I overperformed to cover up any trace of who I was. I made a point to rely heavily on learning new skills. Sadly, all this served as a grand deflection scheme, which ultimately allowed me to move up the academic ladder. If I got invited to hang out outside of work, I used work as an excuse not to attend the event. I traveled out of town frequently with my then partner so we could spend time together freely and openly. I once again grew out my hair and started wearing more feminine clothing. I was hypervigilant in ensuring that I did not show any characteristics that could allow someone to use my sexual orientation against me.

My employers treated me well, but the fear always remained that if I once again lowered the veil to reveal a small piece of the real me, they would ultimately treat me as a degenerate. I feared this because I knew it was true. While smiling and appearing happy at work, I dealt with depression and anxiety. My only saving grace was finding an online community of other librarians who understood my struggle. We created a safe place for us to be. We discussed books, life, love, career goals, and more. I needed this safe space to come to fruition in my real, everyday life.

After a particularly uncomfortable conversation with a coworker at a previous place of employment, I had an epiphany. I realized that I was applying the same homophobic views others had to myself. I was enshrouded in self-hatred and anger. I was actively participating in creating and enforcing an academic chute not only for myself but possibly for others.

Enough was enough. I was tired of avoiding questions about my life because of the closed-mindedness and homophobia of others. I was tired of feeling like I had to hide a part of me that was so very important and intricate to my being. I knew that I could not be myself wholly at the place where I was employed, so I started to plan my next career move, this time for self. I knew I had to continue playing the game at work to ensure that I would be safe. By this time, I was well versed in what was expected of me to remain the safe choice. I maintained what they expected of me to be able to eventually live freely and happily.

Finally, I am in a place where I can choose my career AND self. And that "place" is within me!

With that in mind, please allow me to reintroduce myself. I am Kelly, a Black queer woman librarian.

RECOMMENDATIONS FOR READERS

Three Recommendations for Readers:

1. Go where you are celebrated, not tolerated.
2. Remember the importance of your life outside of work.
3. Do not become so focused on your job title or salary that you lose yourself.

BIPOC Scholars

31

When Work Is Personal:

Closeness to Research and Its Effect on Well-Being and Productivity

Nasir Almasri and Amirah E. Aly

Research is a deeply personal endeavor. Scholars pour years into projects, and their success often has direct implications for career prospects and self-esteem. Yet some scholars, especially those from marginalized backgrounds, are tied to their research through various facets of their identity and life experiences. "Closeness" to one's research shapes the form it takes and the stakes of its outcomes. In this chapter, we explore a range of related questions. How does being close to one's research affect the scholar and the scholarship? Does closeness to research affect objectivity and serve as a "chute" or can it benefit research and serve instead as a "ladder"? How do real-world events impact scholars who are close to their research?

Lesson #1: *Everyone* Has Biases

All scholars—those "close" to their research and those who are nominally distant—carry some amount of bias. For those with distance, assumptions about norms in a society unconsciously shape their beliefs and introduce bias. A commonly cited example comes from medical research in the United States, where guidelines have often been developed under the assumption that the average American is white. For example, the first line of treatment for hypertension traditionally has been ACE inhibitors until more recently, when researchers found them to be less effective for Black Americans than white ones (Cohn et al. 2004; Ferdinand and Armani 2007). Whether intentional or unconscious, these assumptions occur across many fields of study, from education (Tanner 2017) to international affairs (Howell and Richter-Montpetit 2020). Thus, closeness to research is often seen as an obstacle or a "chute."

Scholars must constantly interrogate assumptions about what is "normal" and "unbiased" and consider seriously how their position in the world—their gender, racial, ethnic, religious, or class identity, or their relation to the community directly impacted by their work—influences their work. Moreover, scholars who lack closeness to their research must answer questions about why they care (or perhaps, do not care) about their research. These reflective activities do not require scholars to openly share their background. Instead, they are a call to seriously consider one's position and how it shapes assumptions underpinning their research.

Lesson #2: Closeness Has Benefits + Distance Has Costs

If everyone is biased, why should we be concerned about scholars who are "too close" to research? Historically, students of philosophy of science have been concerned about the potentially subjective nature of research conducted by scholars who care too deeply about the outcomes of research. Emotional attachment to research has been perceived traditionally as subjective and biased, exemplified historically by popular reception to feminist research (Blakely 2007).

In reality, it is unclear how attachment to a community is more harmful than detachment. In fact, this claim seems to uphold the idea that emotions and personal experiences will not be kept at bay by scholars and that those who do not have a stake in the outcome—those less harmed by the status quo—are the only ones who can properly speak to the issues of affected communities. Yet, as we argued above, scholars more distant from their research carry status quo biases. This does not mean that they cannot engage in research; rather, it is a call for them to be more reflexive about their potential status quo biases and the consequences for the communities they study.

Moreover, scholars who are close to their research have two significant advantages over more detached scholars: their closeness provides first, insights that might be missed, and second, motivations that might otherwise be absent. In this sense, we argue that closeness can be a "ladder." For example, Jeff Carroll, a patient with Huntington's Disease (HD), is working on critical research in HD. "I'd be lying if I said there weren't times I'm scared," Carroll says. "But I find it less damaging to my life to be directly engaging as opposed to running away." Ed Wild, Carroll's colleague and fellow HD researcher, finds motivation in their personal connection: "Deep down, it's Jeff I want to save, and I know I'm not alone in that" (Young 2017).

Scholars who are close to their research are as responsible as those who are more distant to identify their biases and use them to be more reflexive about what their advantages are and what their shortcomings might be. In this sense, closeness can potentially be a "chute" or a "ladder," and it is incumbent upon scholars to be conscious of these potential consequences.

Lesson #3: Closeness to Research Means Real-World Events Can Be Distressing

Many scholars from marginalized backgrounds choose to become researchers in an attempt to understand the plight of their communities and to contribute solutions. Naturally, this closeness to their research brings significant emotional attachment.

Against this backdrop, it is not uncommon for these scholars to be negatively impacted by real-world political, social, and economic developments. Speaking from personal experience, one of the authors recalls a particularly low moment linked to political events in their community. After experiencing emotions ranging from anger to fear to indignance, the author struggled for two weeks with questions about the relevance of their research and their role in working toward justice for their community.

In these moments, it is critical that affected scholars develop coping mechanisms (Almasri and El Kurd 2022) and that their colleagues work to support their mental health and well-being. Beyond ensuring their personal well-being, this form of support has academic consequences: without the contributions of these scholars, academic research would be dominated by those more distant from the research topics, diluting our understanding of the world and likely, reinforcing the status quo that is already harming the communities in question.

Finally, for scholars in the social sciences or humanities, distressing events are important moments to study. Although research is necessary to elucidate causes and consequences of these events, it is important that scholars—especially those with distance but also those with closeness—be self-critical about using these moments merely as opportunities to further their own research agendas. In these circumstances, scholars should at least be open about their approach to reducing harm and supporting affected populations.

Road Not Traveled

Scholars, advisers, and teachers should support their colleagues, mentees, and students, respectively, in understanding their positionality vis-à-vis their research, *regardless* of perceived or stated closeness. If we lived in a world in which scholars constantly and critically engaged the ways that their identities and positionalities shape their research—for better or worse—we would more quickly and readily bring to the surface assumptions that implicitly shape our research. Ideally, classes and seminars that focus on philosophy of science—for undergraduate and graduate students—would prioritize strategies for interrogating biases and seeing how they can serve as chutes or ladders.

RECOMMENDATIONS FOR READERS

1. Regularly reassess your relationship with your research, including your positionality and biases—*even if you are studying your own communities.*

2. Be conscious of the experiences of colleagues who are close to their research, including when reviewing their work for tenure or other promotions.
3. If you feel distant from your research, make a careful and conscientious effort to better understand the communities to which your work speaks.
4. Do not view real-world events as opportunities to further your own research agenda; instead, assess the extent to which you are uplifting the voices of communities affected and ensure that your work is carried out with a focus on benefiting those communities.

32

"What's the 411?":

The Beauties and Burdens BIPOC Women Scholars Have Gleaned through Unveiling the Hidden Curricula within the Ivory Tower

Crystal L. White, LaSheba W. Hilliard, Gina E. Tillis, and Tera Warfield

As university tenure-track faculty, we are required to engage in the promotional trifecta of research, teaching, and service. As BIPoC women scholars, we had marginal access to formal academic apprenticeships that would prepare us for this promotional trifecta. Research indicates that women encounter numerous "chutes" that remove them from academia or provide setbacks to promotion at all stages of their careers (Cardel et al. 2020). For instance, female students from underresourced high schools or who lack support often do not know academic solid preparation and mindset. Therefore, it can cause women of color to be unacquainted with the mandate of the hidden curriculum (the "411").

What's the 411? It is knowing the expectations of the hidden curriculum. Those from historically underrepresented populations, including the first in their families to attend college, multilingual, of color, nontraditional age, lower SES, and immigrant backgrounds, are at risk of not knowing the 411. As the authors of this chapter who identify as first-generation Black and Indigenous women scholars (FGBIWS), who have worked in white academic spaces, we wrote this letter to a future BIPoC scholar to illuminate our lived experiences as we navigate the chutes and ladders in our careers. Thus, in sharing our 411, we hope to provide practical advice to our younger siStars[1] so that they don't end up going down chutes on their journey.

Dear Ebonyé,

While pursuing my undergraduate studies, I was introduced to a face that reminded me so much of myself—a Black professor named Dr. Brown. At the time (the early 2000s), Dr. Brown was the chair of my UG psychology department. During one of my final semesters at this institution, she pulled a few of my peers into her office and flat-out told about 6–7 other black and brown students and me to "never apply for grad school—ever." It broke me! So, when I ultimately decided to pursue my goals, I pursued them while I was lost, confused, and mostly *alone*! I did not have any positive models to consult or follow. I had no one in my community or home to turn to because I was the first to embark on such a prestigious journey. It wasn't until I was accepted into my doctoral program that I met other Black women scholars I could confide in and learn from.

I quickly learned that I had to first find my people, then build my own community. In my department, we did not have any Black women mentors who were ready and willing or had the capacity to embrace us. Further, I felt that we had limited support from home because many of our family members barely made it out of high school, let alone college, and they just did not understand what we were really doing. Although they knew we were doing something meaningful and profound, our families had no real idea that we weren't just working on the same paper for years at a time.

The messages I received from home and within academia were conflicting and unclear. This oftentimes led me to ponder whether it might have be best to pursue the degree or withdraw. Therefore, on my journey of *finding my people* and *building my community*, I found myself communicating with other Black women scholars on this same journey but at different institutions. To my surprise, they, too, felt that even though they may have been enrolled in an HBCU, they were not directly mentored or prepared for the research obligations of academia. Our conversations often felt like we were on a never-ending episode of *Survivor.*

We were essentially thrown to the wolves to figure it all out, and we developed remnants of impostor syndrome (Campbell 2021; Tillis 2017; Wright 2021). Though we are often reminded of the foundations of education (Wilder 2013) and that higher ed was not meant for folks like us, we also knew our ancestors, our community leaders and activists did not come this far for us to not shine in the midst of adversity and within these same spaces as our white counterparts. So, when asked how BIPOC women scholars persevere through the white spaces in academia, we (the authors of this chapter) answer with—we do what we always do—we must suit up and boot up with our heads held high. We must use all the idioms, motivating cliches, and scriptures that our ancestors and community leaders have taught us so that we can unveil the hidden curricula for our future Black sisters, who are also pursuing degrees in academia. We must get rid of the "crabs in a bucket" mentality by being willing to help our younger sisters learn the specific ladders we are using to thrive and shine where we are. Coming from institutions that were proud to be diverse and student-centered, it was surprising that a lot of our first-generation, Black women scholars, just like us, felt that they had no authentic mentoring support and went semester to semester feeling exhausted and overwhelmed.

Reflecting on this, we realized that although Dr. Brown's "advice" cut deeply, she might have been trying to save her younger sisters from the ivory world. Although we have yet to know her truth, these feelings of doubt will always be remembered. Doubt withstanding, we are survivors. So, when we were asked to reflect on how we were able to survive as FGBIWS within the ivory tower with no guide, we created our own with these three main steps:

1. ***Find your people to build a community*** where you feel safe, supported, and together. We do this through socialization and networking. We had to remember our purpose, why we enrolled in grad school. Being first-generation Black scholars was so important for our families' legacies and our communities and futures. This happened because although we did not have the support and guidance we needed within our individual programs and institutions, we could use the testimony method to vent, share our lived experiences, and find ways to talk or push back. We were, as hip-hop feminists Morgan (2017) and Pough (2015) would state, learning how to "bring wreck and fuck with the greys!" We had to build on the communal practice of sharing our own lived experiences so that we could know and understand what we might need help with or advice on.
2. ***Use your inner "Superwoman" complex to build the grit and grind for your own self-empowerment.*** We recognized very early on that we needed guidance and resources; however, because we were not provided with tangible resources (via a hand out/hand up) to be successful, we began working together to create our own toolkits. We did our own research, shared resources among ourselves, and discussed who would be our biggest allies. We lived vicariously through our other Black and brown sisters across the nation who also needed our small community of Black women scholars to jointly put on our capes and empower each other. We noticed that although we were in the same program as our white counterparts, we were perceived to be individuals who could *figure it out on our own.* We were reminded, like our ancestors before us, that if we want something, we must get up and go get it. We could not afford just to sit around waiting because no one was going to "give" us anything. Within our toolkit, we began putting together various elements of an academic portfolio (i.e., professional job documents—CVs, philosophy statements, etc.); different types and formats of academic writings; as well as references and other research materials (e.g., annotated bibliographies and self-made dictionaries). We created things ourselves.
3. ***Challenge your mentors and advisers to PRACTICE WHAT THEY PREACH.*** As FGBIWS, we have an additional need for support, guidance, and resources to navigate the spaces within academia successfully. Therefore, we must critically understand how the ivory tower has revised teaching, research, and service in ways that often reify white supremacy and exploit and exauthorate Black and Indigenous communities. Reflecting on this issue, we propose a professional seminar requirement for all majors. The seminar should include a critical sociopolitical history of our respective disciplines, a series of writing for publication, professional portfolio building, and/or opportunities to research with faculty. Research shows (Mervis 2021) that Black and Latinx students are significantly less likely to receive research assistantships than their peers. Research

assistantships offer practical insight into how to approach, manage, and engage in research. We challenge tenured dissertation chairs to coauthor 3–4 publications with BIPOC scholars before they graduate. These experiences are instrumental to our orientation into academia, how we develop our scholastic identity, and our professional trajectory as thought leaders.

Reflecting on these challenges, we realize that this formalized apprenticeship modeling is also critical for newly hired junior faculty as well, but we are oftentimes not matched with suitable faculty mentors. Therefore, as an extension and final step on this ladder, the mentoring should not cease at graduation but continue at least until each scholar has received tenure in the academy.

If and when we are asked by younger (or newly matriculated) Black women scholars, how *we* persevere in these ivory spaces, we often refer them to the three main steps we used to climb our academic (and now professional) ladders (see Figure 32.1 below).

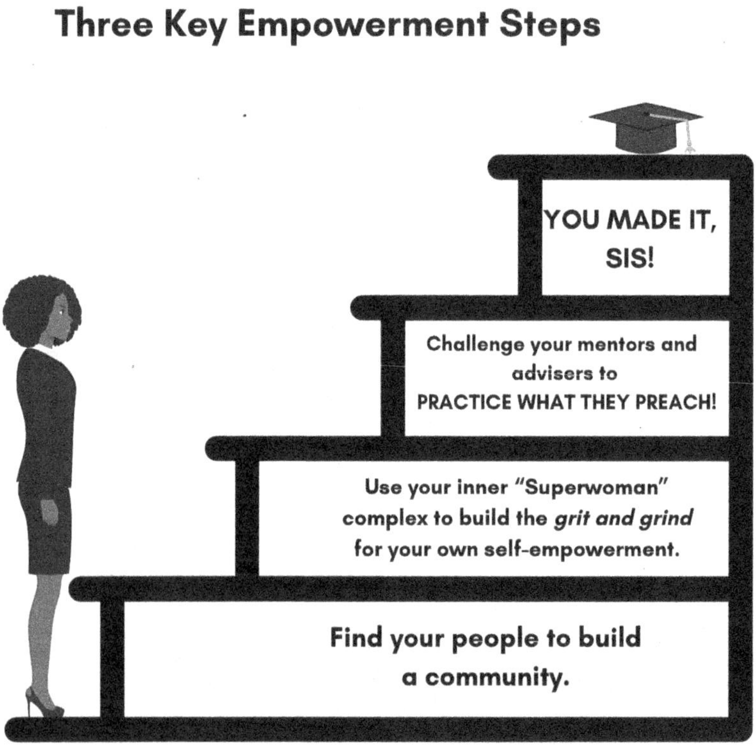

Figure 32.1 Three Key Empowerment Steps. Source: LaSheba Hilliard.

So, Ebonyé, as we prepare to part ways with you (for now), your siStars want personally to remind you that although your journey through the academy will be challenging, remember that we have just given you the key steps to climb your academic and professional ladder while in the ivory tower. As our final parting gift, we would like to leave you with some pieces of advice that will allow you to show up authentically and unapologetically while exuding the expected qualities of the academy with integrity:

RECOMMENDATIONS FOR READERS

To empower readers from a multiplicity of identities, this chapter concludes with ten recommendations to help you navigate the academic landscape, survive its inevitable "chutes," and seize its rewarding "ladders" by understanding and mastering the hidden curriculum.

1. Always remember your purpose for entering the academy in the first place.
2. Consistently reflect on *whose* agenda you are working for or against.
3. Be present and do more than just stay afloat by creating the experience *you* want and need.
4. Be sure to embrace, absorb, and digest what you are reading and learning.
5. Fully commit to the (global/local) community by staying connected and grounded to the work. Don't just talk about it; be about it (talk and walk through both research and service).
6. Find ways to humanize your professors, then challenge them to teach or train you through full immersion and research apprenticeship.
7. Be sure to observe how faculty manage their tasks through a project management strategy.
8. Seek to understand the structure, organizational logistics, and programmatic and problematic practices of the academy.
9. Communicate with your colleagues and peers (often) and support them when you can.
10. As you *persevere*, be sure to carry your own weight, knowing that putting self first is a form of self-love, not selfishness.

Walk in power,
Your Empowered First-Generation Black Big SiSTARs

First-Generation Scholars

33

Being in Limbo as a Working-Class Academic

Daniel J. Mallinson

I have no idea what I am doing. Navigating academia as a first-generation student and scholar is disorienting at each stage. Having a working-class background contributes to feeling like one is in "limbo"—caught between the world we grew up in and the new world we are trying to navigate (Lubrano 2003). Often, we must learn to navigate both worlds, but with little understanding from our companions in each. I have wondered what my construction-working dad would think about what I do now. He died when I was thirteen, of a fourth heart attack precipitated by an addiction to smoking that began on the job site. My mom, the more academic of my parents, did her best, but many things in academia still mystified her.

This chapter is inspired by Alfred Lubrano's (2003) reporting on the "limbo" felt by those who grew up working-class but moved into white-collar work through advancing their education. I will address the feelings that come along with not fitting into blue-collar spaces anymore but not fitting into academia either. Being in limbo affects how we feel, work, and build relationships. It can also result in both chutes and ladders in an academic career. I will discuss feeling in limbo both with one's blue-collar family and white-collar colleagues. I will then present two strengths that limbo scholars bring to their profession. I conclude with how to move forward as a "blue-collar academic."

Feeling in Limbo—Blue-Collar Family

"Why can't you get a job at the [*insert school*] down the street?" "Are you done with your dissertation yet?" "Oh, he's stressed about this test he has coming up [*ah, it's my comprehensive exam …*]." Family gatherings are great places to feel out of place. Seemingly innocuous questions can surface existential crises about our chosen vocation. Feeling misunderstood by family and friends is incredibly common, as are their concerns about changes to our lifestyle that come with branching out and gaining education. For me, it was picking up running, changing my diet, and consequently losing excess weight. As my preferences changed, tensions rose when visiting home. For you it may be tensions over where you live, how you live, how you work, the nature of your work, who you love, and more. Misunderstanding can be helped (at least a bit) with communication, but it still hurts.

Feeling in Limbo—White-Collar Colleagues

Unfortunately, the misunderstandings do not just occur when returning home. Academics with blue-collar roots have had different life experiences than their colleagues. It may be living on public assistance, growing up in a rural/urban environment different than the small college town or big-city university where they now work, juggling part- or full-time work while completing their studies, and much more. We do not easily speak the same language. I have been corrected for mispronouncing places and whiskeys. I struggle in scuttlebutt conversations about academia, such as who is moving where and publishing where and what institutions are rising and falling. Such conversation is baffling. And I hate office politics, whereas some of my better-informed colleagues seem to relish it.

Then there is the vast hidden curriculum that can scuttle careers (Calarco 2020; Lorentz et al. 2022). I, and many other first-gen scholars that I have spoken to, often feel like I am stumbling through this career path, each step of the way trying to uncover what I need to be successful. But much of this vital knowledge is (purposefully) murky. Picking up bits and pieces over time leads to endless reconsidering and questioning, which is exhausting. Moreover, such knowledge would have made a huge difference in my path if I had possessed it earlier. I say this while also acknowledging that as a white cis-gender male I have advantages that reduce certain burdens that colleagues who are not in the same position face.

Recognizing Your Strengths

Although navigating academia as a limbo scholar has its challenges, we must recognize that we have vital skills to draw from that can help create ladders. Foremost are grit and grind. Blue-collar workers know how to grind out the work. Widgets need to be produced. This mentality has unconsciously shaped my work as an academic. I have been able to grit through rejection and grind out work that has made me productive. The downside of this is that I do not know how to celebrate my wins (e.g., an article acceptance) because the next widget (paper) to work on is always there. But in the metrics of academia, this type of grit and grind has been beneficial. Granted, perplexities remain—such as publishing in top journals, considering the best fit for a particular paper, or having a pool of friends to recommend as reviewers to grease the process. These have not been part of my experience.

Relatability is another limbo scholar skill. Admittedly, academics are an awkward bunch, even those of us with a blue-collar background. But I have noticed that my colleagues with better-educated parents struggle in their interactions with staff and students. They can come across as aloof and rude. A broader set of people skills comes with being able to code switch across classes. Not only is this useful, but I find it personally enriching to have good relationships with staff, from maintenance to our administrative support. Again, that has a downside. I still feel like an outsider in both communities. I cringe when staff call me "Dr. Mallinson," and I feel behind when discussing academia with faculty colleagues. But there is an ability to be *personable* in both spaces.

What If?

My big what if is around social media. I was part of academic Twitter at its height. I was also devastated seeing that community slowly bleed dry after Elon Musk took over the platform. Several years later some of that community coalesced around BlueSky, but I cannot imagine what my career would be like if I were starting now. Academic Twitter introduced me to so many people in the profession that I now call friends and collaborators and was an amazing source of information on opportunities that otherwise I would have known nothing about. As I advanced in my career, it also allowed me to engage a wider network with opportunities that I could offer. Academic Twitter was vital for me as a first-generation political scientist.

What to Do?

This chapter is a necessarily brief treatment of a large topic. But I hope it gets you thinking. It is important for you to be true to who you are as you navigate academia instead of simply conforming to its white upper-class norms. Academia is monumentally difficult to change, but I am encouraged by all the different angles by which marginalized voices within and outside the academy are critiquing it. Scholars in limbo have a choice. They can assimilate in ways that reify the structural barriers that hinder those following in their footsteps or they can join in the work to make the academy a more inclusive place. Far more resources are available to support you than when I was in graduate school a decade ago. Start with reading Lubrano's book, *Limbo: Blue-Collar Roots, White-Collar Dreams* in. Benson and Montoya (2022) offer useful advice for first-gen graduate students in *Strategies for Navigating Graduate School and Beyond*, a volume full of revealed hidden curriculum (Lorentz et al. 2022). Not to mention Ayers (2022), *Managing Your Mental Health during Your PhD*, who assesses the mental health challenges of graduate studies and offers strategies for coping. Learn, grow, survive, (hopefully) thrive; it is what we do as scholars in limbo.

RECOMMENDATIONS FOR READERS

1. Understand that you are not alone. Many first-generation scholars feel in "limbo," not feeling completely comfortable in their old life or new.
2. Self-reflect on how as a first-generation scholar, you bring strengths to a career in the academy (grit, grind, and relatability).

3. As a first-generation scholar, you can choose whether to reify existing structural barriers in academia or work to make the academy more inclusive.
4. Good resources exist for learning the "hidden curriculum" in academia, including some referenced in this chapter.

34

Academic Border Crossings:

Ladders for First-Generation Student Success

T. Mark Montoya

Introduction

First-generation (first-gen) college students—the first in their families to attend college—are constantly crossing academic borders: from high school to university, from the hallway to the classroom, and from student to graduate/professional. First-gen students are border crossers with limited access to ladders. Attach to this race and further intersections of class, gender, sexualities, and abilities, and the chutes of the hidden curriculum may hinder any advancement, creating an infinite border. How first-gen students navigate academic borderlands is of utmost importance, not only for first-gens but for the academy itself. Therefore, we must highlight asset-based strategies (Castillo-Montoya and Ives 2021) via borderlands pedagogy to recognize and offer students additional ladders. As our students navigate various borders in their everyday lives (Elenes 1997), these ladders help them to consider their differences in positionality and subjectivity as strengths so that we, as educators, can understand and cultivate first-generation student success.

Grasping for Ladders

The following is a snip of an email I received from a colleague, an outstanding collaborator who also happens to be my spouse. She reached out given my work with first-gen students. The email stated, "My student is worried about the world caving in on her and doesn't feel she has time or money to get the issue addressed. While her parents are supportive, they're putting all their proud energies into her graduating from college." This student was grasping for a ladder; a chute had brought her to this place. Both current first-gen student success research (McCarron 2022) and borderlands pedagogy theories (Ramírez 2002) show us the nexus between catastrophe and triumph. Here, the hidden curriculum draws attention to the grueling academic border-crossing experience of this first-gen student.

The email continued, "Since no one in their family has graduated before, she doesn't feel she can be honest with her parents. She also feels her parents don't understand college. They think it's all classes and parties." Border crossing is not an easy feat, and academic border crossers not only have to deal with the university as an institution but also with the realities of their home lives and families (Bell and Santamaría 2019). Sometimes they are students, sometimes they are children, but usually they are both—navigating the borders of college and home life. The email ends with, "Her parents don't know or understand the amount of stress she is under trying to support herself, hold down a full-time internship, a full class load, and a job." More chutes, indeed. How one navigates the academy without access to the hidden curriculum can be a trying endeavor. Further, those with access to ladders will be recognized or rewarded, whereas those of us confronting the hidden curriculum may feel invisible doing the same work with twice the effort and little to show for it, hence continually sliding down a chute.

The student's plea for help was her attempt to access a ladder. She, likewise, exposed the hidden curriculum by revealing a complex question asked in an unassuming way: "How does one survive college as a poor first-gen Latina?" The query was not seeking a direct answer but instead was asking for guidance. The academy is a border unto itself. Universities bring people together and impede others. The hidden curriculum was blocking her. Too often, first-gen students are encumbered or turned away—shot down a chute—and those few who get ladders may not have the proper mapping to circumnavigate the hidden curriculum. We first-gen faculty and de facto effective border crossers—who may have transcended some but maybe not all academic borders—must continue to guide those who follow. We need to support first-gen students by offering guidance and assistance at every step on the ladder of their journey.

Holding Ladders

As we attempt to understand our lived experiences, we should consider what we as first-gens within the academy can do to hold more ladders for first-gen border crossers. Navigating academic borderlands can be an arduous process, and borders can be difficult to cross, but they are not impossible. Borders are the obstacle, and borderlands are the spaces we strategize and organize. Borderlands pedagogy allows us to consider our uncertainties (e.g., being first-gen) as ladders. Perceived deficits are our strengths; they uphold our many intersectional identities as key to social transformation through alternative forms of citizenship. In short, our strengths draw upon the multiple borderlands we navigate, whether they are racial, gendered, sexual, class-based, or others. In the case of academia's hidden curriculum, our differences—cast as doubts and creating chutes—are actually our steps. Because the hidden curriculum is a border or a chute, we must further understand that the academy was not created, shaped, or reproduced for the various "others" for whom this chapter is written. Accordingly, we must examine the nature and effects of a purposeful hidden curriculum on first-gen students. In other words, the hidden curriculum may be a chute, but like most borders, it is an arbitrary human construct ready to be climbed.

The academy's bias is creating college citizens. This assumes that there must also be noncitizens or second-class citizens. We, with access to ladders, must reveal the rules that guide the game and uncover the processes of the hidden curriculum, encouraging students to practice citizenship even if they are not granted full citizenship rights. Although the hidden curriculum creates chutes, we hold the ladders that challenge the rigidity of college citizenship as a regime. In short, first-gen students practice multiple forms of citizenship in their everyday experiences and become citizens of the academy by having crossed the border. Cultivating first-gen student success is itself a redefinition of college citizenship, encouraging "others" to take up more space within the academy and emphasizing how student empowerment is linked to citizenship.

Our differences are our strengths, and having diverse "citizens" is a new norm for universities. New cultural identities should continue taking form within the academy, as they suggest the need to rethink toxic citizenship regimes generated within universities. Here, first-gen students problematize the nature of college citizenship by forcing the academy to ask new questions *or* at least to ask old questions in new ways. As we continue to expose the hidden curriculum, the possibilities also help highlight how inclusive college citizenship should be the standard to strive for. We should always challenge the chutes we come across. What emerges as a new type of college citizenship, helping us better understand the ways first-gen students "do" college—citizenship practices—is often contradictory to the rigidity of the academy. This may also help find alternative methods for empowerment, especially when it comes to (re) defining and particularly (re)claiming college citizenship. These are ladders. Borders may represent the meeting place of different worlds, but the intricacy of borderlands pedagogy demonstrates that college must allow us to converge. If not, then maybe tunnels might be needed to expose the hidden curriculum. We create a new game.

RECOMMENDATIONS FOR READERS

Learning is a journey, not a destination. When you encounter chutes, such as a lack of resources or support, focus on the ladders you have climbed, such as achieving academic milestones or building a support network. The steps we take on a ladder are our accomplishments.

Every step you take is more than just a move upward—it's a confrontation, challenge, and crossing of a barrier. In our lives and our classrooms, we are afforded ladders of opportunities to see what we will make of them, even when they seem daunting. Be a border crosser. Then be a ladder holder.

Being "good" at a school is a matter of hard work. As you navigate the hidden curriculum, you still may encounter many chutes. Embrace chutes as lessons—they're often our best teachers. Keep climbing. The ladder to your success is already within you. It's you. It's me. We're the ladders, and we need more.

Section Four

Invisible Workloads

Women+ Scholars, Caregivers, and Scholars With Disabilities

The Why

This section uncovers the too-often hidden chutes in academic chutes and ladders: the invisible workloads that scholars at all levels carry while navigating undergraduate and graduate programs, the job market, and the academic career. The academic profession was built by and for the unencumbered, able-bodied scholar who lives the life of the mind without responsibilities off campus competing for time and attention—and often the capacity to ignore or deflect on-campus responsibilities that compete with time spent on research. Although that may be the reality for some academics today, scholars across all ranks and types of institutions face competing demands for their time, attention, and resources. Many scholars navigate higher education and the academic profession while living with a disability (disclosed, invisible, or kept hidden) or chronic illness or while processing the world differently and facing challenges related to neurodivergence. These realities do not need to become insurmountable obstacles or unavoidable chutes; with the right policies, resources, and support systems in place, all scholars can thrive. We can maintain academic rigor *and* accommodate the invisible workloads that encumber many scholars.

The COVID-19 pandemic brought issues related to on- and off-campus workloads to the forefront, as any existing boundaries between campus life and home life vanished overnight for students, faculty, and staff in the swift pivot to virtual teaching and learning. Suddenly, classmates, faculty, mentors, colleagues, and supervisors became familiar with the sights and sounds of each other's homes, and invisible life obligations became more visible. Caregiving responsibilities increased as schools and day cares closed or loved ones of all ages became ill and required care or quarantine away from typical responsibilities and care work (Kelliher 2021; Windsor and Crawford 2020). The uncompensated labor undertaken largely by women was suddenly thrust into the picture—literally, on Zoom—as children interrupted classes and meetings and academic caregivers had to fetch snacks while virtually teaching chemistry or anthropology. Society had a collective realization that women are the "safety net" in the United States (Petersen 2021).

As pandemic-era strains took their toll, women+ scholars submitted fewer manuscripts for peer review, signaling a sharp decline in time for research and writing—the essential ladders to dissertation completion or to tenure and promotion (Murdie et al. 2020; Viglione 2020). Social isolation meant that conferences were canceled, in-person lab work became more difficult, and casual mentorship declined (Crawford and Windsor 2022). Some scholars with disabilities, however, found work more accessible as brick-and-mortar campuses and offices shifted to online workspaces with increased flexibility around working hours and conditions (Peterson 2022). Responses to the pandemic created chutes *and* ladders. Employers also recognized that employees could be equally, if not more productive with flexible working arrangements, and many campuses have embraced remote work to retain—or recruit—talented professionals to jobs that can be done completely online.

Invisible workloads existed long before the pandemic. They may stem from identity-based attributes such as sex, race, or ethnicity. They may be acquired through parenthood or caregiver status. They may manifest as physical or mental health issues that are not readily apparent. The yardstick for measuring "normal" on campus traditionally has been the unencumbered, neurotypical, and heteronormative scholar who does not need a tenure clock extension due to childbirth or adoption or caring for a sick parent. Yet as scholars became more familiar with one another's previously invisible (or at least hushed) workloads, many campuses adapted policies and practices to create flexibility during a time of global crisis. As societies emerged from the emergency phases of the pandemic, campuses began to return to standard operating procedures. Our hope is that campus decision-makers, faculty, mentors, and students remember and institutionalize the lessons learned about invisible workloads during the pandemic and extend the accommodations that make campuses more welcoming and accommodating to all.

This section and the chapters herein are not limited to the pandemic-era questions, constraints, and workloads. Each author highlights their lived experiences as a scholar navigating academic chutes and ladders with an invisible workload. As in previous sections, each chapter offers a set of best practices stemming from both lived experiences and the authors' research.

The Academy Never Accounted (or Made Space) for Our Workloads

Course syllabi detail the professor's expectations for students, such as reading, writing, research, and participation in pursuit of a set of defined learning objectives. Faculty job ads detail the area of expertise sought and the courses to be taught by the ideal candidate. Tenure and promotion standards (ideally) lay out expectations with respect to the number of articles or books a faculty member should publish, the prestige of the journals or presses in which the faculty member should publish those works, the quality of courses in the faculty member's rotation, and the service obligations the faculty member should take on. In an ideal scenario, the expectations we as scholars must meet are clearly communicated, transparent, and equitably applied at every level. Of course, the ideal scenario is not the reality, though we should aspire to it. But even in this ideal scenario, major aspects of our individual workloads remain unaccounted for, unaccommodated, and uncompensated. These invisible workloads can create obstacles and chutes for scholars from the undergraduate years through promotion to full professor when effective support systems are lacking.

Women+ Scholars

In considering women+ scholars, we contemplate the experiences of cisgender and transgender women and nonbinary folks who identify as women. The academy is built on and continues to operate with gendered expectations that constrain some, empower others, and shape the nature of chutes and ladders. As we discussed in the book's introduction, the original "leaky-pipeline" metaphor explores the gender dynamics that traditionally have driven women out of academia and created observable gender gaps in tenure and promotion rates, pay, publishing, and senior faculty and upper-level administrative positions (Clark Blickenstaff 2005; Goulden, Mason, and Frasch 2011; Hesli, Lee, and Mitchell 2012; Hancock, Baum, and Breuning 2013; The London School of Economics and Political Science 2014; Gasser and Shaffer 2014; Miller and Wai 2015; Windsor and Crawford 2021; Windsor, Crawford, and Breuning 2021; Scalera Elliott et al. 2022). Gendered assumptions and expectations often arise from the presumption that young women+ will eventually give birth and need leave time or will leave altogether, but these gendered expectations surrounding eventual or actual parenting responsibilities extend beyond women+ who are actually parents, shaping the experiences of all women+ scholars. Sex, gender, and biology create expectations—colleagues will have to pick up the service slack for women who use FMLA or their institution's parental leave to grow their family. These expectations and perceptions reflect a deficit mindset (rather than a growth mindset)—that hiring someone who could give birth will create a departmental inconvenience. On the other hand, they could lean on the research that shows that women with children outperform their colleagues—not in the short term—but in the long run, in terms of lifetime publications.

Gender dynamics and related obstacles vary widely by discipline, but they often take the form of microaggressions. Microaggressions are comments, questions, assumptions, slights, discriminatory behaviors, or put-downs arising from implicit bias and directed toward people of historically excluded or marginalized groups (Mena and Vaccaro 2017; Sue 2021; Washington 2022). Women+ scholars may encounter comments, behaviors, and exclusionary practices at all ranks from undergraduate through full professor. They also carry the burden of representing women+ in their field, mentoring junior women+ scholars, and carrying a disproportionate service load (Guarino and Borden 2017; Crawford and Windsor 2021). As we discussed in section three, transgender scholars and Black women scholars face additional layers of bias and microaggression, as well as additional service and mentoring demands related to DEI (diversity, equity, and inclusion) initiatives that seek out representatives with marginalized identities to serve on campus boards and task forces (Lesiak 2023; Sabet, Bajaj, and Stanford 2023; Jeffries-EL 2021; Hanna 2016). And as was also mentioned in section three, women are not universally allies for other women but can see them as competition and accordingly, behave poorly.

Overburdening individuals with service is linked to worse academic outcomes that are important for tenure and promotion, including delays in getting articles published. This is especially pernicious for women academics with intersectional identities. Women are bound by gendered expectations—being community-oriented and team players, and they are damned if they do or don't. In "Double Jeopardy? An Empirical Study with Implications for the Debates over Implicit Bias and Intersectionality," Joan Williams describes four processes that systematically work against scholars with multiple identities (Williams 2014). She writes about "Prove-It-Again!," the tightrope, the maternal wall, and tug-of-war (Williams 2014, 189). Prove it again means that women scholars must provide twice as much evidence as men to demonstrate expertise and be viewed as equally competent (Lyness and Heilman 2006). This means that women must work more than twice as hard as their men counterparts to demonstrate equal—believable—competence.

Williams (2014) discusses how agentic and communal traits work against women when they "go against type" in professional scenarios. Agentic traits are commonly viewed as typically masculine—assertive, information-providing, rational, and stoic, whereas communal traits are those viewed as typically feminine—caring, emotional, summative, and passive. Even when women accumulate twice the evidence of expertise as men do, they may be overlooked for admittance, hiring, or promotion because their expertise runs contrary to gendered expectations. They are not a good "fit"—an ill-defined concept linked to implicit bias (White-Lewis 2020).

Women have to both prove it again and walk the tightrope to navigate the workplace and tiptoe around gendered expectations. Women are penalized for personifying agentic traits—being viewed as "too strong"—and for communal traits as well or being "too weak." Others have called this predicament the "gender double bind" (Diekman 2007; Teele, Kalla, and Rosenbluth 2018), and it has been linked to measurable disparities such as the wage gap where women earn less than men counterparts in the same position. The conventional wisdom suggests that it's because "women don't ask" (Mitchell and Hesli 2013), but in reality, women *do* ask. This next point is important: women who bargain and negotiate like their men counterparts are not only more likely to be denied their requests but suffer reputational costs as well (Bowles, Babcock, and Lai 2007; Bowles, Thomason, and Bear 2019). Williams (2014) also writes about the maternal wall, which reflects the intersectional identities that women who are mothers face. It's bad enough to be a woman—it's worse to be a mother, according to Williams (2014). Motherhood sends gender essentialism into overdrive. Tug-of-war is a scarcity mindset phenomenon that pits women against other women. It embodies the perspective that there is only room for one woman; its symptoms include women gatekeeping the progress of other women or undermining their professional advancement.

In her study, Williams (2014) goes far beyond the singular woman identity to explore how race and ethnicity, motherhood, and gender-nonessentialist behavior impact women's advancement. She finds that intersectional identities—being both woman *and* Black—often have compounding negative outcomes for women in the workplace (Livingston, Rosette, and Washington 2012; Rosette et al. 2016; Rosette and Livingston 2012). However, the effects of intersectional identities are not universal across different races and ethnicities. Wong et al. (1998) describe how Asians fill the "model minority" stereotype with comparable advantage to whites, although this may not hold true in times of crisis such as the COVID-19 pandemic (Li and Nicholson 2021).

In approaching the range of women+ scholars' experiences navigating the academic chutes and ladders, the contributing authors in this section speak to intersecting identities related to gender, parenthood, and socioeconomic status. Rachel Blume writes about her experience as a first-generation academic woman who became a mother in her teen years and how those intersecting identities led to obstacles that have persisted even into her years as a full-time faculty member. Her chapter, "Experiences of a Former Teen Parent Working in Academia," is as much a motivational essay for students who have children in tow as it is a call for faculty, staff, administrators, and mentors to do better to support students and colleagues who take a nontraditional path to academia.

In their coauthored chapter, members of the Motherscholar Collective speak to the importance of mentorship and collaboration, particularly for women+ and mothers+, who carry heavy but often unseen workloads. In "Academic Motherhood: Holistic Motherscholars Lifting Each Other Up the Ladders," the authors observe that the Motherscholar Collective formed a career-preserving ladder for its participants through the COVID-19 pandemic and the related, sudden, and drastic increases in academic and household workloads. Their chapter speaks most directly to scholars who identify as women+ and mothers+.

Jessica Salvatore describes the transient nature of academics as they rise through the ranks from graduate student to postdoctoral researcher to faculty member. She challenges readers to recognize the wide variation in academic experiences from undergraduate education through promotion to campus administrator. "Chutes and Ladders in the Rearview Mirror May Be Less Distinct Than They Initially Appeared" speaks to scholars across all ranks but especially to undergraduate and graduate students and early career faculty, with a reminder that chutes and ladders are not always recognizable for what they truly are. She also acknowledges that the recurring transitions in the academic journey make it difficult to turn other (at times competing) dreams into reality: the biological clock and the tenure clock are at odds.

Caregivers

In *The PhD Parenthood Trap*, we focused on the bias and discrimination academic parents, particularly mothers, face at all ranks (Crawford and Windsor 2021).

Parenthood, and especially motherhood, comes with a professional tax that can force scholars down the chutes (Evans and Grant 2008; Pirtle 2018; Ward and Wolf-Wendel 2012). Of course, the lack of support for parents who work outside the home in the United States is not limited to the academy (Budig 2014; Frank 2018; Ingraham 2018; Livingston and Thomas 2019). But "caregiver" is a multifaceted identity. Caregivers devote their time, attention, and labor to loved ones in all stages of life, with a range of abilities, and often with meager support.

The COVID-19 pandemic brought the caregiving workload into the picture—literally. When campuses pivoted to remote work, faculty, staff, and students alike were forced to erase any existing boundaries between work and family, and their loved ones were often in view during meetings, classes, or conference presentations. Suddenly, the invisible care work became visible. Karen Sobel and Melissa Bowles-Terry write about the changes made to campus policies and practices during the early days of the pandemic. They urge campus decision makers and faculty to continue to expand on the initiatives designed to support teaching, research, and well-being; although these changes arose from necessity in March 2020, they do not need to end with the return to "normal." This chapter appeals to campus administrators and department heads specifically, but any reader balancing work and family will connect with the authors' discussion.

Courtney Peters examines the invisible workload caregivers carry, even in "normal," non-pandemic eras. Her chapter, "Navigating Hopeful and Heartbreaking Caregiving in Academia," outlines a three-perspective approach to demystifying the hidden curriculum of pursuing academic success as a caregiver, outlining the roles of caregivers and institutions, and collaboration between the two. Importantly, Peters underscores the range of caregiving identities, from the hopeful new parent to the sibling caring for a disabled sibling, to the caregiver supporting a loved one in their final days. Peters's chapter resonates with graduate students, faculty mentors and department heads, and caregivers at any stage of their career.

The academy must do more to support caregivers, particularly those who are students or precariously employed. Lesley Thornton-Cronin's chapter, "The Bittersweet Fruits of Perseverance," reflects on her experiences as a graduate student undergoing cancer treatment, a new mother in a contingent faculty position during the COVID-19 pandemic, and her perseverance through the many chutes she encountered on the way to (finally) gaining a secure faculty position. The experiences she writes about underscore the ways in which identities and invisible workloads intersect; as a cancer survivor, a parent, and a former adjunct professor, she understands—and calls on all of us to accept—the responsibility for those with job security to advocate for those who lack such security. Thornton-Cronin's chapter speaks to readers across a range of identities, particularly parents or caregivers, precariously employed faculty, and campus decision makers.

Caregiving as part of the hidden curriculum may be confusing because many universities have enacted policies to support caregivers, such as paid parental leave, family leave, bereavement leave, and extending or pausing the tenure clock to account for unforeseen—or planned—events that serve as career diversions. But using these resources may send certain signals—or perceived signals—that dissuades people from using them. Women+ who take paid parental leave may incur inadvertent penalties, such as being expected by their tenure and promotion committees to publish *more* as a result of their "baby vacation," as one colleague called it—because they got more time added to their tenure clock. Women+ may not want to face the stigma of not being able to "do it all" if they use the resources available to them. *This* is the hidden curriculum, the subtle and consequential judgments that are applied inequitably.

Yet caregiving need not be an inevitable chute. When support systems, policies, and practices are in place to ensure that scholars with caregiving responsibilities can continue to pursue their academic and career goals, the workload can become manageable. When chairs and unit heads are taught to enforce antidiscrimination policies and empowered to identify implicit bias, then colleagues with caregiving responsibilities can use the full suite of resources available to them without fear of penalty. As cultural norms change and evolve, more men+ colleagues are assuming active caregiving roles, with a less inequitable distribution of labor than in previous generations. Yet because women+ still are in the minority among university administrators, we still rely on our allies—what Windsor and Thies (2021) call the "men in the middle"—to speak up.

Scholars with Disabilities

Physical, developmental, cognitive, and sensory disabilities complicate the trajectory from undergraduate education through the faculty ranks (Brown and Leigh 2020). Academia is facing a mental health crisis that affects students and scholars at all ranks (Nature Editorial Board 2023; Hammoudi Halat et al. 2023; Nicholas 2021). These challenges compound an individual's workload, particularly when support or accommodation on campus is insufficient. As we consider ways to make higher education and the academic profession more humane, inclusive, and accessible, questions surrounding access for students, faculty, and staff living with mental and physical health challenges must be part of the conversation.

Melanie Savelli discusses the chutes facing scholars with physical disabilities and chronic illnesses, particularly as they navigate on-campus interviews for faculty positions. Savelli's chapter, "On-Campus Interviews: The Invisible Chutes for Disabled Academics," offers concrete recommendations for department heads, administrators, and search committees with the object of making interviews universally accessible; it is also instructive for graduate students and faculty with a disability navigating the job market. Some physical disabilities are visible, but some are not. It can feel precarious to disclose any disability, even though the Americans with Disabilities Act offers protections for disabled people in the workplace. Job candidates, for example, already face cognitively and physically demanding schedules and may feel awkward, intimidated, or ashamed about asking for accommodations for their disability. A job interview involves a packed schedule from breakfast until dinner, with few breaks. The candidate must be "on" the whole time, and they may feel that sharing their disability would imperil their chances of being selected for the position. These fears are not entirely unfounded. Academia lags behind private industry in protections and accommodations for people with disabilities in critically important career moments such as candidate selection and the hiring process.

Invisible disabilities—issues such as migraines, chronic pain, or Crohn's disease—do not have obvious presentations—nor does neurodiversity. Although neurodiversity is not a disability, considerations for neurodiverse individuals often occur in tandem with those addressing individuals with disabilities. It also lacks a single, consistently used definition but refers generally to wide variation in neurocognition in humans (Baron-Cohen 2017; Dwyer and Rogan 2022). Neurodiverse scholars do not share a single diagnosis, but the term may refer to those living with Autism Spectrum Disorder (ASD), ADHD (Attention-Deficit/Hyperactivity Disorder), and hundreds of other diagnoses (Baron-Cohen 2017). Because the scientific community's understanding of neurodiversity continues to evolve and incorporate more nuance, including a broader range of diagnostic criteria that can include behavior or experiences previously not recognized, more people—especially women—are identifying as neurodiverse.

Neurodiverse students, faculty, and staff need support, acceptance, and a seat at the table when discussions are held about policies and resources designed to improve their access and inclusion. Traditional ways of "doing" higher education privilege neurotypical individuals. Students have access to student disability services, but faculty often are on their own to request accommodations for their professional expectations. In the field of occupational therapy, modifications are made for "activities of daily living"— few corollary accommodations exist for neurodiverse academics who are expected to modify their own behavior to fit the needs of the department or institution. Some neurodiverse academics consider that the way they experience the world is less a deficit and more a superpower.

In "OCD Meets PhD: The Fight to Thrive in Academia with an Invisible Illness," Maya Novak-Herzog writes about the fear of being perceived as "crazy" by colleagues and even by readers of the chapter in this book. Novak-Herzog issues a call for camaraderie, allyship, and accommodation; in expressing the determined struggle to thrive in graduate school as a neurodiverse scholar, she reminds campus decision makers, faculty, mentors, and students to make space for scholars living with invisible conditions that compound their workloads. Many people do not disclose their neurodiversity for fear of stigma or facing misperceptions about what their neurodiversity entails.

Eun A Jo, Sally Friedman, and Alan Babcock invite readers to consider the ableism that is rampant in academia. "Disabilities and the Hidden Curriculum" discusses the ways in which higher education and the academic profession rely on a hidden curriculum of ableism. They call on campus decision-makers to increase disability awareness and establish support systems and dedicated offices with sufficient staffing to make campus more accessible to students, faculty, and staff with disabilities. Their chapter speaks most directly to campus administrators and department heads but will resonate more broadly as readers consider the work remaining to make campuses more inclusive and accessible.

The South African disability rights movement issued a call for inclusion and empowerment of people living with disabilities, uniting around the cry "Nothing about Us without Us." The slogan demands full representation of affected populations in the crafting and implementation of any policy designed to address the needs of people with disabilities. Historically, oppression of people with disabilities and denial of equal access mirrors oppression based on race, gender, sexuality, and nationality (Charlton 1998). People from historically excluded groups need and deserve to be in the rooms where policy decisions are made to promote their equal access and inclusion.

Jarod Giger discusses other invisible challenges—mental health in the academy—with a particular focus on the "epidemic of loneliness" that the US surgeon general warned was a prevalent and looming crisis. Giger writes for all scholars, with particular attention to how students might advocate for themselves and how faculty can support students who are struggling with mental health concerns. The pandemic initiated many conversations about isolation and loneliness. Children started kindergarten online and spent their formative first years in a virtual classroom. High-school seniors became the first college freshmen to enter college in quarantine, all online. The pandemic yielded such phenomena as "social distanced drive-by birthday and graduation parties" where the birthday child or recent graduate stood in the front yard, and the partygoers drove by in vehicles, often decorated with streamers and balloons.

But if you think loneliness started with the pandemic, you'd be mistaken. It's been a growing problem for the past several decades as participation in volunteer, civic, and extracurricular activities has declined in the United States. Loneliness is only one manifestation of a larger mental health epidemic that universities are struggling to address. When universities resumed in-person instruction, the pervasive motto was "back to normal," rendering the struggles and challenges from the pandemic invisible. "Back to normal" erased the years of pervasive existential fear of sickness and death and negated the very real losses—in terms of COVID-19 mortality as well as experiential and social losses. "Back to normal" functions as gaslighting, with the expectation that people just move along and move forward, with little substantive care for the collective psychological trauma everyone experienced because of the pandemic.

One consequence of years of virtual learning is that students who entered college during the pandemic missed orientations to university resources for intervention—access to mental health services—and for prevention—the development of social bonds and relationships that foster social and emotional resilience. Faculty are also suffering from burnout, having abruptly transitioned to virtual instruction alongside juggling multiple roles and responsibilities at home. Faculty missed conferences and professional development. They missed opportunities for collaboration and mentorship. The answer to these problems is reestablishing connection, forthright acknowledgment of the trauma everyone experienced, and ample resources for addressing pervasive mental health concerns on campuses across the United States.

Takeaway Points and Best Practices

For Scholars Carrying Invisible Workloads

Cultivate a team or network of advocates and mentors who understand your work ethic and your invisible workload and who will support you along your path.

Ask for the support you need from your department chair and campus administrators.

Ask about and consider using flexible evaluation timelines.

Engage in collaboration with others who share your commitment to a project, initiative, or task.

Leverage any and all capital you have to advance your education or your career and your well-being.

For Established Faculty, Mentors, and Administrators

Welcome adjunct and contingent faculty as colleagues and help them access and use resources available to support teaching, research, and professional development.

Advocate for legal protections, health benefits, paid leave, and gap benefits or contract bridging for adjunct and contingent faculty.

Find ways to consolidate campus interviews for faculty positions, make the campus visit schedule more humane, or use virtual options for campus visits to make the interview process more accessible to scholars with physical disabilities and chronic illnesses.

Facilitate department-level and university-level dialogues to empower neurodiverse students, staff, and faculty and students, staff, and faculty with disabilities or chronic illnesses to express their accommodation needs.

Support students and colleagues as they navigate coursework, dissertation work, or academic career responsibilities while carrying invisible workloads. Offer flexibility and accommodations to empower them to persevere.

Take the lessons learned from the pandemic and continue to provide flexibility and support for caregivers.

Advocate for and model clear boundaries between work life and personal life. Limit academic business to business hours and contribute to a campus culture that embraces work-home balance.

Leverage any and all capital you have on behalf of others who are in more precarious positions (students, contingent faculty, junior faculty, staff).

Conclusion and Transition

The chapters in this section highlight how the invisible workloads are part of the hidden curriculum. Scholars dealing with invisible workloads persist—and often succeed—in spite of the compounding challenges they face. Caregivers do scheduling acrobatics to balance and juggle their personal and professional responsibilities. Women+ scholars defy gendered assumptions and implicit biases that work against their advancement. Faculty and students struggle with anxiety, depression, and loneliness without access to adequate resources. Neurodiverse scholars and those with disabilities continue to advocate for themselves to gain concessions and accommodations. Invisible workloads can lead talented scholars down the chutes or, at the least, delay their progress in the academic game. It doesn't have to be this hard.

As we have observed at several points throughout the book, the chapters and contributing authors herein do not represent the full range of academics' experiences, constraints, or opportunities. Instead, the chapters in this section provide insights into several types of invisible workloads and the need to create a more equitable, inclusive, and humane academy. We seek to inspire change so that the academy will embrace all scholars at all ranks, not only *in spite of* the invisible workloads they carry but *because of* the lessons they learn and the scholars they become through their lived experiences.

Guiding Questions

For Students:

1. What invisible workload do you carry? If you have more than one, how do you manage them?
2. Have you identified resources on campus to support you—such as student disability services or the counseling center—and are you prepared to use them?

For Job Seekers:

1. How do your invisible workloads affect your scholarship, including which jobs you apply for?
2. What is most scary—or empowering—about asking for accommodations for your invisible workload, whether having an infant in tow or having a disability?

For Faculty, Mentors, and Campus Leaders:

1. What provisions or considerations do you make universally for people with invisible workloads, and how does your leadership set the tone for your classroom, department, or unit for people with invisible workloads?
2. What accommodations are available in your workplace for your invisible workloads, and are they adequate to easily meet the needs of faculty and students?

Women+ Scholars

35

Experiences of a Former Teen Parent Working in Academia

Rachel Blume

Background

Society often paints teen parenthood as the death of a mother's education, career, and relationships. My mother was the result of an affair between my grandma and a Cherokee man; therefore, she was born into a white family. By fifteen, she was a mother, as was her mother before her. I would follow in their footsteps. Despite struggling with childcare, finances, time management, and being a first-generation college student, I completed my education through a master's degree and became an academic librarian. I find that many people assume because I've made it this far, the issues I've faced from having been an adolescent mother are behind me. Yet teen parenthood is still an almost daily obstacle for me in finding and feeling a sense of belonging in academia. In fact, this is one of the greatest "chutes" of my academic experience; if not for the "ladders" created by the excellent mentors I've had along the way, I'm not sure I'd still be in this profession.

Unfortunately, the negative experiences I had early on my journey to motherhood often revolved around the health care I received. I can remember applying for government assistance when finding out I was pregnant and feeling humiliated by the Department of State Health Services (DSHS) worker:

"What's your plan for birth control after the baby comes?" she asked me.

"I don't know; I have a lot of time to decide," I joked.

"Well, you don't want this to happen again, do you?" she asked critically.

Throughout the pregnancy, I endured countless comments from strangers and family or friends. The juxtaposition between the love you feel for your baby and the apparent shame the people around you impose upon you is confusing. At the hospital, when it was time to give birth to my son, things were no different. My boyfriend was asked if he wanted a paternity test. During the crisis of a possible emergency C-section, I wasn't told what was happening and was left to cry in agony for an hour while the nurse tapped loudly on her computer in the corner.

"Should I be pushing?" I asked in between sobs.

"You can if you want to," she responded.

Unfortunately, my experience is not unique. Young mothers face so much stigma and judgment that some nursing schools have made efforts to study student empathy levels toward teen mothers to improve the level of care offered to adolescent mothers and other marginalized groups (Kim et al. 2013). The prevalence of these empathy training programs combined with my personal experience has often led me to wonder when the shame and judgment from society will be sufficient. When have I and others like me been adequately punished? After fifteen years as a mother, society does not seem to be finished disgracing me yet.

I became a librarian because the public library made me feel equal. As a child, I lived in poverty. While my peers went home to eat Fruit by the Foot and chat on MSN Messenger, I went to a home without any electronics, almost no food, and no one to greet me. At my public and school library, however, I was the same as everybody else. As Russell and Huang state, "accessibility provided by libraries is often the only information source for many low-income families or the unemployed who do not have access at home" (Russell and Huang 2009). Libraries are an incredible equalizer. During library school, I decided early on that I wanted to be an academic librarian instead of working in a public or school library because an education changed my life. I rose out of poverty, moved away from my hometown, challenged and evolved my intellect, and even got health insurance for the first time in my life. It was a culture shock, however, when I entered the field and experienced academic culture.

The Academic Experience

The cultural norm in academia often assumes that every academic professional fits a certain mold. They have a particular look, speak a certain way, and have a similar background. In the book *Presumed Incompetent: The Intersections of Race and Class for Women in Academia*, Gutiérrez y Muhs et al. write, "The nation's most prestigious universities were not established to educate women, people of color, or the working class. On the contrary, they were designed to serve the interests of wealthy white men" (2012). This represents one of the greatest barriers to diversity, equity, and inclusion in academia and has contributed strongly to my struggle to "fit in" and the constant chute I find myself perched above ready to slide down.

In many circumstances, feeling part of a community can improve a sense of belonging for marginalized groups, something that often seems impossible for me. No matter where I turn, other parents are either in different stages of parenthood or from a different generation. Many of my coworkers have children. However, the people my age don't have teenagers. Those who have children the same age as mine are often significantly older than me. This creates considerable barriers for me to connect. It is painfully isolating listening and watching from the outside as the mothers at work create support systems for each other. This dynamic, combined with the prevailing academic stereotype of the typical middle-class white family means that I often struggle to relate to my colleagues. Validating my perception, Gutiérrez y Muhs et. al. write:

> Women from the lower or working class face enormous obstacles in the academy, due not only to material deprivation but also to the alienation of working-class academics from their origins and native communities. These academics face enormous pressures to pass as middle or upper-class, and they must carefully evaluate the potential repercussions of "coming out" as working class.
>
> (*Presumed Incompetent: The Intersections of Race and Class for Women in Academia* 2012, 10)

I am painfully aware of the casual way I speak and the word choice I use in contrast with those around me. When I first meet colleagues, I clench up when they ask how old my children are, knowing the comments and questions that will come next: "I can't believe you have a fifteen-year-old! Your family must be so proud of you!" To survive academia, I hide much of who I am to "fit in." This dynamic leads to impostor syndrome and a feeling of loneliness and isolation.

The culture of academics, unfortunately, feeds directly into the insecurities and pressures that I face because of my background. One of the major differences in academia compared to other work settings is that the university often expands far beyond the typical nine-to-five. On campus, my children attend summer camp, we go to dinner and swim, I use the gym, and so on. Being a salaried faculty at a university with service expectations also means that engagement with activities outside work hours is encouraged. From one perspective, these amenities provide the benefit of close childcare and access to bonus activities, but it also means that the lines between work and personal life become blurred, and it is difficult to set healthy boundaries for myself. I am set in an impossible circumstance, therefore, where I want to prove everyone wrong and give my children a better chance than I had but feel immense guilt if I spend too much time on my career. Experiencing the constant doubt from others that I would be able to handle it all, the many comments over the years that I would have been a better mother had I waited, has left a lasting mark. Women already feel pressure to "do it all": get married, have babies, a successful career, and stay thin. If I fail, society will blame it on teen parenthood.

Given the obvious chutes that I have encountered along the way, it's easy to miss the ladders that have kept me around in the world of academics. More than anything, what has propelled me forward are the female mentors I've had along the way. Through both formal and informal mentorship programs, I have had invaluable support from these women that has pushed me to keep going, helped me to see the importance of staying and challenging the stereotype of who belongs here, and given me the confidence to let the discomfort of other people be their problem. Yet the constant advocacy is tiring.

Although my mentors have been instrumental to my perseverance in this environment, some aspects could have been approached differently to improve my experience. To make the biggest impact, I would need to change people's perceptions of who is a professional, what it means to have been an adolescent mother, and how to create a sense of belonging in the workplace for people from nontraditional backgrounds. The steps to achieve this feel daunting and impossible. However, small changes could have made a significant difference. One of the most painful and isolating aspects of my experience has been seeing other moms form relationships and support networks at work while I struggled to relate or feel included. If those moms had thought to include me and been more aware of the damage cliques can cause, I would have felt more welcome. In addition, I have received countless inappropriate and hurtful comments at work that contributed to my feelings of "otherness." Our words are powerful, and if even half of those comments had been withheld, I would have felt less judged. Both of these circumstances could have benefited from more emphasis in the workplace on building community. Now that I am in a department that is supportive of taking time to speak with coworkers and supporting programs such as book clubs or walking groups, I find I have had opportunities to speak with colleagues about my experiences, which has been the best compassion training possible. Finally, it's important to note that with age and experience in this profession, I have gained confidence—not to feel less judged but to care less about others' opinions. This progression has fueled my passion to mentor others so they might reach this place sooner than I did.

RECOMMENDATIONS FOR READERS

Much work is yet to be done to help others understand the lifelong struggles of teen parents and the importance of supporting them. Unfortunately, academia is not structured to adequately support those of us with diverse backgrounds and experiences. However, departments and individuals can start small by implementing compassion training, setting flexible and reasonable expectations for commitments, and genuinely promoting work-life balance. In addition, those of us with similar experiences can use our positions to help build a supportive community for students who share these backgrounds. My recommendations include:

1. Offer or require compassion training for university employees.
2. Management should set reasonable expectations for outside work engagement and be flexible in support of work-life balance.
3. If you were a teen parent, seek out mentoring opportunities.
4. Managers should emphasize community building to provide opportunities for connection.

36

Academic Motherhood:

Holistic MotherScholars Lifting Each Other Up the Ladders

Lynn Bielski, Emily T. Cripe, Katharina A. Azim, Stacey H. Bender, Maggie Campbell-Obaid, Kathryn E. Frazier, Janet Garcia-Hallett, Jennifer H. Greene-Rooks, Amanda Harmon, N. A. Heller, Colleen C. Myles-Baltzly, Summer Melody Pennell, Ivanna Richardson, and Alexandra K. Frazer

Caregivers, particularly those from underrepresented groups, often face "chutes" in the forms of challenges in meeting academic expectations for teaching and research, and gendered norms of care work exacerbate the challenges that women+ feel.[1] As a result, mothers+ engage in more "invisible" service work (e.g., providing emotional support to students), produce less scholarship, and take longer to advance in their careers than colleagues without care responsibilities—especially during the pandemic (Docka-Filipek and Stone 2021; Górska et al. 2021; King and Frederickson 2021; Oleschuk 2020). This mirrors the hidden curriculum of academia that often pits motherhood against notions of the "ideal academic" who is fully intellectual (not emotional) and individual (not relational).

The MotherScholar Collective as a Ladder

During the pandemic's height, when teaching, research, and service expectations became particularly overwhelming for caregivers, the MotherScholar Collective (MSC, of which all authors are members) was created to make space for participants to exist meaningfully as both scholars and mothers of young children. The MSC resists academic pressure to compartmentalize the personal and professional (which often creates chutes for mothers), instead enabling authentic integration of mother and scholar identities. A shared investment in each other's success—based on genuine mutual care, both personally and professionally—produces a strong desire to research and write together. The MSC's working format creates a ladder for research and publications by allowing participants to contribute what they can, when they can, ensuring that projects reach completion even when some members need to step away. The result has been consistent productivity, well-received research, and continuously growing membership. Further, many members have continued to work in our group despite leaving academia for industry positions.

Implementing the MotherScholar Collective's Model to Benefit Women+ in Academia

Through working together since 2020, we have developed several practical methods through our adherence to a radical feminist flexibility (MotherScholar Collective et al. 2021, 2023). These methods provide ladders to participation in academic research to mothers+ who were otherwise struggling to work during the pandemic. These strategies can be applied beyond the pandemic, and we hope that academic institutions will use these practices to uplift marginalized voices by creating flexible research groups. Our practical strategies include:

Writing Practices

As academic mothers+, we all understand that academic work does not always come first, and that an ebb and flow to productivity is dependent on contextual and social factors, including familial caretaking responsibilities. Rather than reinscribing this feature of life as an academic chute, due to this mutual understanding and trust, we instead use a "hop on, hop off" approach to writing. Anyone who is interested in working on a manuscript participates as they can. This may mean that someone begins working on a text section and needs someone else to edit, finish, or refine it. We write together without judgment for how much time we can give, acknowledging that each writing and thinking task is an integral part of the scholarship process, allowing the collective to function as a ladder in our writing process.

Authorship

As explained, our research and writing practices allow for flexible contributions. This often means that traditional ways of quantifying input to determine authorship are less relevant. We also acknowledge that traditional academic structures can often result in those who have more power or capital being prioritized in authorship lists. Everyone who works on a manuscript gets authorship, and the author order is influenced by who has the greatest need. This is intentionally negotiated by all authors on every publication, and priority for first or second authorship is given to those in need of a ladder for their career stage (e.g., on the job market, working on tenure or promotion materials, or seeking new opportunities). In addition, when allowed by editors, the MotherScholar Collective as a whole is listed as the first author and applies to our entire active membership.

Facilitating Access: Stepladders

We work to bring multiple voices to our research. Our coding procedures, for example, allow for substantive participation by having a team open code the data set first, then create a summary document for feedback from the other coders as well as the larger authorship group. This process also allows those who want to learn new skills to receive mentorship from other members, creating stepladders that set up our members for success. When we conduct research on our own membership, such as our ongoing research on the effects of the pandemic, we offer multiple ways to participate, ranging from journaling or voice memos to more formal focus groups to structured questionnaires. No matter the format, we are committed to practices and procedures that allow motherscholars with limited time or bandwidth to participate.

Using Our Strengths

Unlike research collectives based in an academic field, our interdisciplinary group allows us to focus on our strengths across fields. Strong writers write, those with strong editing skills edit, and those who are good at organizing keep us on schedule. During meetings, those who are good synthesizers capture our ideas as outlines and rough abstracts. Our decentralized, inclusive, flexible model makes us more efficient and productive, as it encourages each individual to strengthen the efforts and outcomes of the group by leveraging their expertise and skills for the benefit of the collective good. Simultaneously, if members wish to acquire new skills, such as thematic analytic skill, they are guided by those with expertise in that area. Through these efforts and collaboratively constructed ladders, we are able to share knowledge, create connections across our disciplines, and conduct innovative work that is widely applicable to multiple fields and intersectional scholarly identities (see, e.g., our research on the experiences of academic mothers+ with disabilities [Wagner et al. 2022], women of color [Blanks Jones et al. 2021], and LGBTQ+ mothers+ [Pennell et al. 2021]).

RECOMMENDATIONS FOR READERS

1. Self-work is a productive first stepladder when seeking to create your own supportive network. Reflecting upon, and in some cases, unlearning the ways

academia has shaped your understanding of productivity, value, and shared commitment can support an approach to collaboration in which all tasks are equally valuable and so are their contributors with their diverse, intersecting identities and experiences.

2. Provide a ladder for scholars by grounding collaborations in shared commitment, both in your shared desire to successfully complete a project and in your personal determination of when to tap into or out of a task and when to take a break and prioritize self-care.
3. Eliminate chutes based on inequitable assumptions about substantial and meaningful scholarship. Help create ladders for others by advocating for institutional change to recognize and value participatory action research collaboratives, which should be weighted the same as other types of research during the hiring, promotion, and tenure processes.

37

Chutes and Ladders in the Rearview Mirror May Be Less Distinct Than They Initially Appeared

Jessica Salvatore

The people who make post-tenure moves to better-resourced institutions tend to be academic superstars. I am not an academic superstar, but a few years ago, I was fortunate enough to move from a very small liberal arts college to a thriving university, leading me to reflect on the decades leading up to that unusual move. Life *as I had lived it* had involved a mix of what this book calls ladders and chutes, but I couldn't help noticing that with enough hindsight, some of those blended or even switched places (see also McAdams et al., 2001). Let me illustrate with some examples.

An early ladder was an opportunity to do serious mentored biochemistry research starting in high school. My first publication was only a conference abstract, but it had undergone a form of peer review, and I was thrilled when it appeared in the *FASEB Journal* just before I turned sixteen. It's clear that this *was* a ladder: most public high-schoolers do not have access to such opportunities, but I was enrolled in a STEM magnet program in one of the wealthiest public school systems in the country, with ample research opportunities nearby in the DC metro area. Various forms of capital collided to my benefit there, including resources for finding opportunities, an environment that communicated the expectation of capitalizing on those opportunities, and my mother's ability to make sacrifices in her job to ensure that I was able to get to that lab during the school day. I am certain that this experience helped get me into a college where I was fortunate to work with faculty members who invested heavily in me. At the same time, I experienced extended sexual harassment at the research institute (though outside my lab), another PI recommended applying for scholarships he knew I wasn't eligible for (I didn't), and my own lab's PI never gave up trying to convert me to evangelical Christianity. It was an early lesson in the tricky power dynamics of the all-important ecosystem of letters of reference.

Later on, I again was fortunate in the timing of my grad school applications, receiving an Ivy League offer because a relatively new faculty member with priority to recruit happened to be seeking, at just the right moment, a first graduate student with interests like mine. But this incredible blessing was also complicated by the degree of pressure that she was under in a context where tenure historically had been awarded stingily. To build her case, my adviser spent both my first and my third years at research institutes in other states. As I worked to develop a dissertation proposal, I eventually wound up supervised by another faculty member as a natural outgrowth of this distance. The change was not due to a lack of underlying support from my initial adviser, and what initially felt like a "chute" (having to switch advisers) in hindsight reads to me as the opposite, as I wound up with two powerhouse mentors in my corner for many years.

But the peripatetic realities of academia at all ranks continued to complicate my experience as I moved into a first postdoc in the United Kingdom: two of the three principal investigators on the grant I'd been hired to work on left my new institution within months of my arrival. Further, per the perverse logic of grantsmanship, the work promised in the grant was really already done, which left me floundering at first. I finally found local "sea legs" after developing some unexpected collaborations (and friendships) that remain strong even now—which might never have happened had my initial understanding of the postdoc not been dizzyingly upended.

In fact, *global* upendings were also rampant around that time; another terrifying experience for many, including me, was the sudden academic hiring freeze that accompanied the financial collapse of 2008. A campus interview offer that I was particularly excited about—a definite ladder, if I could land it—was abruptly rescinded shortly before my flight. I was lucky eventually to land a second postdoc back in the United States, a reprieve from needing to leave academia. In that postdoc, I benefited from talented students, plentiful resources, and once again caring feminist mentors, which together helped me envision and launch the beginnings of a large, lengthy project that continues to sustain me intellectually more than a decade later. With that said, the inherently marginal and contingent nature of a time-limited academic position meant that the scope was limited for developing programmatic work. Without a continuing contract, for example, like most postdocs under most institutions' rules, I was not eligible to seek external funding independently.

I only really felt legitimized when I finally landed a tenure-track job after five cycles on the junior-level job market. In a small liberal arts environment, I was grateful for the larger network I had spent years cultivating, which allowed to me thrive in a "small pond" without sacrificing active scholarship. But the job turned out to be far less secure than I hoped: after only a year and a half, the institution announced its intent to close, and all employees were told that our jobs would be terminated. I needed to again rely heavily on my generous mentors and network immediately to mobilize my portfolio and references as I dived back into the job market in the spring.

Although this is unambiguously a "chute"—and *was* truly scary—an exhilarating sense of new possibilities quickly kicked in alongside that fear and uncertainty. I turned down another good postdoc offer in favor of one year as a visiting professor. This year in limbo found me desperately applying for wildly inappropriate administrative and alt-ac jobs with minimal relevant experience but also pushed productively to acknowledge the various emotionally complicated forms of privilege that buffered this nosedive off the tenure track, such as a lack of family care responsibilities tying me to a specific location, as well as the safety net held up for me by those in my networks.

Ultimately, something surprising happened: the small college did not close after all, and I returned. When I was tenured there soon after, I'm a little embarrassed to say that I felt great liberation, because tenure had always been its own goal for me: I realized that after many professional ups and downs, I'd deeply desired to prove to myself simply that it was possible. But in transparency, during this period I also felt some ambivalence about aging (Cecil et al. 2023), including resentment about how my inability to stay for long in any one place made it difficult to imagine having children at any certain moment before it was functionally too late in my life to do so. What had functioned as privilege in the past (giving me flexibility to draw on when I needed it) had, over time, come to mean something more mixed.

After tenure, I settled in a bit more at my institution. I took on internal leadership roles, began doing academic coaching, and served a term on the board of a professional organization. I was increasingly in a position to credibly champion others for awards and work to support students in their career aspirations, which typically were not in academia. These experiences helped me land a role as the head of a department about the same size (~1300 majors) as my entire undergraduate institution. For three years, it has been an honor, and extremely rewarding, to be able to facilitate opportunities for others at this larger scale. And as I write this, I've made the decision to step away from a job focused mainly on administration—my life's most recent reminder to me to expect and accept mixed, and perhaps unanticipated, meanings from each new development.

RECOMMENDATIONS FOR READERS

1. Chutes can be exhilarating—like a waterslide. Climbing ladders can be an exhausting workout that leave you a little too high up for comfort. It is not always clear in the moment what will be an advantage or a disadvantage in the longer term.
2. Building on that thought, challenge yourself to stay flexible and resilient when things change. An academic career can appear to have many "single points of failure," but there may be many possible alternatives or variations on the future you had envisioned initially.
3. Brazenly leverage all the forms of capital and privilege at your disposal. If you are established in your career, seek ways to leverage these on behalf of others.

Caregiver Scholars

38

Caregiving and Academia without a Filter:

When a Pandemic Made Invisible Dependents Visible

Karen Sobel and Melissa Bowles-Terry

Introduction

What a day, I thought, directing my university's faculty center over Zoom while my first grader used Google Classroom next to me. *At least the shutdown is just for two weeks*. My husband struggled with Microsoft Teams from his basement desk. Three family members, three online platforms, one new world. (Both authors have the same basic pandemic story: we direct university faculty centers and spent the early shutdown at home with one first grader and one spouse each.)

Several years later, we've long since returned to our faculty centers. Although many things have returned to normal, we still talk with faculty members daily about the pandemic's effects. Many conversations have to do with the sudden ways in which families became a workplace reality. Instead of dropping children off at school or arranging for a midday home health aide's visit to an aging parent, these arrangements became fragile or nonexistent.

Both authors feel driven to support our faculty caregivers in their struggles and pursuits—the "chutes" of full-time caregiving when it intersects with career responsibilities or ambitions and the "ladders" of building a mentorship and care network that makes it all possible. In this chapter, we will share major lessons that we, as faculty development professionals and faculty members, learned during the COVID-19 pandemic. We hope this will help colleagues across higher education to support each other.

Concrete Challenges of Caregiving while Being a Scholar and Teacher

Faculty members speak of the challenges of living the dualities of teacher and scholar. There's often a degree of conflict between the high-contact, time-intensive nature of teaching and the need for copious quiet time, proper equipment, and more to support one's scholarship. Layer that with full-time caregiving, and the degree of difficulty in achieving success becomes almost unsolvable. Both our personal experience and recent scholarly analysis suggests that women's workplace success was affected more than men's (McNulty and Lufler 2022).

During the pandemic, faculty members struggled with academic journals' schedules. Many journals fell months behind due to lack of availability of reviewers. This places tremendous stress on faculty who need a certain number of publications per year. An article from June 2022 in *Inside Higher Ed* describes "The Peer-Review Crisis." Journal editors found that in the early days of the pandemic, they were able to find reviewers for articles as some academics were working from home with extra time on their hands. But in 2021–22, participation in peer-review dropped off as professors found burnout catching up with them (Flaherty 2022). The delay in review and publication is a special problem for those who struggled to finish research and write due to caregiving duties.

Finding workable conference presentation opportunities proved a struggle as well. Many conferences moved toward virtual mode during the pandemic. However, numerous other conferences were canceled or downscaled. Others came back in person in 2021, when many caregivers were still unable to travel.

Some universities made meaningful attempts to support faculty and provide ladders by adjusting research expectations for faculty going through tenure processes and during pandemic-era annual reviews. However, this supported faculty of different ranks unequally. Long-term effects have not been accounted for. Caregivers, with their overlapping, ever-changing load of situations and responsibilities, were arguably affected to a greater degree than others.

As teachers, faculty of all ranks struggled with the order to move in-person courses online almost instantaneously. These challenges, and the social and educational implications of this shift, are already well documented (Daumiller et al. 2021). Years later, faculty continue to discuss the change in students' classroom social skills and in specific areas of learning and classroom behavior resulting from a year spent learning online.

Years after the big March 2020 pandemic modality shift, some universities still ask that faculty be "flexible" in response to their students' needs. However, universities have removed much of the flexibility that we once offered in terms of evaluating and supporting our faculty.

The multilayered, intersectional struggle that faculty members are experiencing contributes a great deal of stress to faculty members' lives. Caregivers still struggle with the after-effects of both shifts in teaching and research, layered with home responsibilities that do not feel settled.

Authentic Support for Caregivers

What have we learned through this pandemic that helps us better support faculty caregivers in the long run? This is an incomplete list, and these activities, or ladders to propel faculty forward, should be supported through both policy and funding.

Social Support

Providing a place for faculty to share concerns and strategies in a friendly environment goes a long way. We'll emphasize, though, that social support needs to be combined with more pragmatic support that's consistent across the university.

It can be helpful to offer a group where faculty caregivers from all departments are welcome. Host open conversations on what's happening, what people are feeling, and what would be helpful. Lesson learned by a faculty development professional: do not push the group to do "projects" or to have specific outcomes.

On a practical level, consider working with administrators to identify viable options for faculty caregivers. Make these available to department chairs and other leaders across your institution. This can help create greater equity and stronger support, particularly in units run by leaders who are not caregivers. Guidelines can include, for example, ways to structure time for faculty who must perform school pickup but who could teach online afterward.

Supporting Research

The following strategies can help support faculty in their research or creative work. We are not advocating for lowering the standards. In this situation, rather, we advocate for greater flexibility of timelines, where scholarly or creative output may be assessed and "averaged" over a longer period of time. This allows for ebbs and flows of productivity. Although faculty developers do not control these evaluation timelines, we often have connections with the groups at our institutions that do.

On the topic of timelines, advocating for reenvisioning requirements related to publication may benefit all. If your institution requires publications to be "accepted" or even published before faculty may take credit for tenure, promotion, or review, consider whether your institution might restructure that requirement to include "works in progress." This adjustment can take a great deal of pressure off caregivers and others.

Supporting Teaching

The conversation about supporting teaching is at a different place from the conversation surrounding research. Much of the support needed for pandemic teaching shifts occurred immediately out of necessity. The more relevant questions about supporting teaching at this point are: What changes do we need to keep in our teaching supports? How do we create and maintain the level of agility needed to support faculty through potential future upheaval?

Some lessons that have emerged from supporting pandemic teaching involve the need to provide technology, technology support, and training for online teaching. Our centers can help provide some of this support and advocate for other parts.

Late-pandemic, faculty often speak of the challenges of supporting the "flexibility" that they're asked to provide students while not being supported with flexibility themselves. Moving forward, many faculty intuitively support this need for greater flexibility yet feel overwhelmed by the lack of guidelines. We, as faculty development professionals, can support faculty and administrators as they redefine those boundaries.

Conclusion

Moving forward, our hope is that academia will take advantage of this moment to explore our cultural assumptions of how faculty must "filter" images of their lives as caregivers. Making invisible care work visible is a potential step toward valuing it more as a society. In a 2021 article about the costs of caring for America's elderly, Anne Helen Petersen points out how care work—both paid and unpaid—has been feminized and racialized, which means we either don't think of it as work, or we don't think of it as valuable work (Peterson 2021). If administrators can consciously create pathways or ladders to mitigate the emotional labor of caregiving as a faculty member through policies such as flexible work hours or adjustments to tenure clocks, that is one step toward recognition of the vital societal work of caregiving that can no longer be hidden in the off-screen parts of our lives.

RECOMMENDATIONS FOR READERS

1. Work with your institution to better support caregivers through policies. Support flexibility in teaching arrangements as well as in promotion and tenure guidelines.
2. Continue to provide support for faculty who are learning to teach online.
3. Discuss caregivers' needs open and active on campus. Normalize discussing family and personal situations.
4. Help campus administrators understand ways to support faculty caregivers.
5. Support flexibility in evaluation timelines. Productivity ebbs and flows for everyone.

39

Navigating Hopeful and Heartbreaking Caregiving in Academia

Courtney B. Peters

Caregivers. This word can mean many things. Caregivers can be celebrating the most joyous occasions in life—welcoming a new biological, foster, or adoptive infant or child. Caregivers could also be facing some of the hardest days—providing continuing or end-of-life care for a loved one. Caregiving spans the time between these two occasions with some seasons being more demanding than others. Regardless of the situation, caregiving presents additional obstacles to achieving success in academia that is often amplified by other identities that caregivers hold.

The hidden curriculum of academia can act as an unforgiving structure, where the lack of institutional flexibility can function as a *chute*, resulting in caregivers struggling or falling behind, whereas strategic mentorship, supportive policies, and building community can act as *ladders* that help scholars continue advancing in their careers. The importance of recognizing potential pitfalls and developing strategies for avoiding them and leveling up are irreplaceable. To navigate the hidden curriculum in the area of caregiving, I suggest a three-perspective approach:

1. **From the caregiver's perspective**—The academic community is slow to change. We must accept this while also advocating for necessary improvements and continuing to make the incremental changes necessary for success. In the meantime, we must also survive (and, hopefully, thrive). To do this, we must create advocates, find mentor(s), and build teams.
2. **From the institutional perspective**—Flexibility must be prioritized. Institutions should reevaluate rigid and traditional tenure timelines and expectations and build policies that promote equity across diverse lifestyles as well as different seasons of life.
3. **From the individual + institutional perspective**—Norms must change. Unhealthy workstyles should no longer be the expectations. We must create a structure that promotes work-life balance for all and especially for caregivers.

My own experience illustrates these chutes and ladders, and my reasoning for these perspectives is influenced by my personal role as a caregiver, which has spanned both the joyous and the heartbreaking but not in the traditional order. As my mother and father both passed away before I began my PhD program at the age of twenty-seven, I became the primary caregiver to my disabled older sister. Caregiving made the task of applying and being accepted into a PhD program that much more difficult. This is where I realized the importance of *creating advocates*—someone who has witnessed my work ethic and could support me when I faced setbacks. My sister passed away during the second year of my program, and I was very strained by my class load while providing the best end-of-life care that I could—care that took me almost three hours away from my university for the last three weeks of the semester. This time was made easier because of the advocates I had—those who knew my work ethic and were willing to provide me with the structure, space, and time needed to finish out the semester. This allowed me to hold onto the ladder rather than falling down a chute.

Shortly thereafter, I came to realize the importance of *mentors*. During the third year of my program, my husband and I welcomed a beautiful baby girl to the world during a global pandemic. With one course left prior to work on my dissertation, I went back to virtual classes—having missed only two classes. Had I not finished that semester with my tiny newborn attending her first PhD seminar at three weeks old, I would have been almost a year and a half behind in my program due to the structure of class schedules. Although many suggested I take this leave, I knew it would function as a chute delaying my career progression significantly. The scheduled structure of academia is not conducive to "interruptions." I held on because of the mentors who told me I could do it. Although not ideal and something I hope will change in the future, the reality is that change takes time. To prevent me from falling down the chute, I leaned on my mentors and pushed through. My professor for this specific class was extremely supportive. I attended a weeklong virtual workshop over the class topic prior to my absence to make up for the two weeks I was out with my daughter. This professor helped arrange this to ensure that I had the opportunity to learn the material properly while also not lowering any expectations of performance. This scenario was not ideal, but it highlights how supportive mentorship can serve as a ladder, enabling caregivers to persist within academia's rigid structure.

Now, having defended my dissertation and started my career as a tenure-track professor, I recognize the importance of *building a team*. Both my advocates and my mentors continually reiterated the importance of academic relationships. Building a team of coauthors and more simply, friends within and across my university and my discipline, is the goal. Because academic structure does not lend itself ideally to caregivers, it is of utmost importance to have a hand that can help guide you to and up the ladder rungs while avoiding any chutes. In short, relationships are vital.

This brings me to the institutional perspective. Although change in academia is slow, I think for the future that academia should consider ways and processes for providing more flexibility to caregivers by letting go of traditional timelines and expectations. We need to focus on building policies that promote equity across not only diverse lifestyles but also in diverse seasons of life. The academic tenure system as we know it was designed more than eighty years ago in a time that is very different from today ("Tenure" 2006). Academic literature surrounding the impacts of caregiving in academia has expanded significantly, especially since the beginning of the COVID-19 pandemic. Academic literature suggests crafting new and removing and/or adapting old criteria that disservice caregivers such as considering the impacts of assigning specific timelines to tenure expectations and funding (Meirmans, Lamatsch, and Neiman 2022). Institutions should critically examine tenure expectations and other structures that inadvertently create chutes for caregivers. By embedding flexibility in academic policies, universities can ensure ladders are created that foster long-term retention and career advancement for caregivers.

From an individual and institutional perspective, we, as individuals, must shape the institution's processes by changing the norms. Rather than waiting for systemic reforms, we must lead by example—rejecting unhealthy workstyles, advocating for policy changes, and mentoring others to avoid the chutes we have faced. These changes happen through sustained and incremental collective action, starting with everyday conversations, implicit bias awareness, and a commitment to making changes from the bottom to the top. Together, we can serve as advocates and mentors today to shape a better tomorrow for our future colleagues.

The challenges of caregiving made the physical and mental toll of a PhD program that much more difficult for me; navigating the challenges and rewards of caregiving has encompassed a process of learning when to ask for help. It involves hanging on to the ladders and avoiding the chutes when the challenges have driven climbing to a halt. Discernment in making these moves is difficult, but the strategies of *creating advocates*, *finding mentors*, and *building a team* have proven invaluable in my personal journey. These tools continue to serve me, and I hope they can serve others as mechanisms for navigating academia's hidden curriculum.

RECOMMENDATIONS FOR READERS

1. **Build a support network.** Success in academia is not a solo endeavor; cultivating relationships can help you navigate the chutes.
2. **Seek mentors and advocates.** Identify mentors who understand the challenges of caregiving. Allow them to advocate for you in more difficult seasons of life.
3. **Advocate for systemic change.** Be what you want the system to be and pass that on to those entering the field of academia.
4. **Recognize the chutes and ladders.** Barriers exist within academia, but identifying and leveraging opportunities that can help you progress is paramount.

40

The Bittersweet Fruits of Perseverance

Lesley Thornton-Cronin

Many women academics receive the same cliched advice: never mention your partner, or wanting children, take off your ring when you interview … When I first heard it from a mentor in the United Kingdom in 2015, it already sounded anachronistic. After nearly falling down my first *chute*, however, I took this advice to heart, and it shaped my approach to my academic career.

The implicit message is obvious: departments don't want to hire you because as a female-presenting person of "childbearing age," you will run off and have babies, which is inconvenient. Astonishingly, I once lost an academic position in my home country of Canada in the final round to a candidate whose LinkedIn profile indicated in no uncertain terms that she would not need parental leave. Of course, I can never know for certain why I wasn't chosen: as is typical, I was given no explanation. It does, however, speak volumes about the culture that this candidate felt the need to disclose such personal information, which employers in Canada are legally prohibited from asking about.

Similar advice is shared in relation to other facets of our identities, such as gender and sexual identity or visible and invisible disabilities. My first *chute* was medical. During my PhD, I was diagnosed with cancer. I was on a generous international scholarship as a Canadian student in the United Kingdom with a very tight funding window in which to complete my doctorate without paying exorbitant international fees. After disclosing my diagnosis, within the academic space my cancer was mostly discussed in terms of *inconvenience* (missed conferences, publishing, teaching opportunities, etc., that would affect my ability to secure a postdoc). I received no institutional support: no discussion of funding extensions, medical leave, or counseling. I skipped the conferences, published minimally, taught, and worked through the night to submit a *stellar* thesis on the deadline. I aced my defense and passed unconditionally—at the expense of my mental and physical health.

At the time, I was so proud of myself for *powering through*, for not making a fuss and for gritting my teeth and getting the job done. It would later be jarring to find that my efforts would go unrewarded: to face the job market and the reality that academia owed me nothing. In hindsight, it was a privilege to live into my late twenties without experiencing ableism.

Upon moving back to Toronto, I had an exciting postdoctoral project lined up with a "big-name professor." We applied for funding through a federal granting agency, and I naively used the opportunity provided in the "allowable inclusions" section of the application to explain the circumstances of my cancer treatment and the impact on my publishing record. To our shock, the application was rejected due to my "capability to complete the project." My appeal was rejected. I've since been warned by disabled scholars to never mention one's health status on *any* application; the question itself is a trap.

I felt compelled to share my story in part because it relates to Canadian mythmaking. Canada is often characterized as a "socialist utopia"—a liberal counterpoint to America's comparatively draconian healthcare and parental leave policies. Canada's identity often rests on not being "as bad as the United States." But, like academia, Canada has much better international PR than actual practice.

I am now a full professor in a polytechnic college in Toronto. This means that I have job security, benefits, a pension, and academic freedom. Only 25 percent of professors in the Ontario college system have such protections. Some 75 percent of my college colleagues across the province of Ontario are hired as *adjuncts* on precarious, exploitative short-term contracts that last only 15–17 weeks at a time. I worked as an adjunct for more than six years. In addition to being egregiously underpaid, for those six years as an adjunct I was technically unemployed between contracts (e.g., between semesters, over winter break, and over the summer). Consequently, I lost access to coverage for prescription medication and birth control, physiotherapy and other pain management, dental, and medical and parental leave outside those contract dates.

I love teaching and wanted desperately to be a full-time professor, but I knew that was unlikely to happen if I was *inconvenient*. Even though a permanent academic career seemed unlikely after six years of unsuccessful applications and precarity, I knew that pregnancy could further threaten my options. When my partner, who is also an academic, and I decided to become parents, neither of us told our workplaces for fear of discrimination. This magical moment in our lives had to be treated as a dirty secret.

My daughter was born over the 2020 winter break, on the night after I submitted final grades and my contract ended. She arrived between contracts, so I wasn't eligible for *any* maternity or parental benefits: I wasn't technically employed, despite working for the same college for six years and on either side of that winter break. I had no job security, so I kept my head down and persevered. I learned from cancer not to ask for help, so I returned to work at the start of the new semester at ten days postpartum. My employer still did not know that I had had a child.

My other choice would have been to decline my contract for that semester—a risky career move. My seniority would have been compromised, and I would have had no guarantee of rehiring after a break. It would also have meant giving up a paycheck for at least eight months. I've since met other women, even within my own department, who chose the unemployment option postpartum and faced financial and career consequences for their decisions.

I've been called strong more times than I can count, for both the cancer and for sacrificing maternity leave. But it wasn't strength; it was desperation. Is it really *strength* and *sacrifice* to take the only realistic option available? To overcome exploitative conditions that shouldn't exist in the first place? When I lectured virtually with my ten-day-old infant on my lap, students called me *amazing*, but they didn't know that I was wearing a diaper—stitched up and in pain from a traumatic birth, not to mention struggling with the crushing isolation of navigating the pandemic as a new mom. In the case of both *chutes*, my choice was clear: compromise my health *or* compromise a potential academic career.

My decision to return to work immediately is the direct result of my own chutes and ladders. The cancer chute taught me that the only way to achieve academic success was to never complain, show weakness, or ask for anything; instead, demonstrate at all costs that I am an unproblematic candidate who does outstanding work and won't cause a fuss. As uncomfortable as it is to discuss the early months of the pandemic as a *ladder*, the increase in asynchronous teaching was the only way that I could have pulled off my return to work so quickly. The flexibility meant that my partner and I were both always home and could alternate equally between work and childcare (there was no sleeping). The impact on my physical and mental health would have been dramatically worse if I had had to return to work in-person so quickly postpartum.

After a hellish postpartum semester, I was ready to give up on academia. The personal costs were too high. I was burned out and angry at the state of academia. Against all odds, however, my final application was successful. I felt immense relief at achieving job security in the field that I love—but I didn't feel *validated*. Any vindication was canceled out by my experiences of institutional exclusion. My daughter, then about six months old, cried as I accepted the offer over the phone, and I did not feel the need to keep her private anymore.

It is bleak to imagine *what if it hadn't paid off*, although this could easily have happened. It is the norm not only for most emerging art historians but for most academics that perseverance and excellence do not guarantee career success (or even a career). To have persevered through cancer and childbirth and still not have "made it" in academia, I imagine, would have been soul-crushing. I would not have been able to afford to live on an adjunct salary and would have needed to switch careers. Likely, I would have needed to leave my home country. With a severe housing and cost-of-living crisis, it would have been an extreme struggle to raise a child in Toronto with a career in the arts, let alone navigate the challenge of switching careers in one's thirties.

Further, with the defunding and devaluating of the arts, it is likely that I would have faced the same challenges in industry that I had in academia: underpay, precarity, and discrimination. Similarly, it is disheartening to imagine the what ifs had I *not* fallen down the chutes. If I had never had cancer and had chosen not to have a child, an academic career could still have been just as easily out of sight. Only 19 percent of PhD holders in Canada have tenure or tenure-track positions. Further, within five years of finishing the PhD, male academics make 19 percent more than their female colleagues in Canada, with women, people with disabilities, and racialized academics far more likely to be working in academia part-time or as adjuncts ("Degrees of Success" 2021).

When I became tenured, I didn't feel validated or rewarded, but I felt the weight lift from my chest. I felt a profound relief for my family, my paycheck, *and* a fiery responsibility to fight for adjunct professors. Faculty with permanent positions must use our security and academic freedom to advocate for our peers: we cannot expect the oppressed to risk their future employment by fighting for their rights and for better treatment. After all, can we really expect change if those with institutional protections fail to both reveal the existence and address the consequences of such inequities?

RECOMMENDATIONS FOR READERS

1. Those with the privilege of secure employment cannot ignore how our adjunct peers are treated. Be an ally and fight for a more equitable academia. Vote with them in mind, talk to your deans, and get out on the picket line.
2. "Adjunctification" isn't stopping. In fact, it is getting worse. In the time between writing this chapter and its publication, the percentage of adjunct faculty in the Ontario college system has risen from 70 percent to 75 percent. We need to properly welcome adjunct colleagues into the faculty and provide them with the resources they need to excel. I didn't even have a desk or know where the printer was as an adjunct; I took meetings in the cafeteria. When administrators reinforce this hierarchical distinction between tenured and nontenured faculty, those of us with job security must push back.
3. Parental discrimination cannot be a women's-only issue. The fight for disability justice cannot be fought only by those with disabilities. To make lasting systemic change requires meaningful allyship.
4. Acknowledge how short-term contracts and the resulting lack of benefits and job security threaten women's equality, maternal health, and equality for disabled people and people requiring medication *across all industries*. Fight for legal protections, unionization, paid leave, and bridging benefits for contract workers. Importantly, we need to be transparent with graduate students about the state of the academic job market and the prevalence of such discriminatory *chutes*.

Scholars with Disabilities

41

On-Campus Interviews: The Invisible Chutes and Missed Ladders for Disabled Academics

Melanie R. Savelli

The Rules of the Game

In the academic version of Chutes and Ladders, disabled candidates encounter far more chutes, steep drops in opportunity, than ladders to advancement. The on-campus interview, especially, is rife with hidden chutes that derail otherwise qualified candidates from progressing in the academic pipeline. Disabled PhD candidates face obstacles related to physical accessibility, accommodations, social exclusion, and systemic barriers. Once people with a disability have brutally navigated all the chutes in earning a PhD, they must scale the rough terrain of the sought-after but dreaded campus interview before being able to break into professorship. On-campus interviews are a marathon of obstacles, with added pressure for those with disabilities or chronic illness. They must disclose their disability, cope with implicit bias and discrimination, and navigate logistical challenges related to accommodations. Some are not even allowed to participate due to travel or health issues.

Disclosure and Implicit Bias

Getting to and surviving the interview has the hidden chute of disability disclosure. The decision to disclose a disability is one of the most precarious chutes disabled candidates face. Disclosure can offer a ladder in the form of accommodations, but too often it leads to bias and lost opportunity. The decision of whether to disclose a disability is similar to disclosing a pregnancy in that it can come with risks and benefits. Candidates may choose not to disclose a disability due to concerns about discrimination or stigmatization. Candidates also must wonder if their requests to level the playing field are seen as "too high maintenance" or "too demanding" and impact their likelihood of a job offer. Just because something is illegal, doesn't mean that it is not done. Disclosure, however, may also help ensure that appropriate accommodations are provided during the interview process. Specific examples of challenges faced by candidates with disabilities may include navigating inaccessible buildings or coping with sensory overload during in-person interviews.

Disabilities are related to implicit bias in that they can trigger negative stereotypes and assumptions on the part of search committees. This bias can be a liability for both candidates and committees, as it can lead to discrimination against candidates or legal challenges against the institution for failing to make appropriate accommodations. Gender biases that women face, such as concerns about pregnancy or maternity leave, may align with the insecurities that search committees face when considering candidates with disabilities. To address these issues, universities must make good on their DEI efforts by providing support for candidates with disabilities and ensuring that search committees are trained to recognize and overcome their biases.

The Format of the Traditional Job Interview

Typically, academic job searches culminate in inviting the top three candidates to campus for a marathon of interviews, assessments, and events. The process costs the university a lot of time and money, but it also requires candidates to pack up their lives for several days for an interview that may not land them a job. Candidates are expected to do this repeatedly if they are fortunate enough to land several interviews.

This is stressful and exhausting under the best of circumstances, but people with disabilities have additional struggles that often go unnoticed or unacknowledged. Although it is evident that the traditional on-campus interview process is due for major revisions, it cannot be emphasized enough that the revisions are born out of necessity for disabled candidates, not just the preferences of able-bodied ones. Because we can all benefit from such changes, it is imperative that the process is revamped so that we can increase the accessibility of academic jobs to disabled candidates. Refusing to do so means going against the "diversity, equity, and inclusion" values that most universities claim to have.

RECOMMENDATIONS FOR READERS

The following suggestions are designed to eliminate some of the invisible chutes embedded in the traditional academic interview process and to create more ladders for disabled candidates to ascend. Each recommendation addresses hidden aspects of the academic hiring process, norms and expectations that are often unspoken but powerfully exclusionary. These suggestions benefit able-bodied individuals by improving their experience, but for disabled candidates, these ladders may be the only way to participate in the academic job search at all.

Ladder 1: Consolidate and Virtualize

The traditional model of fragmented interviews across multiple days is an exhausting chute for disabled candidates, draining their energy and often worsening chronic conditions. Consolidating interviews and moving them online creates a ladder toward inclusion by making the process more accessible and equitable. Throughout the on-campus interview, job candidates are interviewed separately by a variety of entities such as departmental colleagues, the dean, the provost, students, and other interest groups. Instead, one main interview should be conducted with all interested parties. If a certain party feels that they have different questions aimed at ascertaining different information, meetings with them should only be about this extra information that was not already explained in the group interview. This will also save the time of the interviewers. In fact, virtual meetings come with the added benefit of recording sessions so they can be viewed by stakeholders/decision-makers who may not have been able to attend the original interview.

For virtual interviews, the search committee should offer closed captioning for the candidate. They should also type the question in the "chat" for the candidate. All candidate interviews should be held in the same format, lest one candidate be privileged over another for incidental opportunities for the committee to evaluate/chat with/get to know a candidate. Virtual interviews, although increasing efficiency, also depersonalize the interview.

Ladder 2: Request Recorded Teaching and Research Presentations

Teaching and research presentations are time-consuming for search committees and their colleagues. Faculty members often then must yield scarce classroom time with their students to the job candidate. Instead, candidates could provide a recording of their own classes.

This solution offers four main benefits. First, candidates already have a rapport with their own students, providing a more realistic perspective on their teaching style. Second, faculty can view the presentation on their own time. The third benefit is that recording a teaching demonstration is efficient for the candidate, as well, as they can send the same recording to multiple schools. Lastly, allowing candidates to record themselves at their own institutions offers the often-overlooked value of candidates teaching in an environment that is already equipped with any accommodation that they may need. These same guidelines and benefits can also extend to research presentations. Recording research presentations allows candidates to demonstrate how things work in their own labs, with their own equipment. Using recorded teaching and research presentations makes the academic interview more inclusive of disabled and chronically ill candidates. This shift doesn't just support accessibility; it builds a ladder for disabled candidates to present their best selves in familiar environments, leveling the playing field.

Ladder 3: Make the Offer Contingent upon the Visit

At some point, the candidate should be invited to campus so that the candidate and school can see if they are a good fit for each other. Being in-person allows candidates to see the actual campus and its facilities. They can meet students and potential colleagues in a less formal setting.

By making campus visits only necessary when a job has been offered, candidates will then only be packing up their medications, assistive devices, and sometimes caregivers when a serious job offer is on the table. For instance, candidates with chronic health conditions such as diabetes, lupus, or multiple sclerosis may require medications, special diets, or rest periods during the visit. Candidates with sensory disabilities, such as blindness or deafness, may require accommodations such as interpreters, captioning, or Braille materials. Candidates with mobility disabilities may need to bring assistive devices such as wheelchairs, walkers, or crutches. They may also require accommodations such as accessible transportation and lodging. It makes these sacrifices much more worthwhile, and theoretically, they will only have to go through the process once. Requiring travel only after a conditional offer is a small but impactful ladder, one that signals respect for candidates' time, bodies, and dignity.

Ladder 4: Make Traditional On-Campus Visits More Humane

To make traditional on-campus visits more humane for candidates, universities can take several steps. First, they can offer accommodations proactively to all candidates, including those with disabilities, to ensure that their needs are met during the visit. Second, they can shorten meetings to prevent candidates from experiencing exhaustion or burnout. Third, they can lengthen breaks to give candidates time to recharge and reflect on the experience. Finally, universities can review legal and illegal questions with all faculty and graduate students involved in the interview process to ensure that candidates are not subjected to discriminatory or inappropriate questions. These steps can help create a more welcoming and inclusive environment for all candidates and ensure that the interview process is fair and equitable. These humane adjustments can transform what is often a discriminatory chute into a ladder that lifts all candidates, disabled or not, into a fairer, more inclusive interview experience.

42

OCD Meets PhD:

The Fight to Thrive in Academia with an Invisible Illness

Maya Novak-Herzog

I have OCD—obsessive compulsive disorder. This diagnosis is often trivialized in common parlance or attributed in positive or desirable ways as increased "attention to detail," but in reality, it's a disability that makes an academic career quite difficult.

If you have OCD, you are 41 percent less likely to finish a degree and 48 percent less likely to finish postgraduate education (Pérez-Vigil et al. 2018). If you are a woman, you are 16 percent less likely than your male counterparts to finish graduate school and 18 percent more likely to drop out in your first year (Bostwick and Weinberg 2022). Female students with OCD face a disproportionate number of "chutes"—obstacles such as stigma, lack of accommodations, and isolation—on their path toward gaining their degree and securing a job in academia: a struggle that speaks to larger issues of inequality for neurodivergent and mentally ill women in academia. How can we create support systems to allow this neglected group to thrive?

In writing this chapter, I had too much to say, too many ways to say it, and, most of all, too many ways to say it wrong. Could I speak for the OCD community in academia? *Was there even an OCD community in academia?* I could feel the immense weight of my own experiences piling up on the page, truly unspeakable. Deep down, the prominent thought was, "They're going to think I'm crazy."

Unwanted obsessions and compulsions characterize OCD. Obsessions are unwanted thoughts that cause individuals stress, anxiety, or fear. Compulsions are repetitive rituals individuals engage in to alleviate those obsessions (Veale and Roberts 2014). The World Health Organization ranks OCD as one of the ten most devastating conditions based on the decreased quality of life.

As I attempted to write this chapter, the fear of being seen as crazy, a term I intellectually knew to be rooted in mental health stigma and gendered complexities but emotionally feared like no other, cascaded through my head until even the idea of laying the words out on the page became both urgent and impossible. I became obsessed with it. Can I really tell strangers that I refresh my emails so many times per second that my fingers start to cramp; that my eyes start to blur, and I start seeing that stupid red bubble pop up with overflowing numbers even when it isn't there? Can I really tell strangers that I've had to attend conferences with Band-Aids on each finger because I've picked my nailbeds off the night before?

And the potential hypothetical judgments from ungenerous readers of this chapter reminded me of the way I had perceived my peers and professors for the past four years—four years of vulnerability in standing before men with tenure and men without it whose eyes always already tell me that I am wrong and doing it wrong before I even speak. Every email I received in the past four years a reflection of my weakness, my embarrassing womanhood, and inabilities smattered in writing and piling up unattended—no, who am I kidding, piling up so attended that every word has been read and examined one thousand times so that I have imagined every possible disapproval. This chapter reflected back to me the overwhelming feeling that I wasn't understood.

And with these thoughts playing in a never-ending loop in my head, I faced myself for the first time. *Oh* ... I sat poised over the computer, my heart racing in its most familiar pattern, and realized *I'm feeling shame.*

Researchers have found shame to be a significant barrier in OCD sufferers seeking treatment or help (Laving et al. 2023). Shame, what Brené Brown calls the "unspoken epidemic" for women, was a very familiar feeling (Brown 2006). It brought me back to every instance of paralysis, unable to exit my bed for fear of the judgment that awaited me. One way that OCD interacts with shame is through cognitive dissonance (Elliot and Devine 1994). I know this feeling/action is irrational, yet I must think/do it anyway. Paralysis ensues. So, the inability to exit my bed is colored by the inability to stay there. I must move; I can't move for fear of the judgment that awaits me; for fear that *this* presentation, *this* conference, *this* section would be the one where the mask would finally fall, and the razor-thin threads holding the facade together would split, and finally, this time, I would come undone, and my insanity would be exposed. After all, the thoughts in my head can only get so loud before you start hearing them, too, right?

My experience of shame is colored by my experience with OCD. And although one's experience of OCD may be very different depending on who they are as well as their identity markers (if you've met one person with OCD, *you've met one person with OCD*, and that's it), I venture to say that shame is the defining mark of both academia and this wretched disease. How can I write this paper if my worth as a person relies on it? How can I explore the intricacies of research if I am just barely holding the intricacies of my insides from exploding onto you? There's always some aspect of sacrifice: if I don't tell you, you think I'm incompetent. If I do tell you, you think I'm crazy.

When I had completed a draft of this chapter, I ran it by a fellow at Northwestern University's writing center. I've been bringing my work to the center for years now, and I brought it there again, intending to find out whether I sounded too crazy before I shared it with the masses. Instead, after the fellow read it, she stared at me in disbelief. "It's so funny that you came in on this day," she said. "I have OCD. I didn't know anyone else experienced grad school like this." The moment was astounding: for the first time in four years of graduate school, the shame lifted. At that moment, I realized that she had done something more important than reassure me that I didn't sound crazy:

she reassured me that I wasn't alone—that the experiences plaguing me were familiar. It took immense effort not to cry or reach across the desk and hug her.

My struggle with OCD has defined my journey in academia, but I will not let it limit me. On the contrary, I am determined to help pave the way for emerging neurodivergent and female scholars to triumph.

RECOMMENDATIONS FOR READERS

1. Create institutional ladders by implementing infrastructure at the university level to support incoming graduate students with OCD (and all invisible disabilities), such as classroom and conference accommodations.
2. Foster ladders of awareness through structured dialogue at the department level between (compensated) students with OCD and the broader academic community to discuss pathways for change and bring awareness to invisible disabilities more generally.
3. Advocate for easily accessible, free counseling services at the university level with therapists trained in supporting students with invisible disabilities.

43

Disabilities and the Hidden Curriculum

Eun A. Jo, Sally Friedman, and Alan Babcock

Students and scholars with disabilities face shared challenges of ableism in academia: *ways of working and metrics of success that systemically favor abled bodies*. Overcoming prejudices around vulnerability and expectations of meritocracy becomes infinitely harder for disabled individuals with intersectional identities: first-generation, low-income scholars may struggle to identify resources for necessary self-care; LGBTQIA+ scholars may find the disclosure process particularly invasive; and BIPOC or women+ scholars may be subject to additional stigma for seeking accommodations. Disability affects some more than others, precisely because the academic system is to varying degrees ableist, and it exists alongside other privileged and penalized identities, amplifying systemic elitism, racism, and gender bias (Brown and Leigh 2020).

Understanding the hidden curriculum of ableism allows scholars to better address the "leaky pipeline" facing students and faculty members with disabilities. To this end, we identify the "chutes"—how issues of access, discrimination, and implicit bias afflict scholars with disabilities—as well as the "ladders"—how they can avoid and address them.

But before we proceed, we begin with a critical caveat: we talk about people with disabilities as a group, but the needs and interests of individuals with disabilities vary by many factors beyond the disabilities themselves. We explore disabilities and the hidden curriculum in the broadest possible strokes, in the hope that such an exploration provides a unified framework for thinking about disability in academia.

Recognizing the Chutes

Navigating academia can be doubly difficult for scholars with disabilities—broadly defined as a physical or mental impairment that limits life activities ("Americans with Disabilities Amendments Act of 2008," Section 4[a]). Disabilities can be more or less visible and demand different levels of intervention at any point in time. Different aspects of academic life may pose barriers to individuals with disabilities: existing facilities may be inaccessible for those with limited mobility; technologies may be inoperable for the visually impaired; and practices, such as testing times, may be inhospitable to the neurodivergent.

Beyond issues of "access," students and scholars with disabilities face severe discrimination and implicit bias. They may be excluded from certain events due to inadequate accommodation—intentionally or not—and denied equal opportunities. Such constraints on participation can be architectural (e.g., wheelchair accessibility), technological (e.g., computer-assisted transcription services on browsers), and communicational (e.g., assistive listening systems). Worse, such patterns of exclusion may bolster an already acute sense of "impostor syndrome," as scholars with disabilities question whether they deserve accommodation or even belong in academia.

Academic bureaucracy has reinforced these problems by raising additional barriers. The responsibility generally falls on individuals with disabilities to seek out accommodations and prove their needs. According to a recent study, only about a third of students with disabilities inform their college (Welding 2025). All of this can be especially difficult for those with "invisible" disabilities, including individuals with learning disabilities and mental health challenges.

Locating the Ladders

Knowing where and how to find help addresses some of these issues. At the university, seeking accommodation often begins at the office of disability services (ODS). Here, a disability specialist is tasked with explaining options for auxiliary services and accommodation. But the process of formulating a complaint can also begin informally, by speaking with any person relevant to the process including a department chair or the office of human resources. A formal complaint can then be prepared and submitted as needed.

Such accommodations for scholars with disabilities is a legally mandated provision under the Americans with Disabilities Act (1990) and the Rehabilitation Act (1973). Failing to make necessary architectural modifications or provide sufficient aids and services—including sign language interpreters and low-vision formats of learning materials—is *illegal*. It can be empowering to remember that accommodation is a right, not a favor, and violation can be subject to legal recourse.

Still, formal institutional channels are often difficult to navigate alone. Finding friends and allies—disabled and nondisabled alike—can provide much-needed comfort and support. In fact, research suggests that most scholars with disabilities seek help through their social networks before resorting to formal accommodations (Castrodale and Zingaro 2015). People find these social supports purposively—via disability-related websites and gatherings—and organically, by talking to friends and finding allies. Where full disclosure of disability can be subject to social sanction, and the administrative burden of proof needs are prohibitive, such social networks can offer immediate—if sometimes temporary—remedy.

Social networks are important for another reason—that is, to advocate for scholars with disabilities and collectively mobilize for broader institutional reform. Various disability advocacy groups have sections aimed at academia. For example, the two major advocacy groups for blindness, National Federation of the Blind and American Council of the Blind, have divisions for students and professionals in education. These groups could provide scholars with tailored advice and support, as well as tools to seek reform in respective institutions. Various advocacy groups for disability rights more generally also provide resources, information, and agenda-setting.

Bringing Disabilities into Conversation

In addition to the obvious benefits of increasing equity and accessibility, it is fair to say that disciplines including political science would benefit from researching through the lens of disability. Applying a "hidden curriculum" to what we research and teach in classes—even a few, brief examples—can show how disability-related content can enrich our understanding of key themes, such as in American politics.

Disability, for instance, is a perfect topic to study the interaction of laws and legislation at the level of governmental institutions and what happens on the ground to ordinary citizens. Laws such as the Americans with Disabilities Act are clearly in place. But what happens to ordinary citizens in real-world situations as they engage with bureaucratic institutions to negotiate the provision of needed services and other people to navigate educational opportunities, employment, and social situations?

Examining how today's candidates present their disabilities also says much about change (or the lack of it) in social attitudes toward disabilities (Scotch and Friedman 2014). In the 1930s and 1940s, for instance, President Franklin Roosevelt went to extreme efforts to hide his disability from the public (Gallagher 1999). Similarly, even as we rightly focus on the importance of the 1964 Civil Rights Act, we know much less about the landmark politics of the 1990 Americans with Disabilities Act. Among other things, the tactics of interest groups and social movements—ranging from the more ordinary to the surprisingly militant (Shapiro 1994)—that disability-rights advocates mobilized in this and other instances are notable.

Unmasking the Hidden Curriculum

Beyond what individuals can do to address this hidden curriculum, institutions must do better to equalize the playing field for students and scholars with disabilities. At a basic level, institutions must explicitly commit to disability awareness. This begins with acknowledging disability in all official statements of university inclusivity, as well as making disability resources more visible and easier to access. Meanwhile, dedicated entities, such as the ODS, should be adequately staffed and resourced, such that their services can be accessed in a timely, meaningful manner.

More broadly, these institutional reforms must follow a new framework that sees disability services not as a form of accommodation but as a provision of equal opportunities. This would help set disability in a larger context of fairness and would help eliminate the stigma of asking for something that appears "special" or "extra." This simple language reframe may allow institutions to design accommodation as a more equitable process rather than as a set of administrative hoops that individuals with disabilities must jump through to get what they already deserve. The overall aim of unmasking this hidden curriculum should thus be to make higher education more inclusive for all, at whatever stage in their academic career.

RECOMMENDATIONS FOR READERS

Recognizing the Chutes

1. Engage in discussions about ableism in academic culture and actively work toward dismantling harmful stereotypes.
2. Support and fund research on the experiences of disabled students and scholars. This can help institutions better understand the unique obstacles that individuals with disabilities face and create targeted solutions.
3. Ensure that dedicated entities, such as the ODS and HR, are adequately staffed and resourced to provide timely services.

Locating the Ladders

1. Encourage faculty, administrators, and peers to create and adopt inclusive practices that address both visible and invisible disabilities. This includes providing flexible accommodations and ensuring equal access to resources and opportunities.
2. Advocate for simplified, transparent processes for requesting accommodations that are not burdensome for individuals with disabilities. Institutions should make sure that scholars know how to access support without stigma.

44

It Took My Village:

How the Pandemic Worsened Decades of Social Isolation and Increased Loneliness

Jarod Giger

The kids are not OK. For that matter, the adults aren't doing that great either. The pandemic has come and gone, and life has resumed its normal pace. But it is marked by an unspoken heaviness, obligation, and drudgery in classrooms and on campus. Of course, we have things to be excited about—people are going to college sporting events and homecomings and graduations. But many faculty aren't going to their offices, campus events are poorly attended, and many students aren't coming to class. The pandemic gave us ample ways to connect online, but life has never felt so lonely.

The surgeon general agrees. In May 2023, Dr. Vivek Murthy worried about all of us:

> Our epidemic of loneliness and isolation has been an underappreciated public health crisis that has harmed individual and societal health. Our relationships are a source of healing and well-being hiding in plain sight—one that can help us live healthier, more fulfilled, and more productive lives. Given the significant health consequences of loneliness and isolation, we must prioritize building social connections the same way we have prioritized other critical public health issues such as tobacco, obesity, and substance use disorders. Together, we can build a country that's healthier, more resilient, less lonely, and more connected.

The pandemic was not the start of the trend in isolation and loneliness. More than twenty years ago, Robert Putnam wrote about declining civic and communal participation in the United States (Putnam 2000). *Bowling Alone* showed how people in the United States were withdrawing from collective activities and spending increasing amounts of time by themselves. These collective activities ranged from civic-minded activities, such as Rotary Club or Veterans of Foreign Wars, to social groups such as bowling leagues that once drew people together for a common fun purpose. Regardless of the group's identity, the collective gathering of people for a common purpose served many functions, not least of which was providing accountability and connection—two important ingredients for individual and social resilience.

College campuses are microcosms of society. Results from the recent Student Voice survey show that one in three college students engages in no campus extracurricular activities (Flaherty 2023b, 2023a). Instructors and professors have lamented the proliferation of two competing trends: students' classroom absenteeism, and their impatience with not getting answers "right" on their first try. Students skip class more often, and they are easily frustrated if the tasks are multistep or require greater-than-average critical thinking. It's not that they don't want to do the work—it's more likely that they are cognitively unable. Their nervous systems are overstimulated, their lives are overcomplicated, and their resilience is underdeveloped. They don't know how to cope because we haven't taught them—either because we haven't modeled it for them or because we simply assign readings to students regarding higher education trends and best student and emerging faculty practices but fail to implement this knowledge into actionable steps (Nguyen and Yao 2023). Or perhaps we don't know how to cope effectively.

There is a full-blown mental health crisis in higher education today ("Stressed Out: The Mental Health Crisis in Higher Education" n.d.; Flannery n.d.). A recent survey found that more than 60 percent of college students meet the criteria for at least one mental health disorder ("Healthy Minds Study" n.d.). Seeking professional mental healthcare is less stigmatized today than in previous generations, but for some identity groups, talking about feelings of depression or anxiety is still taboo. In some racial and ethnic populations, the rates of psychiatric disorders may be undercounted because they are less likely to seek mental health services (Chen et al. 2019). Many students—especially first-generation students—have additional responsibilities beyond school (Ardoin and Erb 2022). Many hold part-time (or more) jobs while carrying a full courseload. Many are veterans of recent wars. Many are parents. Many are in the "sandwich generation" and are caring for both older and younger dependents (Lei, Leggett, and Maust 2023). Many want help but lack the hours in the day or the bandwidth to do the research to find a provider who can see them in a timely manner. Or no providers are in the area. Or there just aren't enough hours in the day to do everything that must get done plus find time to spend fifty minutes with a therapist.

But those problems are on the demand side of the equation. Imagine you find the time and money to talk to a therapist on campus: you may have a long wait, because on the supply side, campus counseling centers themselves have been in crisis (Gorman et al. n.d.). Staff turnover rates are high, recruitment for mental health professionals is challenging, and licensing guidelines have limited provision of services to students. Students most frequently sought treatment for anxiety, depression, family concerns, academic problems, relationship problems, and loneliness. The issues troubling students are not out of the ordinary; the magnitude of the impact they are having on students' lives, careers, and well-being—and the sheer volume of students affected by these issues—is extraordinary. The tidal wave of students in need of mental health services is taxing the capacity of campus and community providers to support them.

Faculty are also experiencing a collective mental health crisis (Hammoudi Halat et al. 2023). We are told to focus on our "work-life balance" but also expected to do all the things and do them perfectly. For faculty parents and caregivers, we are expected to work and perform like we don't have a family and parent (or provide care) like we don't have a job. Some have advocated instead for "work-life *boundaries*" or "life-work balance," but deadlines still loom, deliverables still need to be met, manuscripts need to get published, and classes still must be taught. These are individual problems—as in, individual people are experiencing real problems—but they have to be addressed at an institutional and societal level.

People in crisis see fewer options and possibilities than those who are relaxed (Dionne et al. 2018). We are snippy with our significant others and dependents, we are checked out at work, we are overstimulated with cascading responsibilities, and we are coping with the quiet hum of lingering pandemic stress that is occasionally punctuated by the sounds of bullets flying across our campuses. There's often barely enough time to catch our breath and recover from the most recent crisis—whether a violent incident or natural disaster that disables essential services such as water and electricity. As academic faculty, many of us are far-flung from family and loved ones—crucial support systems that are or could be a safety net. Many of us don't get to choose where we live. We are isolated in a random academic village, far from help, and just doing the best we can.

It does take a village to care for everyone. And it's not entirely the pandemic's fault that higher education is having a mental health crisis—among both students and faculty. Some of us coped by "quiet quitting," realizing that academia eats its young. Isolation is the manifestation of a deeper problem—one of divestment from participating in activities for the public good and engaging in things that increase social resilience. We need to take better care of each other so we can take better care of ourselves. The myth of American exceptionalism, of "pulling ourselves up by our own bootstraps," shows how little we recognize the communal foundations of individual success. There's no parting platitude or upside here. We just have to do better. Together.

RECOMMENDATIONS FOR READERS

1. **For students:** If you are struggling, please reach out to your professors. They often know which campus resources to connect you with. It's better to let them know sooner rather than later. You can also look up resources on campus on your own for help, and many student groups and campus organizations may be able to provide tangible academic support alongside mental health professionals. Also check your email and learning management system (LMS); this is how people in academia get in touch with you.
2. **For faculty:** If you are not a licensed healthcare professional, or if clinical work is not within your professorial scope of work, do not attempt to provide clinical counseling for your students experiencing mental health crises. It's one thing to be supportive, but stay in your professional lane. Legal and moral consequences can ensue from operating outside your area of expertise, even if it is validating or feels good that students confide in you. You're likely not their therapist, so be the best professor and role model you can be for them. Help the students in the way you are best equipped to—by being accommodating and understanding of their challenges and helping them learn to the best of their ability. Connect them with

campus resources, check in with them, and offer options for how to manage the demands of college coursework while they seek professional resources to cope with the psychological and emotional stressors in their lives. Including a brief description in your syllabus or LMS about your role as instructor of record (i.e., content expert) can go a long way in setting a supportive tone for students and being transparent about what you can do or offer a student in crisis. As academic faculty, we are one cog in a big machine, and that machine has policies and procedures. One does not want to explain to a student in the throes of a crisis that "XYZ is outside the scope of my role as instructor of record."

3. **For all:** If you are concerned about someone in your life, never be afraid to ask them this question: Are you thinking of hurting or killing yourself? If yes, ask if they have a plan. If yes, ask if they have the means to carry out that plan. These triage questions can determine what level of care and intervention someone needs and on what timeline.
4. **For all:** Self-care is not a weekend activity or something you do only when things are really bad. Self-care does not have to be expensive or extravagant. The cure (for stress) is not a pedicure or a new TV. Self-care can be small acts of mindfulness that help reset your baseline, center yourself, and reduce your reactivity. Square breathing is effective (Contributors n.d.), as is "sigh" breathing ("How to Breathe Correctly for Optimal Health, Mood, Learning & Performance—Huberman Lab" n.d.). These help to reset and regulate your autonomic nervous system.
5. **For all:** Build better life-work boundaries. Rarely in academia will people tell you to close your computer—overworking humblebrags are all too common. You will become more efficient when you stop working all the time. Work when you work best. Don't work when you're not supposed to be working.

Conclusion

In our first book, *The PhD Parenthood Trap*, we introduced the concept of academic chutes and ladders, making the case that it is a more fitting metaphor than the leaky pipeline for the nonlinear trajectory many scholars follow to and through the academic profession. Academia is like a game board where some players know the rules and others don't, and some can bend the rules to their advantage where others can't. Some players start the game already at a disadvantage, which makes progression and matriculation all the more difficult. Many colleges and universities are upending these rules by making tuition free for families earning less than a certain amount, one step in a promising direction. This does not guarantee academic success, however, because many invisible assumptions (e.g., that students will be able to afford the price of books) still hit students with "sticker shock." Things beyond our control affect our academic and life trajectories in both helpful and less-than-helpful ways. Part of the hidden curriculum is learning how much is beyond our control, and part of it is "paying it forward" with the generalizable lessons that we can help clear the path, lighten the load, and point out the ladders for others.

Our hope, in taking on this work, is that all members of the academic community—students, faculty, staff, administrators, and mentors—will reconsider the policies, norms, and support systems needed to make campuses more diverse, equitable, inclusive, and accessible. We seek to start the conversations that will lead to a more humane academic environment and provide evidence that the wide variety of experiences discussed in this book are not idiosyncratic or particular. Rather, the accounts the contributors have shared in this book tell the story of an increasingly diverse higher education population from many backgrounds and identities. We believe higher education should be accessible to all who want to learn, to deepen their understanding of their field and the world, and to make contributions through teaching, research, and service to help academia and our communities become better for everyone. We believe the academic profession should embrace the whole scholar—invisible workloads, lived experiences, nonlinear trajectories, and all.

In our first book, we wrote about three key principles of sound decision-making and good policies: norms, procedures, expectations, and policies should be (1) clearly communicated, (2) transparent, and (3) equitably applied. These principles are at the root of efforts to demystify the hidden curriculum as well. The hidden curriculum stays hidden in environments where expectations, opportunities, and consequences are not clearly communicated. This doesn't mean just sending an email to everyone and assuming that a policy or decision is understood or relying on historical norms and routines. This means checking for comprehension—the difference between a multiple-choice exam or an open-ended exam, in essence. One gives you a range of potential options (where you may occasionally guess correctly) and the other demands that you show what you know. In mathematics and the physical sciences, this is called "showing your work." The hidden curriculum thrives in the world of assumptions. Clear communication requires a feedback loop, comprehension checks, and some creativity that may take more time on the front end but will save time, energy, and grief in the long run.

If you don't know the rules of the game, it probably isn't obvious how to learn them—what questions to ask, which people can help you, or what resources to look for or request. The defining feature of the hidden curriculum is that *you don't know what you don't know*. It's not enough that you lack information or resources about college or higher education in general—you also probably lack the knowledge about where to go to get answers. This is a frustrating place to feel stuck. This lack of information, knowledge, and access is not inconsequential. For example, not understanding the nuances and obligations of financial aid can have lasting effects on lifetime earnings, debt, and psychological stress. Similarly, not knowing which types of publications count toward tenure and promotion can create major career setbacks.

When expectations are clearly communicated, they also become more transparent. The hidden curriculum flourishes in opaque places but wilts in the sunlight of transparency and discussion. This is true about syllabi, about family-leave policies, about performance evaluation expectations, about research opportunities, and about the distribution of faculty service assignments. A pervasive myth is that some people have succeeded in their endeavors due solely to their own hard work and efforts; this very well may be true in some cases, but it's also possible that they are oblivious to the advantages that have contributed to their successes or, at least, not created additional impediments in their path. All things are not equal, and transparency makes this evident. It shows where the hidden advantages and disadvantages are and empowers people to advocate for better, more equitable policies.

When resources are equitably applied, people in academia are more likely to get what they need to succeed. A metaphor for the differences between equal and equitable involves three people trying to look over a fence to watch a baseball game. Each person is standing on a block that is supposed to help them see over the fence; one person is tall and could see easily even without the block, one person is medium (without the block they would not be able to see, but with it they can see over), and one person is short and can't see over the fence at all, even standing on the block. The distribution of resources is equal: one block per person. An equitable distribution would be for the shortest person to have two blocks because the tallest person doesn't need one at all. This metaphor provides several important takeaways: first, we each have unique endowments that help us or hinder us in different ways; second, the allocation of blocks assumes a fixed resource, which isn't necessarily or always the case in higher education; and third, giving people access to a resource doesn't ensure that they will use it effectively or at all.

In academia, an equitable application of resources and policies is predicated on clear communication so that information is not sequestered either deliberately or unintentionally. This also promotes transparency, which itself contributes to an atmosphere of shared governance and inclusivity that is conducive to better outcomes and overall satisfaction. One faculty member we talked with described the cascade of understanding and learning about how things on campus work from being the department's representative on the Faculty Senate. This included budgeting decisions, university policies, and faculty handbook revisions—including such important processes as tenure and promotion appeals. Their experience highlights one of the many ways in which exposure to the bigger picture on a campus can help someone understand how decisions are made and why things work the way they do.

At the undergraduate level, a student's service on a campus-wide organization, such as student government, can help foster connections with campus leaders and administrators, which can make norms and processes more visible, much like a faculty senator experienced. We can't all get what we want all the time, but we can get better answers and a clearer picture when we know what the landscape and terrain is, and where to find information. Of course, roles in the Faculty Senate and student government are finite, so the task for all of us is to determine how to make the rules, norms, and processes more transparent, clearly communicated, and equitably applied for everyone on our campuses, regardless of their direct access to key positions and leaders. The environment in higher education will never be perfect, but it can be clearer in ways that make life easier or at least less difficult. When we all do our best to be mindful of these three principles, better outcomes become more likely for everyone; we help scholars dodge the chutes and scale the ladders.

When we consider higher education and the academic profession through the lens of academic chutes and ladders, we gain an increased understanding of the idiosyncratic nature of opportunities (access to networking, mentorship, funding, and tenure-track jobs) and the need for greater protection from the obstacles and biases that threaten to derail progress through undergraduate and graduate school, the academic job market, or tenure and promotion. The course of normal life events—such as bringing children into the family—can present temporary barriers to access for people on both sides of the podium, students and faculty alike. Increasing awareness of issues such as invisible disabilities or medical problems—migraines, chronic pain, mental health challenges, or infertility—have made accommodations not only more available but more acceptable to use. Through the application of these three principles, we can transform the *idiosyncratic* into the *systematic*.

Academia is not a one-size-fits-all enterprise anymore, which means approaching situations with patience, creativity, and open-mindedness. We should remember that all students and faculty do not follow a linear path to campus with the same lessons learned from their lived experiences. When we remember this, we begin to understand more completely the need for clearly communicated, transparent, and equitably applied policies, support systems, and norms. In other words, when we understand the wide variation in identities and backgrounds of the students in our classrooms and colleagues in our departments and cohorts, we begin to see the importance of demystifying the hidden curriculum. And the enlightened self-interest rationale for this is that higher education is a major economic driver and critical component to the thriving success for local communities and at the national level.

Higher education is important for strong, resilient, and innovative local and national economies. Universities are often among the largest employers in their area. They generate revenue for local businesses through contracts for supplies along the value chain. They contribute hundreds of billions to the economy through technology transfer—innovations created in laboratories and workshops on campus. They train an educated workforce who contribute to society through their employment and the tax revenue they generate. To compete in the global economy, we all need universities to incubate new technologies, train literate and skilled workers, and serve as stable community anchors. There should be a place for anyone who wants to learn because this makes the entire society stronger. Although we write from the perspective of scholars in the United States, colleges and universities provide economic, social, and cultural benefits everywhere in the world; for this reason, many countries invest heavily in higher education and strive to make it accessible to all. Although higher education is undeniably strengthened, better funded, and more accessible when a country chooses to invest in its colleges and universities, that isn't the reality for all of us; at the time of publication (2025), it certainly isn't the reality for us in the United States as we navigate a period of immense uncertainty for students, scholars, and campus communities. Nevertheless, each of us can work with the resources we have to help our peers, students, and colleagues identify the chutes and ladders.

Reader: After considering what you've learned about in this book, are there things that you now understand better about yourself or others? Perhaps you see some part of your own story in these pages. At some point, you probably either benefited from or were penalized by some aspect of the hidden curriculum. You climbed a ladder because you knew it was there or someone pointed it out. You sidestepped a chute because you'd developed skills or strategies to help you navigate the uneven terrain of higher education. Or perhaps you slid down a chute right at the start because your diploma wasn't from an elite high school, your family couldn't pay for test prep courses, and your only college acceptance came from the state school, which then limited your graduate school—and, later, tenure-track job—prospects. Or maybe your caregiving responsibilities limited the scope of your academic job search, and tenure-track jobs in your region were simply unavailable. We, as a profession and as a society, can do better. By "demystifying" the hidden curriculum, we mean to expose the unwritten and unevenly communicated and applied rules, norms, and expectations for success at all levels of higher education and the academic profession.

Our goal in this book has been to start conversations about ways to do exactly this on campuses everywhere by elevating the real-world experiences of colleagues who have provided personal insights into how the hidden curriculum has impacted their lives. We—and they—are sharing these stories to demonstrate how the hidden curriculum looks in specific circumstances. Perhaps you have experiences that resonate; perhaps you disagree in part or whole with their—and our—perspectives. This is an opportunity to reflect on how you interpret and understand how unwritten rules manifest throughout higher education, from college freshmen to senior tenured scholars. *Why do you believe what you believe about how things are, or should be, in higher education? Why do you behave the way you do in your academic ecosystem? What underlying principles inform your perspective, and how has this book challenged, reinforced, or informed them? What, if anything, will you do differently in the future? How will you use the hidden curriculum "lens" to look at the way you approach academic life?*

We hope to get campus decision-makers thinking about, discussing, and then implementing changes that make undergraduate and graduate programs more accessible to students; that reduce the roles of implicit and explicit bias in hiring practices and tenure and promotion processes; and that make academia more compatible with personal challenges and responsibilities off campus. We hope to empower students to ask questions, cultivate supportive mentoring relationships and peer groups, and to understand that they belong in academia if they wish to be there. We hope to inspire all faculty to "pay it forward" through mentorship and advocacy on behalf of students and precariously employed colleagues. All these efforts start with the simple recognition that we must and can do better to create a more humane academia.

We have not, of course, detailed the complete set of obstacles, opportunities, and nuances within every discipline or for every identity group, type of academic institution, or academic rank. No book can do that. What we and our contributing authors have set out to do, and what we hope we have accomplished, is to communicate a range of experiences within academia and recommendations for best practices gleaned from both research and lived experience. Each chapter has, no doubt, resonated differently with different readers. Every academic journey involves unique obstacles, opportunities, and outcomes; we hope the journeys shared in this book will inspire discussion, advocacy, and action to create the support systems, shape the policies and processes, and ensure that everyone who sets out in pursuit of an academic career has the opportunity to thrive in the profession.

Key Takeaways and Next Steps in Establishing Best Practices

In each of the preceding chapters, the author or team of authors has shared a short list of takeaway points or best practices for creating a more diverse, equitable, inclusive, accessible, and humane academic profession. Bookmark these lists and revisit them often, particularly if they pertain to your unique role or situation. Here, we conclude with summary takeaways that form common threads across the chapters in this book.

- Lift while you climb.[1] Everyone at every rank and of every identity has a role to play in the effort to support success in academia. From individual undergraduate students to university presidents, we can all make small (or major) changes on our campuses that make the journey easier for those who come after us.
- Mentorship is a ladder and a lifeline. Training is available for mentors but not required. Mentorship can help scholars navigate unexpected or recurring obstacles and workloads and identify the ladders and opportunities that will

help them pursue their academic and career objectives. This can happen in the classroom, during office hours, in the form of research collaboration, and through professional development and guidance at all student and faculty levels.

- Mentors can normalize variation in academic experiences, such as sharing stories and experiences of how personal and/or professional challenges helped to shape their careers. Departments and offices on campus, off-campus networks, professional associations, and even individuals can play valuable roles in cultivating mentorship initiatives and programs. Sometimes your best mentor may come from outside your department or institution.
- Mentorship does not require formal training, although sometimes that is helpful. At the core of good mentorship is mindfulness and the willingness to seek information and solutions and meet your students and colleagues where they are at. Both men+ and women+ benefit from good mentorship, and it is critically important that everyone participate in this conversation about making higher education more transparent and accessible for all who wish to learn.
- Mentorship is also *not* many things. It is important for mentors not to overstep boundaries or exceed their professional expertise. Connecting students and colleagues with the appropriate resources, especially regarding physical and psychological well-being, is part of being a good mentor—not thinking you are a one-stop shop. And it's important to consider the many roles different mentors can play. It's OK (and ideal) to have more than one person in your corner. You may seek mentorship in various forms from different people.
- Bias in its many forms—including human and machine biases—opens chutes and creates processes and outcomes that can drive talented scholars out of the academy. Implicit bias, especially, is pernicious in its ability to undermine and thwart careers. There are best practices that admissions committees, faculty search committees, fellowship committees, classroom instructors, and campus decision-makers can adopt to identify the potential roles and sources of implicit bias in decision-making processes and the appropriate steps to minimize the effects of bias.
- Policies, procedures, and available resources should be transparent, clearly communicated, and equitably applied at all levels, from undergraduate student through university administration. For example, hiring committees should all agree upon and work from the same set of questions for each candidate to ensure apples-to-apples comparison across responses and make notes of if and when the conversation deviates or new questions arise.

By reading about, reflecting on, and discussing the academic chutes and ladders and the potential barriers to success on our campuses, each of us is already taking the first vital step in the effort to make academia more diverse, equitable, inclusive, accessible, and humane. We hope you avoid the chutes and scale the ladders along your academic journey and that you find tangible and concrete ways to help others do the same. Most importantly, don't create chutes for others by gatekeeping, and *do* create ladders where you can. Each of us can make the academy better for those around us. Hold the door open for others and lift while you climb.

Notes

Chapter 4

1 First-generation students can struggle picking a major and classes, and understanding the purpose of office hours.
2 First-generation students are proactive in making college a viable option. They are often optimistic about the impact a college education will have on their future, and they are reflexive (self-aware) of their strengths.
3 The McNair Scholars Program is a two-year program that prepares underrepresented low-income, first-generation college students for graduate school by providing numerous research and conference opportunities for undergraduates. The Summer Research Opportunity Program is offered at the Big Ten universities that gives undergraduates access to research opportunities as well as various workshops on taking the Graduate Record Examination (GRE) and applying to graduate school.
4 Since the COVID pandemic in 2020, some universities have opted to not require the GRE. It is unknown how long this GRE requirement discontinuation will last. Therefore, prospective graduate students should look at their prospective programs to determine whether they need to take the GRE.
5 Link to the ETS GRE Fee Reduction Form: https://www.ets.org/content/dam/ets-org/pdfs/gre/gre-fee-reduction-request-form.pdf.
6 Link to the Free App Fee Waiver Program: https://btaa.org/resources-for/students/freeapp/introduction.
7 Traditionally underrepresented in graduate education, including racial and ethnic minorities, women in STEM, first-generation college students, and individuals who have faced adversity, such as societal, economic, or academic disadvantages.
8 Prospective students can look at the curriculum vitae of faculty to see whether they regularly coauthor with students. Many faculty members will include notes on their publications stating whether it was coauthored with a graduate student.
9 NerdWallet offers a cost-of-living calculator that allows users to compare costs of living between their current city and another city of their choice: https://www.nerdwallet.com/cost-of-living-calculator.
10 Many programs list the placements of their recent graduates on their websites. Here is a link to questions to ask the director of graduate studies during an interview: https://www.thoughtco.com/graduate-admissions-interview-questions-to-ask-1686245.

Chapter 7

1 This draws mostly on the American model but applies more generally to the Canadian, British, and Australian models.

Chapter 12

1 Promotions for teaching-focused contingent positions may still require evidence of research engagement.
2 NTT positions often include heavier teaching, service, and student advising requirements. They may also be excluded from sabbaticals or other course-release programs designed to increase research productivity for tenure-track faculty.
3 "Percentages of Full-Time Faculty Members Who Were Non-Tenure-Track, by Institutional Classification, 2018–19," *The Chronicle of Higher Education*, August 16, 2020. https://www.chronicle.com/article/percentages-of-full-time-faculty-members-who-were-non-tenure-track-by-institutional-classification-2018-19.

Chapter 14

1 See Bradner (2022) on the hurdles that NTT face.
2 See Haviland et al. (2023) for the way to redress some of the problems noted above.

Chapter 32

1 This is a very endearing term often used within the Black community to describe a woman or female-identifying nonrelative with whom someone relates and builds community. SiStars, another variation of sisters, can be a group of friends, colleagues, or complete strangers with whom one is building a communal relationship through love and mentorship.

Chapter 36

1 We define women+ as transgender and cisgender women, as well as nonbinary and gender nonconforming people who identify as women.

Conclusion

1 To paraphrase Mary Church Terrell, who served as the first president of the National Association of Colored Women.

References

"100 Million 'Destination Vanderbilt' Initiative Launched to Recruit Top Faculty, Address Essential Challenges." 2020. Vanderbilt University. https://news.vanderbilt.edu/2020/09/23/100-million-destination-vanderbilt-initiative-launched-to-recruit-top-faculty-address-essential-challenges/.

Agathangelou, Anna M., and L. H. M. Ling. 2002. "An Unten(ur)able Position : The Politics of Teaching for Women of Color in the US." *International Feminist Journal of Politics* 4 (3): 368–98. https://doi.org/10.1080/1461674022000031562.

Allen, Tammy D., and Lillian T. Eby, eds. 2007. *The Blackwell Handbook of Mentoring: A Multiple Perspectives Approach*. Blackwell Publishing. https://doi.org/10.1111/b.9781405133739.2007.x.

Allen, Tammy D., Lillian T. Eby, and Elizabeth Lentz. 2007. "Mentorship Behaviors and Mentorship Quality Associated with Formal Mentoring Programs: Closing the Gap between Research and Practice." *Journal of Applied Psychology* 91 (3): 567–78. https://doi.org/10.1037/0021-9010.91.3.567.

Almasri, Nasir, and Dana El Kurd. 2022. "Mental Health and Well-Being in Grad School: Dealing with Isolation, Depression, Anxiety, and Turmoil." In Kevin G. Lorentz II, Daniel J. Mallinson, Julia Marin Hellwege, Davin Pheonix, and J. Cherie Strachan, eds. *Strategies for Navigating Graduate School and Beyond*. American Political Science Association, 455–62.

Alsubaie, Merfat Ayesh. 2015. "Hidden Curriculum as One of Current Issue of Curriculum." *Journal of Education and Practice* 6 (33): 125–8.

American Association of University Professors. 2021. "2020–21 Faculty Compensation Survey Results." https://www.aaup.org/2020-21-faculty-compensation-survey-results.

"Americans with Disabilities Amendments Act of 2008." 2008. US Equal Employment Opportunity Commission. https://www.eeoc.gov/statutes/ada-amendments-act-2008.

Andersen, Kristi, and Dana Michael Harsell. 2005. "Assessing the Impact of a Quantitative Skills Course for Undergraduates." *Journal of Political Science Education* 1 (1): 17–27. https://doi.org/10.1080/15512160490921824.

Ardoin, Sonja, and Maria Dykema Erb. 2022. "First-Generation Graduate Students: Reducing Barriers with Support Mechanisms." In David J. Nguyen and Christina W. Yao, *A Handbook for Supporting Today's Graduate Students*. Routledge, 55–69.

Ayers, Zoë J. 2022. *Managing Your Mental Health during Your PhD: A Survival Guide*. Springer Cham.

Baba, Yoko, and Megumi Hosoda. 2014. "Home Away Home: Better Understanding of the Role of Social Support in Predicting Cross-Cultural Adjustment among International Students." *College Student Journal* 48 (1): 1–15.

Baker, Vicki L., Laura Gail Lunsford, and Meghan J. Pifer. 2017. *Developing Faculty in Liberal Arts Colleges: Aligning Individual Needs and Organizational Goals*. Rutgers University Press.

Banda, Roselyn. 2018. "Changing the Things I Cannot Accept: My African Experience of a U.S. Classroom." *Journal of International Students* 8 (1): 488–95. https://doi.org/10.32674/jis.v8i1.176.

Baron-Cohen, Simon. 2017. "Editorial Perspective: Neurodiversity – A Revolutionary Concept for Autism and Psychiatry." *Journal of Child Psychology and Psychiatry* 58 (6): 744–7. https://doi.org/10.1111/jcpp.12703.

Beagan, Brenda L., Tameera Mohamed, Kim Brooks, Bea Waterfield, and Merlinda Weinberg. 2021. "Microaggressions Experienced by LGBTQ Academics in Canada: 'Just Not Fitting In … It Does Take a Toll.'" *International Journal of Qualitative Studies in Education* 34 (3): 197–212. https://www.tandfonline.com/doi/full/10.1080/09518398.2020.1735556.

Becker, Megan. 2020. "Importing the Laboratory Model to the Social Sciences: Prospects for Improving Mentoring of Undergraduate Researchers." *Journal of Political Science Education* 16 (2): 212–24. https://doi.org/10.1080/15512169.2018.1505523.

Bell, Amani, and Lorri J. Santamaría, eds. 2019. *Understanding Experiences of First Generation University Students: Culturally Responsive and Sustaining Methodologies*. Bloomsbury.

Benson, Thomas S., and T. Mark Montoya. 2022. "Concerns for First-Generation Political Science Graduate Students." In K. G. Lorentz, D. J. Mallinson, J. Marin Hellwege, D. Phoenix, and J. C. Strachan, eds. *Strategies for Navigating Graduate School and Beyond*, 405–10. American Political Science Association.

Berheide, Catherine White, Megan A. Carpenter, and David A. Cotter. 2022. "Teaching College in the Time of COVID-19: Gender and Race Differences in Faculty Emotional Labor." *Sex Roles* 86 (7): 441–55. https://doi.org/10.1007/s11199-021-01271-0.

Besas, Marianne. 2021. "Tenured Faculty Continue Being Replaced by Adjuncts across U.S." *The College Post*. https://thecollegepost.com/tenured-faculty-replaced-adjuncts/.

"Big Ten Academic Alliance." 2025. https://en.wikipedia.org/w/index.php?title=Big_Ten_Academic_Alliance&oldid=1278823309.

Bilimoria, Diana, and Abigail J. Stewart. 2009. "'Don't Ask, Don't Tell': The Academic Climate for Lesbian, Gay, Bisexual, and Transgender Faculty in Science and Engineering." *NWSA Journal* 21 (2): 85–103.

Blair-Loy, Mary, Olga V. Mayorova, Pamela C. Cosman, and Stephanie I. Fraley. 2022. "Can Rubrics Combat Gender Bias in Faculty Hiring?" *Science* 377 (6601): 35–7. https://doi.org/10.1126/science.abm2329.

Blakely, Kristin. 2007. "Reflections on the Role of Emotion in Feminist Research." *International Journal of Qualitative Methods* 6 (2): 59–68.

Blanks Jones, Jasmine L., Jessica P. Cerdeña, Chonika Coleman-King, and Mahauganee D. Shaw Bonds. 2021. "Coping through Kinship during COVID-19: Lessons from Women of Color." *American Educational History Journal, Snapshots of History: Portraits of the 21st Century Pandemic*: 51–8.

Boafo-Arthur, Susan. 2014. "Acculturative Experiences of Black-African International Students." *International Journal for the Advancement of Counselling* 36 (2): 115–24. https://doi.org/10.1007/s10447-013-9194-8.

Bostwick, Valerie K., and Bruce A. Weinberg. 2022. "Nevertheless She Persisted? Gender Peer Effects in Doctoral STEM Programs." *Journal of Labor Economics* 40 (2): 397–436. https://doi.org/10.1086/714921.

Bowles, Hannah Riley, Bobbi Thomason, and Julia B. Bear. 2019. "Reconceptualizing What and How Women Negotiate for Career Advancement." *Academy of Management Journal* 62 (6): 1645–71. https://doi.org/10.5465/amj.2017.1497.

Bowles, Hannah Riley, Linda Babcock, and Lei Lai. 2007. "Social Incentives for Gender Differences in the Propensity to Initiate Negotiations: Sometimes It Does Hurt to Ask." *Organizational Behavior and Human Decision Processes* 103 (1): 84–103. https://doi.org/10.1016/j.obhdp.2006.09.001.

Boyer Commission on Educating Undergraduates in the Research University. 1998. "Reinventing Undergraduate Education: A Blueprint for America's Research Universities." https://eric.ed.gov/?id=ED424840.

Bradner, Alexandra. 2022. "The Cruelty of the Adjunct System." In Steven M. Cahn, ed. *Academic Ethics Today: Problems, Policies, and Prospects for University Life.* Rowman & Littlefield, 145–55.

Breuning, Marijke, Paul Parker, and John T. Ishiyama. 2001. "The Last Laugh: Skill Building through a Liberal Arts Political Science Curriculum." *PS: Political Science & Politics* 34 (3): 657–61. https://doi.org/10.1017/S1049096501001056.

Brown, Brené. 2006. "Shame Resilience Theory: A Grounded Theory Study on Women and Shame." *Families in Society* 87 (1): 43–52. https://doi.org/10.1606/1044-3894.3483.

Brown, Jennifer, Jennifer A. Ferretti, Sofia Leung, and Marisa Méndez-Brady. 2018. "We Here: Speaking Our Truth." *Library Trends* 67 (1): 163–81.

Brown, Nicole, and Jennifer Leigh, eds. 2020. *Ableism in Academia: Theorising Experiences of Disabilities and Chronic Illnesses in Higher Education.* UCL Press. https://doi.org/10.14324/111.9781787354975.

Bryant, Jessica, and Chloe Appleby. 2025. "These States' Anti-DEI Legislation May Impact Higher Education." *Best Colleges.* https://www.bestcolleges.com/news/anti-dei-legislation-tracker/.

Budig, Michelle J. 2014. "The Fatherhood Bonus and the Motherhood Penalty: Parenthood and the Gender Gap in Pay." *Third Way.* https://www.thirdway.org/report/the-fatherhood-bonus-and-the-motherhood-penalty-parenthood-and-the-gender-gap-in-pay?tpcc=nlbroadsheet.

Byrd, W. Carson, Rachelle J. Brunn-Bevel, Sarah M. Ovink, Antron D. Mahoney, Marcela G. Cuellar, R. Nicole Johnson-Ahorlu, Terry-Ann Jones, et al. 2019. *Intersectionality and Higher Education: Identity and Inequality on College Campuses.* Rutgers University Press.

Calarco, Jessica McCrory. 2020. *A Field Guide to Grad School: Uncovering the Hidden Curriculum.* Princeton University Press.

Campbell, Cara. 2021. "The Struggle Is Real: The Imposter Syndrome." PhD Diss., California State University, Chico.

"Can Rubrics Combat Gender Bias in Faculty Hiring?." 2025. *Science.* https://www.science.org/doi/full/10.1126/science.abm2329.

Cardel, Michelle I., Emily Dhurandhar, Ceren Yarar-Fisher, Monica Foster, Bertha Hidalgo, Leslie A. McClure, Sherry Pagoto, et al. 2020. "Turning Chutes into Ladders for Women Faculty: A Review and Roadmap for Equity in Academia." *Journal of Women's Health* 29 (5): 721–33. https://doi.org/10.1089/jwh.2019.8027.

Cassese, Erin C., Mirya R. Holman, Monica C. Schneider, and Angela L. Bos. 2015. "Building a Gender and Methodology Curriculum: Integrated Skills, Exercises, and Practices." *Journal of Political Science Education* 11 (1): 61–77. https://doi.org/10.1080/15512169.2014.985106.

Castillo-Montoya, Milagros, and Jillian Ives. 2021. "Transformative Practices to Support First-Generation College Students as Academic Learners: Findings from a Systematic

Literature Review." *Journal of First-Generation Student Success* 1 (1): 20–31. https://doi.org/10.1080/26906015.2021.1890948.

Castrodale, Mark Anthony, and Daniel Zingaro. 2015. "'You're Such a Good Friend': A Woven Autoethnographic Narrative Discussion of Disability and Friendship in Higher Education." *Disability Studies Quarterly* 35 (1). https://doi.org/10.18061/dsq.v35i1.3762.

Caterine, Christopher L. 2020. *Leaving Academia: A Practical Guide*. Princeton University Press. https://www.degruyterbrill.com/document/doi/10.1515/9780691209869/html.

Cecil, Vanessa, Louise F. Pendry, Katherine Ashbullby, and Jessica Salvatore. 2023. "Masquerading Their Way to Authenticity: Does Age Stigma Concealment Benefit Older Women?" *Journal of Women & Aging* 35 (5): 428–45.

Charlton, James I. 1998. *Nothing about Us without Us: Disability Oppression and Empowerment*. University of California Press.

Chen, Justin A., Courtney Stevens, Sylvia H. M. Wong, and Cindy H. Liu. 2019. "Psychiatric Symptoms and Diagnoses among U.S. College Students: A Comparison by Race and Ethnicity." *Psychiatric Services* 70 (6): 442–9. https://doi.org/10.1176/appi.ps.201800388.

Chisadza, Carolyn, Nicky Nicholls, and Eleni Yitbarek. 2019. "Race and Gender Biases in Student Evaluations of Teachers." *Economics Letters* 179 (June): 66–71. https://doi.org/10.1016/j.econlet.2019.03.022.

Choy, Susan P. 2002. "Students Whose Parents Did Not Go to College: Postsecondary Access, Persistence, and Attainment." United States Department of Education. https://doi.org/10.1037/e492182006-021.

Cipriano, Robert E., and Jeffrey L. Buller. 2021. "Faculty Job Dissatisfaction in the New Normal." *The Department Chair* 32 (2): 14–15. https://doi.org/10.1002/dch.30412.

Clark, Cole. 2023. "Trend No. 2: The Value of the Degree Undergoes Further Questioning." Deloitte Insights. https://www2.deloitte.com/us/en/insights/industry/public-sector/articles-on-higher-education/value-of-college-degree.html.

Clark Blickenstaff, Jacob. 2005. "Women and Science Careers: Leaky Pipeline or Gender Filter?" *Gender and Education* 17 (4): 369–86. https://doi.org/10.1080/09540250500145072.

Clement, Laurence, Jennie B. Dorman, and Richard McGee. 2020. "The Academic Career Readiness Assessment: Clarifying Hiring and Training Expectations for Future Biomedical Life Sciences Faculty." *CBE – Life Sciences Education* 19 (2): ar22. https://doi.org/10.1187/cbe.19-11-0235.

"COE – Characteristics of Postsecondary Faculty." 2025. Annual Reports and Information Staff (Annual Reports). https://nces.ed.gov/programs/coe/indicator/csc/postsecondary-faculty.

Cohn, Jay N., Stevo Julius, Joel Neutel, Michael Weber, Prasad Turlapaty, Yannan Shen, Victor Dong, Alicia Batchelor, Weinong Guo, and Hjalmar Lagast. 2004. "Clinical Experience with Perindopril in African-American Hypertensive Patients: A Large United States Community Trial." *American Journal of Hypertension* 17 (2): 134–8.

Colby, Glenn, and Chelsea Fowler. 2020. "IPEDS Data on Full-Time Women Faculty and Faculty of Color" (Data Snapshot). American Association of University Professors. https://www.aaup.org/sites/default/files/Dec-2020_Data_Snapshot_Women_and_Faculty_of_Color.pdf.

Colby, Glenn, and Chelsea Fowler. n.d. "Data Snapshot: IPEDS Data on Full-Time Women Faculty and Faculty of Color."

"Content Not Found: Ingenta Connect." April 18, 2025. https://www.ingentaconnect.com/content/prin/csj/2014/00000048/00000001/art00001.
"Coping through Kinship during Covid-19: Lessons from Women of Color - ProQuest." April 18, 2025. https://www.proquest.com/openview/d47514866b655bcd3ff4a59a7eec7c4a/1?cbl=29702&pq-origsite=gscholar.
CourseHero. 2025. "Faculty Wellness and Careers." February. https://www.coursehero.com/blog/faculty-wellness-research/.
Crawford, Kerry F., and Leah C. Windsor. 2021. *The PhD Parenthood Trap: Caught between Work and Family in Academia*. Georgetown University Press.
Crawford, Kerry F., and Leah C. Windsor. 2023. "Call Me, Maybe? Gender, Bias, and Virtual Mentorship in Post-Covid Academia." *International Studies Perspectives* 24 (2): 189–229.
Crenshaw, Kimberlé. 1989. "Demarginalizing the Intersection of Race and Sex: A Black Feminist Critique of Antidiscrimination Doctrine, Feminist Theory and Antiracist Politics." *The University of Chicago Legal Forum* 140: 139–67.
Crick, Kent A., Lisa M. Larson, and Matthew T. Seipel. 2020. "Non-Tenure Track Faculty Satisfaction: A Self-Determination Model." *Journal of Career Assessment* 28 (3): 425–45. https://doi.org/10.1177/1069072719870681.
Cuddy, Salina. 2022. "Code-Switching: The Pressure on People to Change How They Speak." *The Conversation* (blog). http://theconversation.com/code-switching-the-pressure-on-people-to-change-how-they-speak-194302.
Culpepper, Dawn, Damani White-Lewis, Kerry AnnO'Meara, Lindsey Templeton, and Julia Anderson. 2023. "Do Rubrics Live up to Their Promise? Examining How Rubrics Mitigate Bias in Faculty Hiring." *The Journal of Higher Education* 94 (7): 823–50. https://doi.org/10.1080/00221546.2023.2168411.
Currier, Carrie Liu. 2022. "Breaking the Bamboo Ceiling: Challenges for APA Women in and Outside of the Classroom." *Journal of Political Science Education* 18 (2): 203–19. https://doi.org/10.1080/15512169.2022.2058956.
Daumiller, Martin, Raven Rinas, Julia Hein, Stefan Janke, Oliver Dickhäuser, and Markus Dresel. 2021. "Shifting from Face-to-Face to Online Teaching during COVID-19: The Role of University Faculty Achievement Goals for Attitudes towards This Sudden Change, and Their Relevance for Burnout/Engagement and Student Evaluations of Teaching Quality." *Computers in Human Behavior* 118 (May): 106677. https://doi.org/10.1016/j.chb.2020.106677.
Deal, Terrence E., and Allan A. Kennedy. 1982. *Corporate Cultures: The Rites and Rituals of Corporate Life*. Addison-Wesley.
"Degrees of Success." 2021. Council of Canadian Academies. "https://cca-reports.ca/reports/the-labour-market-transition-of-phd-graduates/.
DePhillips, Frank A., William M. Berliner, and James J. Cribbin. 1960. *Management of Training Programs*. Richard D. Erwin. http://archive.org/details/managementoftrai0000deph.
Dewey, Jessica, Michelle C. Pautz, and Martha K. Diede. 2024. "How Do We Address Faculty Burnout? Start by Exploring Faculty Motivation." *Innovative Higher Education* 49 (3): 521–39. https://doi.org/10.1007/s10755-023-09685-2.
Diekman, Amanda B. 2007. "Negotiating the Double Bind: Interpersonal and Instrumental Evaluations of Dominance." *Sex Roles* 56 (9): 551–61. https://doi.org/10.1007/s11199-007-9198-0.

Dionne, Shelley D., Janaki Gooty, Francis J. Yammarino, and Hiroki Sayama. 2018. "Decision Making in Crisis: A Multilevel Model of the Interplay between Cognitions and Emotions." *Organizational Psychology Review* 8 (2–3): 95–124. https://doi.org/10.1177/2041386618756063.

Docka-Filipek, Danielle, and Lindsey B. Stone. 2021. "Twice a 'Housewife': On Academic Precarity, 'Hysterical' Women, Faculty Mental Health, and Service as Gendered Care Work for the 'University Family' in Pandemic Times." *Gender, Work & Organization* 28 (6): 2158–79. https://doi.org/10.1111/gwao.12723.

Dutt-Ballerstadt, Reshmi. 2019. "Academic Prioritization or Killing the Liberal Arts?" *Faculty Publications*. https://digitalcommons.linfield.edu/englfac_pubs/71.

Dwyer, Rachael, and Libby Flynn. 2018. "'If These Walls Could Talk': Looking in, Walking out, and Reimagining a Broken System." In Alison L. Black and Susanne Garvis, eds. *Lived Experiences of Women in Academia*, 55–64. Routledge.

Dwyer, Sophie, and Alice Rogan. 2022. "Seeing the Unseen: Neurodiversity in the Emergency Department." *Emergency Medicine Australasia* 34 (4): 609–12. https://doi.org/10.1111/1742-6723.14038.

Ehrich, Lisa C., Brian Hansford, and Lee Tennent. 2004. "Formal Mentoring Programs in Education and Other Professions: A Review of the Literature." *Educational Administration Quarterly* 40 (4): 518–40. https://doi.org/10.1177/0013161X04267118.

Elenes, C. Alejandra. 1997. "Reclaiming the Borderlands: Chicana/o Identity, Difference, and Critical Pedagogy." *Educational Theory* 47 (3): 359.

Elliot, Andrew J., and Patricia G. Devine. 1994. "On the Motivational Nature of Cognitive Dissonance: Dissonance as Psychological Discomfort." *Journal of Personality and Social Psychology* 67 (3): 382–94. https://doi.org/10.1037/0022-3514.67.3.382.

Ellsworth, Diana, Jonathan Law, and Duwain Pinder. 2022. "US Racial and Ethnic Equity in Higher Education." McKinsey & Company. https://www.mckinsey.com/industries/education/our-insights/racial-and-ethnic-equity-in-us-higher-education.

Ertem, Hasan Yücel, and Gokce Gokalp. 2022. "Role of Personal and Organizational Factors on Student Attrition from Graduate Education: A Mixed-Model Research." *Journal of College Student Retention: Research, Theory & Practice* 23 (4): 903–28. https://doi.org/10.1177/1521025119881391.

Evans, Elrena, and Caroline Grant, eds. 2008. *Mama, PhD: Women Write about Motherhood and Academic Life*. Rutgers University Press. https://www.degruyterbrill.com/document/doi/10.36019/9780813544984/html.

Fasching-Varner, Kenneth J., Katrice A. Albert, Roland W. Mitchell, and Chaunda Allen. 2014. *Racial Battle Fatigue in Higher Education: Exposing the Myth of Post-Racial America*. Rowman & Littlefield.

"Fee Reductions." 2025. Educational Testing Service. https://www.ets.org/gre/score-users/reducing-barriers/fee-reductions.html.

Ferdinand, Keith C., and Annemarie M. Armani. 2007. "The Management of Hypertension in African Americans." *Critical Pathways in Cardiology* 6 (2): 67–71.

Fernandes, Jason D., Sarvenaz Sarabipour, Christopher T. Smith, Natalie M. Niemi, Nafisa M. Jadavji, Ariangela J. Kozik, Alex S. Holehouse, et al. 2020. "A Survey-Based Analysis of the Academic Job Market," edited by Helena Pérez Valle, Peter Rodgers, and Adriana Bankston. *eLife* 9 (June): e54097. https://doi.org/10.7554/eLife.54097.

Figley, Charles R. 1995. *Compassion Fatigue: Coping with Secondary Traumatic Stress Disorder in Those Who Treat the Traumatized*. Routledge.

First Gen Forward. n.d. "Defining First-Generation." https://firstgen.naspa.org/blog/defining-first-generation.

Flaherty, Colleen. 2016. "More Faculty Diversity, Not on Tenure Track." *Inside Higher Ed.* https://www.insidehighered.com/news/2016/08/22/study-finds-gains-faculty-diversity-not-tenure-track.

Flaherty, Colleen. 2020. "Students, Professors and Politics. *Inside Higher Ed.* https://www.insidehighered.com/news/2020/03/03/some-students-do-feel-political-pressure-their-professors-few-change-their-views.

Flaherty, Colleen. 2021. "The Skinny on Teaching Evals and Bias." *Inside Higher Ed.* https://www.insidehighered.com/news/2021/02/17/whats-really-going-respect-bias-and-teaching-evals.

Flaherty, Colleen. 2022. "Prestige Hiring across Academe." *Inside Higher Ed.* https://www.insidehighered.com/news/2022/09/23/new-study-finds-80-faculty-trained-20-institutions.

Flaherty, Colleen. 2023a. "Student Views on the College Experience." *Inside Higher Ed.* August 2023. https://www.insidehighered.com/news/student-success/college-experience/2023/08/21/student-assessments-their-college-experience.

Flaherty, Colleen. 2023b. "Survey: Inequities in Student Involvement." *Inside Higher Ed.* https://www.insidehighered.com/news/student-success/college-experience/2023/09/22/survey-barriers-college-students-campus.

Frank, Hillary. 2018. "The Special Misogyny Reserved for Mothers." *The New York Times.* https://www.nytimes.com/2018/12/31/opinion/childbirth-injury-motherhood-misogyny.html.

Frueh, Jamie, David L. Blaney, Kevin Dunn, Patricia Goff, Eric K.Leonard, and Simona Sharoni. 2008. "Political Beliefs and the Academic Responsibilities of Undergraduate Teaching." *Journal of Political Science Education* 4 (4): 447–62. https://doi.org/10.1080/15512160802413725.

Fry, Richard. 2021."First-Generation College Graduates Lag behind Their Peers on Key Economic Outcomes." Pew Research Center. https://www.pewresearch.org/social-trends/2021/05/18/first-generation-college-graduates-lag-behind-their-peers-on-key-economic-outcomes/.

Gable, Rachel. 2021. *The Hidden Curriculum: First Generation Students at Legacy Universities.* Princeton University Press.

Gabriel, Kelly P., and Herman Aguinis. 2022. "How to Prevent and Combat Employee Burnout and Create Healthier Workplaces during Crises and Beyond." *Business Horizons* 65 (2): 183–92. https://doi.org/10.1016/j.bushor.2021.02.037.

Gallagher, Hugh Gregory. 1999. "FDR's Splendid Deception: The Moving Story of Roosevelt's Massive Disability and the Intense Efforts to Conceal It from the Public." Eweb:198450. https://repository.library.georgetown.edu/handle/10822/918947.

Gallardo, Marta. 2020. "Does Maternity Affect Women's Careers? Perceptions of Working Mothers in Academia." *Educación XX1* 24 (November): 405–28. https://doi.org/10.5944/educXX1.26714.

Garcia, Gina Ann. 2019. *Becoming Hispanic-Serving Institutions: Opportunities for Colleges and Universities.* Johns Hopkins University Press.

García-Gallego, Aurora, Nikolaos Georgantzís, Joan Martín-Montaner, and Teodosio Pérez-Amaral. 2015. "(How) Do Research and Administrative Duties Affect University Professors' Teaching?" *Applied Economics* 47 (45): 4868–83.

Gardner, Paul. 1998. "Teaching at Its Best: A Passionate Detachment in the Classroom." *PS: Political Science & Politics* 31 (4): 802–4. https://doi.org/10.2307/420721.

Garriott, Patton O., Aaron Hudyma, Chesleigh Keene, and Dana Santiago. 2015. "Social Cognitive Predictors of First- and Non-First-Generation College Students' Academic and Life Satisfaction." *Journal of Counseling Psychology* 62 (2): 253–63. https://doi.org/10.1037/cou0000066.

Garrison, Nancy J., and Douglas S. Gardner. 2012. "Assets First Generation College Students Bring to the Higher Education Setting." Association for the Study of Higher Education Annual Conference. https://eric.ed.gov/?id=ED539775.

Gasser, Courtney E., and Katharine S. Shaffer. 2014. "Career Development of Women in Academia: Traversing the Leaky Pipeline." *Professional Counselor* 4 (4): 332–52.

Gelber, Katharine, Katie Brennan, David Duriesmith, and Ellyse Fenton. 2022. "Gendered Mundanities: Gender Bias in Student Evaluations of Teaching in Political Science." *Australian Journal of Political Science* 57 (2): 199–220.

George Mwangi, Chrystal A., Nyaradzai Changamire, and Jacqueline Mosselson. 2018. "An Intersectional Understanding of African International Graduate Students' Experiences in U.S. Higher Education." *Journal of Diversity in Higher Education* 12 (1): 52–64.

Gewin, Virginia. 2021. "Pandemic Burnout Is Rampant in Academia." *Nature* 591 (7850): 489–92. https://doi.org/10.1038/d41586-021-00663-2.

Ghosh, Rajashi. 2013. "Mentors Providing Challenge and Support: Integrating Concepts from Teacher Mentoring in Education and Organizational Mentoring in Business." *Human Resource Development Review* 12 (2): 144–76.

Gino, Francesca, and Katherine Coffman. 2021. "Unconscious Bias Training That Works." *Harvard Business Review* 99 (5): 114–23.

Goffman, Erving. 1959. *The Presentation of Self in Everyday Life*. Vintage.

Goldgeier, James, and Tamara Cofman Wittes. 2023. *Foreign Policy Careers for PhDs: A Practical Guide to a World of Possibilities*. Georgetown University Press.

Górska, Anna Maria, Karolina Kulicka, Zuzanna Staniszewska, and Dorota Dobija. 2021. "Deepening Inequalities: What Did COVID-19 Reveal about the Gendered Nature of Academic Work?" *Gender, Work & Organization* 28 (4): 1546–61. https://doi.org/10.1111/gwao.12696.

Goulden, Marc, Mary Ann Mason, and Karie Frasch. 2011. "Keeping Women in the Science Pipeline." *The ANNALS of the American Academy of Political and Social Science* 638 (1): 141–62. https://doi.org/10.1177/0002716211416925.

Gross, Neil, and Solon Simmons. 2014. *Professors and Their Politics*. Johns Hopkins University Press.

Guarino, Cassandra M., and Victor M. H. Borden. 2017. "Faculty Service Loads and Gender: Are Women Taking Care of the Academic Family?" *Research in Higher Education* 58 (6): 672–94. https://doi.org/10.1007/s11162-017-9454-2.

Gutiérrez y Muhs, Gabriella, Yolanda Flores Niemann, Carmen G. González, and Angela P. Harris, eds. 2012. *Presumed Incompetent: The Intersections of Race and Class for Women in Academia*. University Press of Colorado.

Hammoudi Halat, Dalal, Abderrezzaq Soltani, Roua Dalli, Lama Alsarraj, and Ahmed Malki. 2023. "Understanding and Fostering Mental Health and Well-Being among University Faculty: A Narrative Review." *Journal of Clinical Medicine* 12 (13): 4425. https://doi.org/10.3390/jcm12134425.

Hanasono, Lisa K., Ellen M. Broido, Margaret M. Yacobucci, Karen V. Root, Susana Peña, and Deborah A. O'Neil. 2019. "Secret Service: Revealing Gender Biases in the

Visibility and Value of Faculty Service." *Journal of Diversity in Higher Education* 12 (1): 85–98. https://doi.org/10.1037/dhe0000081.

Hancock, Kathleen J., Matthew A. Baum, and Marijke Breuning. 2013. "Women and Pre-Tenure Scholarly Productivity in International Studies: An Investigation into the Leaky Career Pipeline." *International Studies Perspectives* 14 (4): 507–27. https://doi.org/10.1111/insp.12002.

"Hang Together or Hang Separately." 2017. AAUP. https://www.aaup.org/article/hang-together-or-hang-separately.

Hanna, Alex. 2016. "Being Transgender on the Job Market." *Inside Higher Ed*. https://www.insidehighered.com/advice/2016/07/15/challenge-being-transgender-academic-job-market-essay.

Hansen, W. Lee. 1983. "Impact of Student Financial Aid on Access." *Proceedings of the Academy of Political Science* 35 (2): 84–96.

Haviland, Don, Nathan F. Alleman, Cara Cliburn Allen, and Jenny Jacobs. 2023. *Inclusive Collegiality and Nontenure-Track Faculty: Engaging All Faculty as Colleagues to Promote Healthy Departments and Institutions*. Taylor & Francis.

Heffernan, Troy. 2022. "Sexism, Racism, Prejudice, and Bias: A Literature Review and Synthesis of Research Surrounding Student Evaluations of Courses and Teaching." *Assessment & Evaluation in Higher Education* 47 (1): 144–54. https://doi.org/10.1080/02602938.2021.1888075.

Heilman, Madeline E., and Tyler G. Okimoto. 2008. "Motherhood: A Potential Source of Bias in Employment Decisions." *The Journal of Applied Psychology* 93 (1): 189–98. https://doi.org/10.1037/0021-9010.93.1.189.

Henningsen, Levke, Lisa K. Horvath, and Klaus Jonas. 2022. "Affirmative Action Policies in Academic Job Advertisements: Do They Facilitate or Hinder Gender Discrimination in Hiring Processes for Professorships?" *Sex Roles* 86 (1): 34–48. https://doi.org/10.1007/s11199-021-01251-4.

Herman, Judith. 1998. "Recovery from Psychological Trauma." *Psychiatry and Clinical Neurosciences* 52 (Suppl.): S145–50.

Herrington, Jan, Thomas C. Reeves, and Ron Oliver. 2009. *A Guide to Authentic E-Learning*. Routledge. https://doi.org/10.4324/9780203864265.

Hesli, Vicki L., and Jae Mook Lee. 2011. "Faculty Research Productivity: Why Do Some of Our Colleagues Publish More Than Others?" *PS: Political Science & Politics* 44 (2): 393–408.

Hesli, Vicki L., Jae Mook Lee, and Sara McLaughlin Mitchell. 2012. "Predicting Rank Attainment in Political Science: What Else Besides Publications Affects Promotion?" *PS: Political Science & Politics* 45 (3): 475–92. https://doi.org/10.1017/S1049096512000364.

"High-Impact Practices." n.d. American Association of Colleges and Universities. https://www.aacu.org/trending-topics/high-impact.

Hirshfield, Laura E., and Tiffany D. Joseph. 2012. "'We Need a Woman, We Need a Black Woman': Gender, Race, and Identity Taxation in the Academy." *Gender and Education* 24 (2): 213–27. https://doi.org/10.1080/09540253.2011.606208.

Ho, Helen K., Katharina A. Azim, Summer Melody Pennell, Colleen C. Myles-Baltzly, N. A. Heller, Maggie Campbell-Obaid, Meike Eilert, et al. 2023. "Forming a Motherscholar Research Collaborative." In Melissa Castillo Planas and Debra A. Castillo, *Scholars in COVID Times*. Cornell University Press, 15–38.

Holloway, Pippa. 2009. "'A Chicken-Stealer Shall Lose His Vote': Disfranchisement for Larceny in the South, 1874–1890." *The Journal of Southern History* 75 (4): 931–62.
Howell, Alison, and Melanie Richter-Montpetit. 2020. "Is Securitization Theory Racist? Civilizationism, Methodological Whiteness, and Antiblack Thought in the Copenhagen School." *Security Dialogue* 51 (1): 3–22.
Hoyt, Jeff E. 2012. "Predicting the Satisfaction and Loyalty of Adjunct Faculty." *The Journal of Continuing Higher Education* 60 (3): 132–42. https://www.tandfonline.com/doi/abs/10.1080/07377363.2013.722417.
Hsieh, Betina, and Huong Tran Nguyen. 2020. "Identity-Informed Mentoring to Support Acculturation of Female Faculty of Color in Higher Education: An Asian American Female Mentoring Relationship Case Study." *Journal of Diversity in Higher Education* 13 (2): 169–80. https://doi.org/10.1037/dhe0000118.
Hsu, Nina S., K. Paul Rezai-zadeh, Michael S. Tennekoon, and Stephen J. Korn. 2021. "Myths and Facts about Getting an Academic Faculty Position in Neuroscience." *Science Advances* 7 (35): eabj2604. https://doi.org/10.1126/sciadv.abj2604.
Hughes, Alan. 2014. "Tenure at Small Colleges." *Inside Higher Ed*. August 10, 2014. https://www.insidehighered.com/advice/2014/08/11/essay-earning-tenure-small-liberal-arts-colleges.
Ingraham, Christopher. 2018. "The World's Richest Countries Guarantee Mothers More Than a Year of Paid Maternity Leave. The U.S. Guarantees Them Nothing." https://www.washingtonpost.com/news/wonk/wp/2018/02/05/the-worlds-richest-countries-guarantee-mothers-more-than-a-year-of-paid-maternity-leave-the-u-s-guarantees-them-nothing/.
Institute of International Education. 2019. "Open Doors 2019 Fast Facts." https://opendoorsdata.org/wp-content/uploads/2020/05/Fast-Facts-2019.pdf. Accessed February 17, 2026.
Institute of International Education. n.d. "IIE Open Doors/International Scholars in the U.S., 2000/01-2020/21." https://opendoorsdata.org/infographic/international-scholars-in-the-u-s-2000-01-2020-21/. Accessed February 16, 2026.
"Intersectionality and Higher Education." 2025. *Rutgers University Press* (blog). https://www.rutgersuniversitypress.org/intersectionality-and-higher-education/9780813597669/.
Ishiyama, John. 2002. "Does Early Participation in Undergraduate Research Benefit Social Science and Humanities Students?" *College Student Journal* 36 (3): 381–7.
Jackson, Philip Wesley. 1968. *Life in Classrooms*. Teachers College Press.
Jafar, Afshan, Simon Feldman, and Joan C. Chrisler. 2017. "Hang Together or Hang Separately." *AAUP* (blog). May 16, 2017. https://www.aaup.org/article/hang-together-or-hang-separately.
Jeffries-EL, Malika. 2021. "POV: Where Are the Tenured Black Female Professors?" Boston University. September 15, 2021. https://www.bu.edu/articles/2021/pov-where-are-the-tenured-black-female-professors/.
Joughin, Louis. 1967. *Academic Freedom and Tenure: A Handbook of the American Association of University Professors*. University of Wisconsin Press.
Kelderman, Eric. 2023. "What the Public Really Thinks about Higher Education." *The Chronicle of Higher Education*. https://www.chronicle.com/article/what-the-public-really-thinks-about-higher-education.
Kelliher, Rebecca. 2021. "The Pandemic's Unequal Toll on Faculty." The EDU Ledger. https://www.diverseeducation.com/faculty-staff/article/15286701/as-omicron-rages-on-so-does-the-pandemics-unequal-toll-on-faculty. Accessed February 18, 2026.

Kelly-Woessner, April, and Matthew C. Woessner. 2006. "My Professor Is a Partisan Hack: How Perceptions of a Professor's Political Views Affect Student Course Evaluations." *PS: Political Science & Politics* 39 (3): 495–501. https://doi.org/10.1017/S104909650606080X.

Kezar, Adrianna, ed. 2010. *Recognizing and Serving Low-Income Students in Higher Education.* Routledge.

Kim, David Youngeil. 2018. "In This Together: The Impact of Mentorship Programs on the First-Generation Student Experience." University of Toronto. https://www.proquest.com/docview/2149673933?pq-origsite=gscholar&fromopenview=true&sourcetype=Dissertations%20&%20Theses.

Kim, Son Chae, Leanne Burke, Chris Sloan, and Shannon Barnett. 2013. "Attitudes toward Teen Mothers among Nursing Students and Psychometric Evaluation of Positivity toward Teen Mothers Scale." *Nurse Education Today* 33 (9): 986–91. https://doi.org/10.1016/j.nedt.2012.10.014.

King, Molly M., and Megan E. Frederickson. 2021. "The Pandemic Penalty: The Gendered Effects of COVID-19 on Scientific Productivity." *Socius Sociological Research for a Dynamic World* 7: 1–24. https://doi.org/10.1177/23780231211006977.

Koch, Chris, and W. Brad Johnson. 2000. "Documenting the Benefits of Undergraduate Mentoring." *Council on Undergraduate Research Quarterly* 20 (4): 172–5.

Kowalski, Kamil. 2016. "What Shall We Do with Our Boys? An Impact of the GI Bill on the US Economy." *Annales. Etyka w Życiu Gospodarczym* 19 (4): 167–80.

LaGesse, Shane. 2023. "What to Know as a First-Generation College Student." *U.S. News and World Report.* https://www.usnews.com/education/best-colleges/articles/what-to-know-as-a-first-generation-college-student.

Lange, Peter, and Anthony J. Olejniczak. 2023. "An Uneven Job Market for Assistant Professors." *Inside Higher Ed.* January 17, 2023. https://www.insidehighered.com/views/2023/01/18/growth-assistant-professorships-uneven-opinion.

Langin, Katie. 2020. "Amid Pandemic, US Faculty Job Openings Plummet." *Science.* https://www.science.org/content/article/amid-pandemic-us-faculty-job-openings-plummet Accessed February 18, 2026.

Langin, Katie. 2022. "U.S. Labs Face Severe Postdoc Shortage." *Science* 376 (6600): 1369–70. https://doi.org/10.1126/science.add6184.

Laving, Michelle, Francesco Foroni, Madeleine Ferrari, Cynthia Turner, and Keong Yap. 2023. "The Association between OCD and Shame: A Systematic Review and Meta-analysis." *The British Journal of Clinical Psychology* 62 (1): 28–52. https://doi.org/10.1111/bjc.12392.

Lebo, Matthew J. 2016. "Managing Your Research Pipeline." *PS: Political Science & Politics* 49 (2): 259–64. https://doi.org/10.1017/S1049096516000160.

Lee, Jungmin, Hyun Ju Jeong, and Sujin Kim. 2021. "Stress, Anxiety, and Depression among Undergraduate Students during the COVID-19 Pandemic and Their Use of Mental Health Services." *Innovative Higher Education* 46 (5): 519–38. https://doi.org/10.1007/s10755-021-09552-y.

Lei, Lianlian, Amanda N. Leggett, and Donovan T. Maust. 2023. "A National Profile of Sandwich Generation Caregivers Providing Care to Both Older Adults and Children." *Journal of the American Geriatrics Society* 71 (3): 799–809. https://doi.org/10.1111/jgs.18138.

Lesiak, Atom J. 2023. "I'm a Trans Scientist – Here's My Advice for Navigating Academia." *Nature.* https://doi.org/10.1038/d41586-023-00923-3.

Levecque, Katia, Frederik Anseel, Alain De Beuckelaer, Johan Van der Heyden, and Lydia Gisle. 2017. "Work Organization and Mental Health Problems in PhD Students." *Research Policy* 46 (4): 868–79. https://doi.org/10.1016/j.respol.2017.02.008.
Li, Yao, and Harvey L. Nicholson. 2021. "When 'Model Minorities' Become 'Yellow Peril'—Othering and the Racialization of Asian Americans in the COVID-19 Pandemic." *Sociology Compass* 15 (2): e12849. https://doi.org/10.1111/soc4.12849.
Liu, Cindy H., Stephanie Pinder-Amaker, Hyeouk "Chris" Hahm, and Justin A. Chen. 2022. "Priorities for Addressing the Impact of the COVID-19 Pandemic on College Student Mental Health." *Journal of American College Health* 70 (5): 1356–8. https://doi.org/10.1080/07448481.2020.1803882.
Livingston, Gretchen, and Deja Thomas. 2019. "Among 41 Countries, Only U.S. Lacks Paid Parental Leave." Pew Research Center. https://policycommons.net/artifacts/616477/among-41-countries-only-us/1597146/.
Livingston, Robert W., Ashleigh Shelby Rosette, and Ella F. Washington. 2012. "Can an Agentic Black Woman Get Ahead? The Impact of Race and Interpersonal Dominance on Perceptions of Female Leaders." *Psychological Science* 23 (4): 354–8. https://doi.org/10.1177/0956797611428079.
Lorentz, Kevin G., Daniel J. Mallinson, Julia Marin Hellwege, Davin Phoenix, and J. Cherie Strachan, eds. 2022. *Strategies for Navigating Graduate School and Beyond.* American Political Science Association.
Lubrano, Alfred. 2003. *Limbo: Blue-Collar Roots, White-Collar Dreams.* Wiley.
Lyness, Karen S., and Madeline E. Heilman. 2006. "When Fit Is Fundamental: Performance Evaluations and Promotions of Upper-Level Female and Male Managers." *Journal of Applied Psychology* 91 (4): 777–85. https://doi.org/10.1037/0021-9010.91.4.777.
Mahali, Saghar Chahar, Phillip R. Sevigny, and Shadi Beshai. 2024. "Multicultural Efficacy Beliefs in Higher Education: Examining University Instructors' Burnout and Mental Well-Being." *Psychological Reports.* https://journals.sagepub.com/doi/full/10.1177/00332941241253599.
Margolis, Eric. 2001. *The Hidden Curriculum in Higher Education.* Psychology Press.
Martin, Jane R. 1976. "What Should We Do with a Hidden Curriculum When We Find One?" *Curriculum Inquiry* 6 (2): 135–51. https://doi.org/10.1080/03626784.1976.11075525.
Martin, Lisa L. 2016. "Gender, Teaching Evaluations, and Professional Success in Political Science." *PS: Political Science & Politics* 49 (2): 313–19. https://doi.org/10.1017/S1049096516000275.
Masket, Seth. 2018. "The Crisis in Political Science Education." *Pacific Standard.* https://psmag.com/education/the-crisis-in-political-science-education/.
Maslach, Christina, Susan E. Jackson, and Michael P. Leiter. 1997. "Maslach Burnout Inventory: Third Edition." In Carlos P. Zalaquett and Richard J. Wood, *Evaluating Stress: A Book of Resources.* Scarecrow Education, 191–218.
Maslow, Abraham H. 1943. "A Theory of Human Motivation." *Psychological Review* 50 (4): 370–96. https://doi.org/10.1037/h0054346.
Mason, Mary Ann, and Marc Goulden. 2002. "Do Babies Matter? The Effect of Family Formation on the Lifelong Career of Academic Men and Women." *Academe* 86 (6): 21–7.
Mason, Mary Ann, Nicholas H. Wolfinger, and Marc Goulden. 2013. *Do Babies Matter? Gender and Family in the Ivory Tower.* Rutgers University Press.

Matias, J. Nathan, Neil A. Lewis, and Elan C. Hope. 2022. "US Universities Are Not Succeeding in Diversifying Faculty." *Nature Human Behaviour* 6 (12): 1606–8. https://doi.org/10.1038/s41562-022-01495-4.

Matthew, Patricia A. 2016. *Written/Unwritten: Diversity and the Hidden Truths of Tenure*. University of North Carolina Press.

Mayo, Liz. 2023. "Women Do Higher Ed's Chores. That Must Change." *The Chronicle of Higher Education*. February 13, 2023. https://www.chronicle.com/article/women-do-higher-eds-chores-that-must-change.

McAdams, Dan P., Jeffrey Reynolds, Martha Lewis, Allison H. Patten, and Phillip J. Bowman. 2001. "When Bad Things Turn Good and Good Things Turn Bad: Sequences of Redemption and Contamination in Life Narrative and Their Relation to Psychosocial Adaptation in Midlife Adults and in Students." *Personality and Social Psychology Bulletin* 27 (4): 474–85.

McAlpine, Lynn, and Cheryl Amundsen. 2016. *Post-PhD Career Trajectories: Intentions, Decision-Making and Life Aspirations*. Springer.

McCarron, Graziella Pagliarulo. 2022. "First and Flourishing?: An Exploration of How First-Generation College Students Make Meaning of Their Well-Being through Purpose, Relationships, and Multiple Identities." *Journal of First-Generation Student Success* 2 (1): 1–17. https://doi.org/10.1080/26906015.2021.2018269.

McClellan, Fletcher, Kyle CasimirKopko, and Kayla L. Gruber. 2021. "High-Impact Practices and Their Effects: Implications for the Undergraduate Political Science Curriculum." *Journal of Political Science Education* 17 (Suppl. 1): 674–92. https://doi.org/10.1080/15512169.2020.1867562.

McLean, Scott, and Jaya Dixit. 2018. "The Power of Positive Thinking: A Hidden Curriculum for Precarious Times." *Adult Education Quarterly* 68 (4): 280–96. https://doi.org/10.1177/0741713618777817.

McNulty, Margaret A., and Rebecca S. Lufler. 2022. "The Glass Ceiling Thickens: How The COVID-19 Pandemic Negatively Impacted Academic Medicine Faculty." *The FASEB Journal* 36 (S1). https://doi.org/10.1096/fasebj.2022.36.S1.R3180.

Meirmans, Stephanie, Dunja K. Lamatsch, and Maurine Neiman. 2022. "Sticky Steps and the Gender Gap: How Thoughtful Practices Could Help Keep Caregivers in Science." *Proceedings of the Royal Society B: Biological Sciences* 289 (1987): 1837. https://doi.org/10.1098/rspb.2022.1837.

Mena, Jasmine A., and Annemarie Vaccaro. 2017. "'I've Struggled, I've Battled': Invisibility Microaggressions Experienced by Women of Color at a Predominantly White Institution." *NASPA Journal about Women in Higher Education* 10 (3): 301–18. https://doi.org/10.1080/19407882.2017.1347047.

Mengel, Friederike, Jan Sauermann, and Ulf Zölitz. 2019. "Gender Bias in Teaching Evaluations." *Journal of the European Economic Association* 17 (2): 535–66.

Mervis, Jeffrey. 2021. "Racial Disparities Mark Ph.D. Financing." *Science* 374 (6571): 1038. https://doi.org/10.1126/science.acx9691.

Miles, Patti, and Deanna House. 2015. "The Tail Wagging the Dog: An Overdue Examination of Student Teaching Evaluations." *International Journal of Higher Education* 4 (2): 116–26.

Miller, David I., and Jonathan Wai. 2015. "The Bachelor's to Ph.D. STEM Pipeline No Longer Leaks More Women than Men: A 30-Year Analysis." *Frontiers in Psychology* 6 (February): 37. https://doi.org/10.3389/fpsyg.2015.00037.

Mills, Charles W. 1999. *The Racial Contract*. Cornell University Press.
Mitchell, Kristina M. W., and Jonathan Martin. 2018. "Gender Bias in Student Evaluations." *PS: Political Science & Politics* 51 (3): 648–52. https://doi.org/10.1017/S104909651800001X.
Mitchell, Sara McLaughlin, and Vicki L. Hesli. 2013. "Women Don't Ask? Women Don't Say No? Bargaining and Service in the Political Science Profession." *PS: Political Science & Politics* 46 (2): 355–69.
Morales, Danielle X., Sara E. Grineski, and Timothy W. Collins. 2017. "Faculty Motivation to Mentor Students through Undergraduate Research Programs: A Study of Enabling and Constraining Factors." *Research in Higher Education* 58 (5): 520–44. https://doi.org/10.1007/s11162-016-9435-x.
Morgan, Joan. 2017. *She Begat This: 20 Years of the Miseducation of Lauryn Hill*. Simon & Schuster.
Motherscholar Collective. Colleen C. Myles-Baltzly, Helen K. Ho, Ivanna Richardson, Jennifer Greene-Rooks, Katharina A. Azim, Kathryn E. Frazier, Maggie Campbell-Obaid, Meike Eilert, and Stacey R. Lim. 2021. "Transformative Collaborations: How a Motherscholar Research Collective Survived and Thrived during COVID-19." *International Perspectives in Psychology: Research, Practice, Consultation* 10 (4): 197–214.
Motherscholar Collective. Katharina A. Azim, Jasmine L. Blanks Jones, Maggie Campbell-Obaid, Meike Eilert, Jennifer Greene-Rooks, N.A. Heller, Helen Ho, Sarah Key-DeLyria, Stacey Lim, Colleen C. Myles-Baltzly, Lucy C. Parker-Barnes, Summer Melody Pennell, and Ivanna Richardson. 2023. "Collective Perspectives: The Formation of a Motherscholar Pandemic Research Collaborative." In M. Castillo Planas and D. Castillo, eds. *Scholars in COVID Times*, 15–38. Cornell University Press.
Murdie, Amanda. 2017. "An Academic Woman's Rant of the Week: Service Discrepancies." *The Duck of Minerva* (blog). April 12, 2017. https://www.duckofminerva.com/2017/04/an-academic-womans-rant-of-the-week-service-discrepancies.html.
Murdie, Amanda, Krista Wiegand, Debbie Lisle, and James Scott. 2020. "Journal Submissions in Times of COVID-19: Is There a Gender Gap?" *The Duck of Minerva* (blog). https://www.duckofminerva.com/2020/05/journal-submissions-in-times-of-covid-19-is-there-a-gender-gap.html.
Murtonen, Mari. 2015. "University Students' Understanding of the Concepts Empirical, Theoretical, Qualitative and Quantitative Research." *Teaching in Higher Education* 20 (7): 684–98. https://doi.org/10.1080/13562517.2015.1072152.
Myles-Baltzly, Colleen C., Helen K. Ho, Ivanna Richardson, Jennifer Greene-Rooks, Katharina A. Azim, Kathryn E. Frazier, Maggie Campbell-Obaid, Meike Eilert, and Stacey R. Lim. 2021. "Transformative Collaborations." *International Perspectives in Psychology* 10 (4): 225–42. https://doi.org/10.1027/2157-3891/a000029.
Nagoski, Emily, and Amelia Nagoski. 2019. *Burnout: The Secret to Unlocking the Stress Cycle*. Random House.
National Education Association. 2024. "NEA Higher Education: Faculty Salary Analysis: 2022–2023." 41 (1). https://www.nea.org/sites/default/files/2024-04/2024-higher-ed-salary-report_0.pdf.
Nature Editorial Board. 2023. "Encourage Whistle-Blowing: How Universities Can Help to Resolve Research's Mental-Health Crisis." *Nature* 617 (7962): 651. https://doi.org/10.1038/d41586-023-01703-9.

Nguyen, David J., and Christina W. Yao. 2023. *A Handbook for Supporting Today's Graduate Students*. Taylor & Francis.

Nicholas, Elenita Makani. 2021. "Q&A: Why Discuss Mental Health in Academia?" Stanford Earth. https://earth.stanford.edu/news/qa-why-discuss-mental-health-academia.

Novkov, Julie, and Scott Barclay. 2010. "Lesbians, Gays, Bisexuals, and the Transgendered in Political Science: Report on a Discipline-Wide Survey." *PS: Political Science & Politics* 43 (1): 95–106.

Nussbaum, Martha C. 2017. *Not for Profit: Why Democracy Needs the Humanities*. Revised edition. Princeton University Press.

Oleschuk, Merin. 2020. "Gender Equity Considerations for Tenure and Promotion during COVID-19." *Canadian Review of Sociology* 57 (3): 502–15. https://doi.org/10.1111/cars.12295.

Olson Jr., Mancur. 1971. *The Logic of Collective Action: Public Goods and the Theory of Groups, Second Printing with New Preface and Appendix*. Revised edition. Schocken Books.

Oprisko, Robert. 2012. "Superpowers: The American Academic Elite." *SSRN Scholarly Paper*. Social Science Research Network. https://papers.ssrn.com/abstract=2280725.

Ott, Molly, and Jesus Cisneros. 2015. "Understanding the Changing Faculty Workforce in Higher Education: A Comparison of Non-Tenure Track and Tenure Line Experiences." *Education Policy Analysis Archives* 23 (90): 1–28. (90). https://doi.org/10.14507/epaa.v23.1934.

Patler, Caitlin. 2018. "To Reveal or Conceal: How Diverse Undocumented Youth Navigate Legal Status Disclosure." *Sociological Perspectives* 61 (6): 857–73. https://doi.org/10.1177/0731121418775092.

Pennell, Summer Melody, Jennifer Greene-Rooks, and Kathryn Wagner. 2021. "Pandemic Academic Parenting: Finding the Radically Queer within Our Mundane, Monotonous, and Sometimes Homonormative Experiences." *American Educational History Journal*: 183–90.

Perez, Caroline Criado. 2019. *Invisible Women: Data Bias in a World Designed for Men*. Abrams.

Pérez-Vigil, Ana, Lorena Fernández de la Cruz, Gustaf Brander, Kayoko Isomura, Andreas Jangmo, Inna Feldman, Eva Hesselmark, et al. 2018. "Association of Obsessive-Compulsive Disorder with Objective Indicators of Educational Attainment: A Nationwide Register-Based Sibling Control Study." *JAMA Psychiatry* 75 (1): 47–55. https://doi.org/10.1001/jamapsychiatry.2017.3523.

Petersen, Anne Helen. 2020. "Other Countries Have Social Safety Nets. The U.S. Has Women." *Culture Study* (blog). https://annehelen.substack.com/p/other-countries-have-social-safety.

Petersen, Anne Helen. 2021. "The Staggering, Exhausting, Invisible Costs of Caring for America's Elderly." *Vox*. https://www.vox.com/the-goods/22639674/elder-care-family-costs-nursing-home-health-care.

Peterson, David A. M., Lori A. Biederman, David Andersen, Tessa M. Ditonto, and Kevin Roe. 2019. "Mitigating Gender Bias in Student Evaluations of Teaching." *PLOS One* 14 (5): e0216241. https://doi.org/10.1371/journal.pone.0216241.

Peterson, Gretchen. 2022. "When a Global Pandemic Makes Life More Accessible to Those with Invisible Disabilities." *Sociation* 21 (1): 34–40.

Pirtle, Whitney Laster. 2018. "Motherhood while Black: The Hard Truth about Race and Parenthood." *The Chronicle of Higher Education*. https://www.chronicle.com/interactives/the-awakening.

Planas, Melissa Castillo, and Debra A. Castillo. 2023. *Scholars in COVID Times*. Cornell University Press.

Ponjuan, Luis, Valerie Martin Conley, and Cathy Trower. 2011. "Career Stage Differences in Pre-Tenure Track Faculty Perceptions of Professional and Personal Relationships with Colleagues." *The Journal of Higher Education* 82 (3): 319–46. https://www.tandfonline.com/doi/abs/10.1080/00221546.2011.11777204.

Pope-Ruark, Rebecca. 2022. *Unraveling Faculty Burnout: Pathways to Reckoning and Renewal*. Johns Hopkins University Press.

Porter, Stephen R. 2007. "A Closer Look at Faculty Service: What Affects Participation on Committees?" *The Journal of Higher Education* 78 (5): 523–41. https://www.tandfonline.com/doi/abs/10.1080/00221546.2007.11772328.

Pough, Gwendolyn D. 2015. *Check It While I Wreck It: Black Womanhood, Hip-Hop Culture, and the Public Sphere*. Northeastern University Press.

Powell, Stina. 2018. "Gender Equality in Academia: Intentions and Consequences." *International Journal of Diversity in Organizations, Communities, and Nations* 18 (1): 19.

Putnam, Robert D. 2000. *Bowling Alone: The Collapse and Revival of American Community*. Simon & Schuster.

Quinn, Ryan. 2025. "Ohio and Kentucky Ban DEI, Reduce Tenure Protections." *Inside Higher Ed*. https://www.insidehighered.com/news/faculty-issues/academic-freedom/2025/04/01/ohio-and-kentucky-ban-dei-reduce-tenure-protections.

Ramírez, Cristina D. 2002. "Mestiza Pedagogies: Borderlands Teaching, Writing, and Community Activism Informing Academic Work." In Laura Gonzalez and Michelle Hall Kells, eds. *Latina Leadership: Language and Literacy Education across Communities*. Syracuse University Press, 222–49.

Ramos, Jennifer M., Jamie Scalera Elliott, Christina Fattore, and Marijke Breuning. 2022. "Anxiety and the Onset of COVID-19: Examining Concerns of Historically Excluded Scholars." *International Studies Perspectives* 23 (3): 313–31.

Redford, Jeremy, and Kathleen Mulvaney Hoyer. 2017. "First Generation and Continuing-Generation College Students: A Comparison of High School and Postsecondary Experiences." American Institutes for Research. http://hdl.handle.net/10919/83686.

Reid, Rebecca A. 2021. "Retaining Women Faculty: The Problem of Invisible Labor." *PS: Political Science & Politics* 54 (3): 504–6. https://doi.org/10.1017/S1049096521000056.

Rennane, Stephanie, Hannah Acheson-Field, Kathryn A. Edwards, Grace Gahlon, and Melanie A. Zaber. 2022. "Leak or Link? The Overrepresentation of Women in Non-Tenure-Track Academic Positions in STEM." *PLOS One* 17 (6): e0267561. https://doi.org/10.1371/journal.pone.0267561.

Rideau, Ryan. 2021. "'We're Just Not Acknowledged': An Examination of the Identity Taxation of Full-Time Non-Tenure-Track Women of Color Faculty Members." *Journal of Diversity in Higher Education* 14 (2): 161–73. https://doi.org/10.1037/dhe0000139.

Rivera, Lauren A. 2017. "When Two Bodies Are (Not) a Problem: Gender and Relationship Status Discrimination in Academic Hiring." *American Sociological Review* 82 (6): 1111–38. https://doi.org/10.1177/0003122417739294.

Rockquemore, Kerry Ann. 2010. "Just Say No." *Inside Higher Ed*. https://www.insidehighered.com/advice/2010/09/27/just-say-no.

Rom, Mark Carl. 2021. "Time to Rethink Your Teaching Ideology?" *PS: Political Science & Politics* 54 (3): 587–92. https://doi.org/10.1017/S1049096521000421.
Ronnenberg, Susan Cosby, and Jennifer Sadowski. 2011. "Recognizing Undergraduate Research in Criteria for Faculty Promotion and Tenure." *Council on Undergraduate Research Quarterly* 31 (4): 10–12.
Rosette, Ashleigh Shelby, and Robert W. Livingston. 2012. "Failure Is Not an Option for Black Women: Effects of Organizational Performance on Leaders with Single versus Dual-Subordinate Identities." *Journal of Experimental Social Psychology* 48 (5): 1162–7. https://doi.org/10.1016/j.jesp.2012.05.002.
Rosette, Ashleigh Shelby, Christy Zhou Koval, Anyi Ma, and Robert Livingston. 2016. "Race Matters for Women Leaders: Intersectional Effects on Agentic Deficiencies and Penalties." *The Leadership Quarterly* 27 (3): 429–45.
Rothbaum, Jonathan, and Ashley Edwards. 2019. "U.S. Median Household Income Was $63,179 in 2018, Not Significantly Different from 2017: Survey Redesigns Make Comparisons to Years before 2017 Difficult." United States Census. https://www.census.gov/library/stories/2019/09/us-median-household-income-not-significantly-different-from-2017.html#:~:text=The%20U.S.%20median%20household%20income,Census%20Bureau%20statistics%20released%20today
Russell, Susan E., and Jie Huang. 2009. "Libraries' Role in Equalizing Access to Information." *Library Management* 30 (1/2): 69–76. https://doi.org/10.1108/01435120910927538.
Sabet, Cameron John, Simar S. Bajaj, and Fatima Cody Stanford. 2023. "Academic Hierarchies Are an Uphill Struggle for Black Women." *BMJ* 382 (August): 1784. https://doi.org/10.1136/bmj.p1784.
Salazar, María del Carmen. 2013. "A Humanizing Pedagogy: Reinventing the Principles and Practice of Education as a Journey toward Liberation." *Review of Research in Education* 37 (1): 121–48. https://doi.org/10.3102/0091732X12464032.
Sampaio, Anna. 2006. "Women of Color Teaching Political Science: Examining the Intersections of Race, Gender, and Course Material in the Classroom." *PS: Political Science & Politics* 39 (4): 917–22. https://doi.org/10.1017/S1049096506061191.
Scalera Elliott, Jamie, Sara McLaughlin Mitchell, Michelle L. Dion, Thomas R. Vargas, Yanna Krupnikov, Kerri Milita, John Barry Ryan, et al. 2023. "Forum: Gendered Dynamics of Academic Networks." *International Studies Perspectives* 24 (2): 189–229. https://doi.org/10.1093/isp/ekac009.
Scotch, Richard K., and Sally Friedman. 2014. "Changing Times: Self-Disclosure and the Representational Styles of Legislators with Physical Disabilities." *Disability Studies Quarterly* 34 (4). https://doi.org/10.18061/dsq.v34i4.4008.
Shapiro, Joseph P. 1994. *No Pity: People with Disabilities Forging a New Civil Rights Movement*. Crown.
Sheltzer, Jason. 2020. "Twitter Post." 2020. https://twitter.com/jsheltzer/status/1293291326969188354.
Simionato, Gabrielle K., and Susan Simpson. 2018. "Personal Risk Factors Associated with Burnout among Psychotherapists: A Systematic Review of the Literature." *Journal of Clinical Psychology* 74 (9): 1431–56. https://doi.org/10.1002/jclp.22615.
Smith, Jessi L., Ian M. Handley, and Rebecca Belou. 2018. "Retention, Tenure, and Promotion Bias-Literacy Training Guide." Montana State University. https://www.montana.edu/nsfadvance/documents/RTP_TrainingGuide_6.18.18.pdf.

Smith, William A. 2014. *Racial Battle Fatigue in Higher Education: Exposing the Myth of Post-Racial America*. Rowman & Littlefield.

Snyder, Benson R. 1973. *The Hidden Curriculum*. MIT Press.

Snyder, Charles R. 2002. "Hope Theory: Rainbows in the Mind." *Psychological Inquiry* 13 (4): 249–75.

Stanulis, Randi N., Lindsay J. Wexler, Stacey Pylman, Amy Guenther, Scott Farver, Amy Ward, Amy Croel-Perrien, and Kristen White. 2019. "Mentoring as More Than 'Cheerleading': Looking at Educative Mentoring Practices through Mentors' Eyes." *Journal of Teacher Education* 70 (5): 567–80. https://doi.org/10.1177/0022487118773996.

Sue, Derald Wing. 2021. "Microaggressions: Death by a Thousand Cuts." *Scientific American*. https://www.scientificamerican.com/article/microaggressions-death-by-a-thousand-cuts/.AccessedFebruary18,2026..

Sullivan, Megan. 2021. "POV: Higher Ed Institutions Would Benefit from Hiring More Faculty and Staff with Disabilities." *Boston University Today* (blog). https://www.bu.edu/articles/2021/higher-ed-institutions-hiring-more-faculty-staff-with-disabilities/.

Taffe, Michael A., and Nicholas W. Gilpin. 2021. "Racial Inequity in Grant Funding from the US National Institutes of Health." *ELife* 10 (January). https://doi.org/10.7554/eLife.65697.

Tanner, Samuel Jaye. 2017. "Permission to Be Confused: Toward a Second Wave of Critical Whiteness Pedagogy." *Journal of Curriculum and Pedagogy* 14 (2): 164–79.

Taraban, Roman, and Richard L. Blanton, eds. 2008. *Creating Effective Undergraduate Research Programs in Science*. Teachers College Press.

Taylor, David G., and Michael Frechette. 2022. "The Impact of Workload, Productivity, and Social Support on Burnout among Marketing Faculty during the COVID-19 Pandemic." *Journal of Marketing Education* 44 (2): 134–48. https://doi.org/10.1177/02734753221074284.

Teele, Dawn Langan, Joshua Kalla, and Frances Rosenbluth. 2018. "The Ties That Double Bind: Social Roles and Women's Underrepresentation in Politics." *American Political Science Review* 112 (3): 525–41. https://doi.org/10.1017/S0003055418000217.

"Ten Years of Opportunity at Vanderbilt." n.d. Vanderbilt University. https://web.archive.org/web/20220910081759/https://giving.vanderbilt.edu/oppvu/ten-years/.AccessedFebruary16,2026.

"Tenure and Contingency in US Higher Education" (Data Snapshot). 2023. https://www.aaup.org/article/data-snapshot-tenure-and-contingency-us-higher-education.

Teräs, Hanna, and Ümit Kartoğlu. 2017. "A Grounded Theory of Professional Learning in an Authentic Online Professional Development Program." *International Review of Research in Open and Distributed Learning* 18 (7): 191–212. https://doi.org/10.19173/irrodl.v18i7.2923.

Thelin, John R. 2019. *A History of American Higher Education*. Johns Hopkins University Press. https://doi.org/10.56021/9781421428826.

Tiede, Hans-Joerg. 2022. "The 2022 AAUP Survey of Tenure Practices." *Notices of the American Mathematical Society* 69 (10): 1. https://doi.org/10.1090/noti2560.

Tierney, William G., and Estela Mara Bensimon. 1996. *Promotion and Tenure: Community and Socialization in Academe*. SUNY Press.

Tillis, Tiffany Vanese. 2017. "When and Where I Enter: A Phenomenological Study of Black Women at a Selective Predominantly White Institution." The University of Texas at Austin. http://hdl.handle.net/2152/61380.

Toby, Jackson. 2010. "How Scholarships Morphed into Financial Aid." *Academic Questions* 23 (3): 298–310. https://doi.org/10.1007/s12129-010-9174-y.

Tversky, Amos and Daniel Kahneman. 1981. "The Framing of Decisions and the Psychology of Choice." *Science* 211 (4481): 453–8. https://doi.org/10.1126/science.7455683.

Urban, Jennifer Brown, and Miriam R. Linver. 2019. *Building a Career Outside Academia: A Guide for Doctoral Students in the Behavioral and Social Sciences*. American Psychological Association.

U.S. Citizenship and Immigration Services. n.d. *Employee Rights*. https://www.uscis.gov/i-9-central/employee-rights-and-resources/employee-rights. Accessed February 16, 2026.

U.S. Equal Employment Opportunity Commission. n.d. "Pre-Employment Opportunities and Citizenship." 2023. https://www.eeoc.gov/pre-employment-inquiries-and-citizenship.

"US Racial and Ethnic Equity in Higher Education." 2025. McKinsey. https://www.mckinsey.com/industries/education/our-insights/racial-and-ethnic-equity-in-us-higher-education.

Uttl, Bob, Carmela A. White, and Alain Morin. 2013. "The Numbers Tell It All: Students Don't Like Numbers!" *Plos ONE* 8 (12): e83443. https://doi.org/10.1371/journal.pone.0083443.

Vallance, Elizabeth. 1974. "Hiding the Hidden Curriculum: An Interpretation of the Language of Justification in Nineteenth-Century Educational Reform." *Curriculum Theory Network*. January 1974. https://www.tandfonline.com/doi/abs/10.1080/00784931.1974.11075752.

Valverde, Kieu Linh Caroline, and Wei Ming Dariotis. 2019. *Fight the Tower: Asian American Women Scholars' Resistance and Renewal in the Academy*. Rutgers University Press.

Veale, David, and Alison Roberts. 2014. "Obsessive-Compulsive Disorder." *BMJ* 348: g2183.

Venet, Alex Shevrin. 2021. *Equity-Centered Trauma-Informed Education*. Norton.

"The Vicarious Trauma Toolkit: What Is Vicarious Trauma." 2025. Mayo Clinic. https://ovc.ojp.gov/program/vtt/what-is-vicarious-trauma.

Viglione, Giuliana. 2020. "Are Women Publishing Less during the Pandemic? Here's What the Data Say." *Nature* 581: 365–6. https://doi.org/10.1038/d41586-020-01294-9.

Wachter, Sandra, Brent Mittelstadt, and Chris Russell. 2020. "Bias Preservation in Machine Learning: The Legality of Fairness Metrics under EU Non-Discrimination Law." *West Virginia Law Review* 123 (3): 735–90.

Wagner, Kathryn, Summer Melody Pennell, Meike Eilert, and Stacey R. Lim. 2022. "Academic Mothers with Disabilities: Navigating Academia and Parenthood during COVID-19." *Gender, Work & Organization* 29 (1): 342–52. https://doi.org/10.1111/gwao.12751.

Walkington, Helen, Kearsley A. Stewart, Eric E. Hall, Elizabeth Ackley, and Jenny Olin Shanahan. 2020. "Salient Practices of Award-Winning Undergraduate Research Mentors – Balancing Freedom and Control to Achieve Excellence." *Studies in Higher Education* 45 (7): 1519–32. https://doi.org/10.1080/03075079.2019.1637838.

Wapman, K. Hunter, Sam Zhang, Aaron Clauset, and Daniel B. Larremore. 2022. "Quantifying Hierarchy and Dynamics in US Faculty Hiring and Retention." *Nature* 610: 120–7. https://doi.org/10.1038/s41586-022-05222-x.

Ward, Kelly, and Lisa Wolf-Wendel. 2012. *Academic Motherhood: How Faculty Manage Work and Family*. Rutgers University Press.

Washington, Ella F. 2022. "Recognizing and Responding to Microaggressions at Work." *Harvard Business Review*. https://hbr.org/2022/05/recognizing-and-responding-to-microaggressions-at-work.

Weaver, Mark. 1998. "Weber's Critique of Advocacy in the Classroom: Critical Thinking and Civic Education." *PS: Political Science & Politics* 31 (4): 799–801. https://doi.org/10.2307/420720.

Welding, Lyss. 2025. "Students with Disabilities in Higher Education: Enrollment Data, Outcomes, and Inclusion." *Best Colleges*. https://www.bestcolleges.com/research/students-with-disabilities-higher-education-statistics/.

White-Lewis, Damani K. 2020. "The Facade of Fit in Faculty Search Processes." *The Journal of Higher Education* 91 (6): 833–57. https://doi.org/10.1080/00221546.2020.1775058.

Wilder, Craig Steven. 2013. *Ebony and Ivy: Race, Slavery, and the Troubled History of America's Universities*. Bloomsbury Publishing.

Williams, Joan C. 2014. "Double Jeopardy? An Empirical Study with Implications for the Debates over Implicit Bias and Intersectionality." *Harvard Journal of Law & Gender* 37 (1): 185–242.

Windsor, Leah, and Kerry F. Crawford. 2020. "Snow Days, Holidays and Pandemic Quarantines: Why We Need to Be Looking after Parents." *International Affairs Blog* (blog). https://medium.com/international-affairs-blog/snow-days-holidays-and-pandemic-quarantines-why-we-need-to-be-looking-after-parents-a3dc38413548.

Windsor, Leah C., and Cameron G. Thies. 2021. "Mentorship: 'Men in the Middle' and Their Role as Allies in Addressing Gender Bias." *PS: Political Science & Politics* 54 (3): 502–4. https://doi.org/10.1017/S1049096521000044.

Windsor, Leah C., and Christian Kronsted. 2022. "Grant Writing and the Hidden Curriculum: Mentoring and Collaborating across Disciplines." *PS: Political Science & Politics* 55 (2): 313–23. https://doi.org/10.1017/S1049096521001827.

Windsor, Leah Cathryn, and Kerry F. Crawford. 2021. "Academe Isn't a Leaky Pipeline." *The Chronicle of Higher Education*. https://www.chronicle.com/article/academe-isnt-a-leaky-pipeline.

Windsor, Leah Cathryn, Kerry F. Crawford, and Marijke Breuning. 2021. "Not a Leaky Pipeline! Academic Success Is a Game of Chutes and Ladders." *PS: Political Science & Politics* 54 (3): 509–12. https://doi.org/10.1017/S1049096521000081.

Woessner, Matthew, and April Kelly-Woessner. 2009. "I Think My Professor Is a Democrat: Considering Whether Students Recognize and React to Faculty Politics." *PS: Political Science & Politics* 42 (2): 343–52. https://doi.org/10.1017/S1049096509090453.

Wong, Paul, Chienping Faith Lai, Richard Nagasawa, and Tieming Lin. 1998. "Asian Americans as a Model Minority: Self-Perceptions and Perceptions by Other Racial Groups." *Sociological Perspectives* 41 (1): 95–118.

Wood, L. Maren. 2021. "Why We Need to Be Honest with Students and PhDs about the Academic Job Market." https://www.linkedin.com/pulse/why-we-need-honest-students-phds-academic-job-market-wood-phd.

Wood, Sarah, and Cole Claybourn. 2025. "The Dismantling of the Education Department." 2025. *US News & World Report*. www.usnews.com/education/best-colleges/articles/what-happens-if-the-education-department-is-dissolved.
World Health Organization. 2019. "Burnout an 'Occupational Phenomenon': International Classification of Diseases." https://www.who.int/news/item/28-05-2019-burn-out-an-occupational-phenomenon-international-classification-of-diseases.
Wright, Nzingha. 2021. "Her Melanin: Creating Courageous Conversations for Combating Imposter Syndrome for Black Women in Higher Education." West Chester University Master's Theses. https://digitalcommons.wcupa.edu/all_theses/214.
Wyse, Adam E., Eric M. Stickney, David Butz, Amanda Beckler, and Catherine N. Close. 2020. "The Potential Impact of COVID-19 on Student Learning and How Schools Can Respond." *Educational Measurement: Issues and Practice* 39 (3): 60–4. https://doi.org/10.1111/emip.12357.
Xu, Yin, and Yike Wang. 2023. "Job Stress and University Faculty Members' Life Satisfaction: The Mediating Role of Emotional Burnout." *Frontiers in Psychology* 14 (February): 1–10. https://doi.org/10.3389/fpsyg.2023.1111434.
Young, Bob. 2017. "Huntington's Disease Is Going to Kill Him, but This Bellingham Scientist Is Tackling It Head-On." *The Seattle Times*.

Index

About the Editors

Kerry F. Crawford is Professor and Department Head of Political Science at James Madison University in Harrisonburg, Virginia. She earned her BA in political science from St. Mary's College of Maryland in 2007 and her PhD in political science from George Washington University in 2014. She took a circuitous path to political science academia as a first-generation college student who started as a music major. Her first child was born just two weeks after she defended her dissertation, and her twins were born just two weeks before she submitted her tenure dossier. She has written several books, including *Wartime Sexual Violence: From Silence to Condemnation of a Weapon of War* (Georgetown University Press, 2017); *Human Security: Theory and Action* (Rowman & Littlefield, with David Andersen-Rodgers—first edition, 2018; second edition, 2023); and *The PhD Parenthood Trap: Caught between Work and Family in Academia* (Georgetown University Press, with Leah Windsor, 2021). She has also written numerous academic and public-facing articles on conflict-related sexual violence, gender and peacekeeping, human security, and bias and discrimination in academia. She wrote many of these publications while teaching a full course load online during the COVID-19 pandemic with three young children out of school and day care.

Leah C. Windsor is Associate Professor of Applied Linguistics in the Institute for Intelligent Systems and Department of English at The University of Memphis. She also has faculty affiliate status with CAESER (Center for Applied Earth Science and Engineering Research) and in the department of political science. She directs the Languages Across Cultures Lab and is PI on an NSF grant studying multimodal signals in world leaders' speeches. Her research broadly examines how what we say reveals who we are. Dr. Windsor received her Bachelor of Science in Linguistics degree from Georgetown University in 1998, her master's degree in Political Science at The University of Memphis in 2005, and her PhD in political science from The University of Mississippi in 2012. From 2014 to 2019, Dr. Windsor served as PI for a DoD Minerva Initiative grant that examined political communication in authoritarian regimes and opaque political groups. She is currently PI on a National Science Foundation grant examining embodied cognition and multimodal communication for international relations research (#2117009). Her book on bias in family formation in academia, *The PhD Parenthood Trap: Caught between Work and Family in Academia* (with Dr. Kerry Crawford), is available from Georgetown University Press. She was a 2020–2023 Non-Resident Fellow for the Krulak Center in the Marine Corps University and currently serves on the boards of the Text-as-Data and Tennessee Higher Education in Prison Initiative. She is a fifth-generation farmer.

About the Contributors

Nasir Almasri is a Postdoctoral Scholar with the Society of Fellows at Boston University. His research critically examines the role of religion and ideology in political violence, and he specializes in the politics of the Middle East and North Africa. He completed a PhD in political science at MIT and served as a predoctoral fellow with the Middle East Initiative at Harvard Kennedy School.

Amirah Aly is a Postdoctoral Scholar at the Centre for Molecular Medicine and Therapeutics at the University of British Columbia. Her main research goals lie in overcoming the blood-brain barrier (BBB) to deliver disease-modifying therapeutics to the brain for treatment of neurodegenerative disorders. She completed a PhD in pharmacology from Northeastern University.

Katharina A. Azim is Associate Professor in Human Sexuality at the California Institute of Integral Studies. Her teaching and research centers around women's reproductive health, agency, and rights in the United States, and specifically on experiences of painful sexual intercourse in young women.

Alan Babcock is Assistant Director of Disability Services at Penn State Harrisburg.

Kelly Bauer is Associate Professor and Director of Undergraduate Studies in the Political Science department at George Washington University. Her research focuses on identity and development politics in Latin America, with recent work exploring Indigenous rights and irregular migration. She also writes about political science pedagogy and teaching careers and is a member of the Red De Politólogas—#NoSinMujeres.

Stacey H. Bender is a Professor of Instruction and Program Coordinator in the Department of Health and Human Performance at Texas State University.

Srobana Bhattacharya is an educator and visual storyteller advocating for refugee rights and welfare. From 2013 to 2024, she was an Associate Professor at Georgia Southern University with a focus on political conflict, migration, and forced displacement. Inspired by her teaching and research, she moved to New York to pursue policy-oriented, hands-on work with refugees. She has a PhD in political science from Southern Illinois University and an MFA in visual narrative from the School of Visual Arts.

Lynn Bielski is Assistant Professor of Audiology at Ball State University. Her research interests include auditory-visual communication and the relation between audition and cognitive function, especially working memory.

Dr. Shannon Lindsey Blanton is a Professor in the Department of Political Science and Public Administration and Inaugural Dean of the Honors College at the University of Alabama at Birmingham. She previously served as vice provost for undergraduate programs, department chair, undergraduate coordinator, and on editorial boards for six of her discipline's foremost journals. She has published articles on US foreign policy and international relations, as well as a highly regarded textbook on world politics.

Rachel Blume has been an academic librarian with a focus on open science and evidence synthesis for ten years. She has a bachelor's in English literature and new media and a Master's of Library and Information Science from the University of Washington. She lives in Arkansas with her husband, four children, and pets.

Melissa Bowles-Terry is a Professor and library liaison to the College of Sciences at University of Nevada, Las Vegas, and former director of the faculty center. Melissa earned a master's degree in library and information science (University of Illinois, Urbana-Champaign) and a master of arts in English (Utah State University). She is coauthor of *Classroom Assessment Techniques for Librarians* and a member of the Association of College and Research Libraries Immersion faculty.

Mark A. Boyer is a Board of Trustees Distinguished Professor (emeritus) at the University of Connecticut. He served as Executive Director of the International Studies Association (ISA) from 2015 to 2024.

Clare R. Brock is Assistant Professor of American Politics and Public Policy at Colorado State University. Her work focuses on the intersection of lobbying, partisanship, and policy making, especially in the food and agricultural space. Prior to joining CSU, she was an assistant professor at Texas Woman's University.

Maggie Campbell-Obaid is Associate Professor of Psychology at Framingham State University. She is a social psychologist with a wide range of research interests, focused primarily on issues related to peace, violence, social responsibility, and political psychology.

Alison M. Clifton is an Associate Professor of French in the Department of Modern Languages at Roanoke College. She received her PhD in French and Second Language Acquisition and Teacher Education (SLATE) from the University of Illinois at Urbana-Champaign. Her teaching and research interests include francophone studies, second language acquisition, project-based service learning and undergraduate mentoring.

Amy Collins, PhD, is Assistant Professor and Teaching and Learning Scholar at the University of Minnesota Rochester. She researches student academic success in the post-COVID era as well as how instructors can support this success, with an emphasis on self-regulated learning. She received a PhD in agricultural communication, education, and leadership from The Ohio State University.

Amy Cooter is Deputy Director at the Institute for Countering Digital Extremism. She has studied nostalgic groups in the United States for nearly two decades and consults globally with experts and practitioners about ongoing and emerging threats. She is the author of *Nostalgia, Nationalism, and the US Militia Movement* and has published in a variety of academic and public outlets about militias, neo-Nazis, and similar groups' structures, motives, activities, and narratives.

Emily T. Cripe is Associate Professor of Communication Studies at Kutztown University of Pennsylvania. She studies organizational and health communication, focusing on breastfeeding and feminist approaches to health using autoethnography, other qualitative methods, and mixed methods.

Carrie Liu Currier is Professor of Political Science at Texas Christian University. She is also Director of the National Consortium for Teaching about Asia in Texas, which facilitates teaching about East Asia in elementary and secondary schools. Her research focuses on the impacts of economic reform in China, China's foreign policy with the Middle East, China's one-child policy, and the experiences of Asian Americans in higher education.

Paul F. Diehl is Henning Larsen Professor Emeritus of Political Science at the University of Illinois at Urbana-Champaign and Ashbel Smith Professor Emeritus of Political Science at the University of Texas at Dallas. He was the founding director of four different programs related to pedagogy and faculty development at three different universities.

Elizabeth I. Dorssom is Assistant Professor of Political Science at Lincoln University of Missouri and Program Coordinator for the MA in Community and Economic Development. She has received multiple teaching awards in recognition of her innovative and technology-driven pedagogy. A dedicated advocate for first-generation and underrepresented students, she holds a PhD in political science from the University of Missouri.

William Duffy is a Professor of Writing, Rhetoric, and Technical Communication in the English Department at the University of Memphis. He is the author of *Beyond Conversation: Collaboration and the Production of Writing* and coeditor of the forthcoming volume *Rhetoric and Religion as Resources for Resistance*.

Jamie Scalera Elliott is Associate Dean of the Keeping Sights Upward Journey Honors College at Kennesaw State University. Her primary research agenda focuses on the legitimacy of international organizations, broadly construed as the appropriate and effective exercise of authority to govern state members. She is also committed to the advancement of women in political science and international studies through her research and service to the profession.

Emily M. Farris is Professor of Political Science and core faculty in Comparative Race and Ethnic Studies at Texas Christian University. Her work focuses on local politics and issues of representation and marginalization.

Alexandra K. Frazer is a cognitive psychologist specializing in psycholinguistics with broad interests in the intersection of memory, attention, language, and learning. Her main lines of research focus on grammatical selection, phonological preparation, and language use in society and by the media.

Kathryn E. Frazier is Associate Professor of Psychology at Worcester State University.

Sally Friedman is Associate Professor of Political Science at the State University of New York at Albany.

Janet Garcia-Hallett is Associate Professor of Criminal Justice at the University of New Haven. She is the author of the award-winning book *Invisible Mothers: Unseen Yet Hypervisible after Incarceration.*

Jarod Giger, PhD, is Associate Professor of Social Work at University of Nevada, Las Vegas, and a fifth-generation farmer with deep roots in rural America. A first-generation college graduate, his work centers on rural health, underserved populations, and data-informed social work practice. He previously served on the editorial board of *The Journal of Rural Health* and held the Vernon Wiehe Endowed Professorship at the University of Kentucky. Giger completed a postdoctoral fellowship at the National Rural Health Association, where he focused on telehealth policy. His expertise spans community-based research, eHealth literacy, and behavioral interventions in rural and underserved communities.

Sean P. Giovanello is Associate Professor of Political Science and Public Policy at Elon University. His research interests center on arms control treaty ratification in the United States, the intersection of domestic politics and national security considerations in American foreign policy, and international relations theory.

Shane A. Gleason is Associate Professor of Public Policy and Law at Trinity College in Hartford, Connecticut. Previously on the faculty at Texas A&M University-Corpus Christi and Idaho State University, Gleason received a bachelor's degree in political science and history from Cleveland State University and a PhD in political science from Southern Illinois University. His teaching includes research methods, the legal system, and identity politics. His research focuses on identity, specifically gender, in the state and federal courts.

Jennifer H. Greene-Rooks is an Associate Professor and school counseling liaison in the professional counseling program at Texas State University. She is interested in motherscholarship, intersectionality, and counseling-related research.

Holley E. Hansen is a Teaching Associate Professor in the Department of Political Science at Oklahoma State University. As a first-generation scholar who got her start in the profession as an undergraduate researcher, Dr. Hansen is passionate about sharing this experience with her students. She has received several teaching and mentoring awards from her university, most recently the 2024 Outstanding Faculty Mentor Award from the College of Arts and Sciences.

Amanda Harmon, LCSW, is a Clinical Assistant Professor at Sacred Heart University. She has been Program Director of the Master of Social Work Program since 2024 and maintains a private psychotherapy practice. Her practice includes working with the LGBTQIA2S+ Community and a focus on infertility, pregnancy, and parenting.

N. A. Heller is Senior Director of Programs and Impact at the New Hampshire Children's Trust. She specializes in children and family policy work and is the mother of two boys.

LaSheba W. Hilliard is Assistant Professor of Teaching at the University of Memphis. Her work focuses on culturally responsive teaching, transition planning, and inclusive practices for students with diverse learning needs. She mentors future educators and advocates for equity and holistic support, particularly for Black women and girls with ADHD, striving to create educational spaces that are inclusive, empowering, and responsive to all learners.

Patrick Homan is a Professor of Political Science and Chair of the Political Science Department at Dominican University in River Forest, Illinois. Dr. Homan's research focuses on international relations, with a specialization in foreign policy analysis and international security and conflict resolution. His research also focuses on teaching and learning in higher education, including helping cofound the International Studies Association's "Teaching Centric Institutions Caucus" to help foster a collaborative environment around pedagogy.

Karen Huxtable-Jester is Associate Provost and Director of the Center for Teaching and Learning at the University of Texas at Dallas and Professor of Instruction in the School of Behavioral and Brain Sciences. She received the UT System Regents' Outstanding Teaching Award and is a Fellow in the UT System Academy of Distinguished Teachers and a Piper Professor of Texas.

Diana K. Ivy has been a Professor of Communication for more than forty years, many spent at Texas A&M University-Corpus Christi where she teaches nonverbal, interpersonal, and gender/sexuality communication courses. Her master's degree and PhD in communication are from the University of Oklahoma; her bachelor's is in speech and theater from Texas Wesleyan University. Ivy is the author/coauthor of three communication textbooks (*GenderSpeak 7e*; *Nonverbal Communication for a Lifetime 4e*; *Communication: Principles for a Lifetime 9e*).

Eun A Jo is Assistant Professor in the Government Department and the Director of Asia Policy Lab at the College of William & Mary.

Christine I. Kugelmann earned a PhD in Texts and Technology from the University of Central Florida (UCF), is a Lecturer of Technical Communication at UCF, and has been teaching in higher education for twenty-five years at two- and four-year public institutions as well as private universities and technical colleges. Her research interests include instructional design, open educational resources, and equity and accessibility in higher education.

Crystal Machado, an Education Professor at Indiana University of Pennsylvania (IUP), personally experienced "chutes" when she began her doctoral degree in 2003. Since then, she helps multiple minoritized student and faculty navigate the hidden curriculum. She started and led a mentoring program for women and male faculty of color at IUP. She enjoyed coauthoring this reflective piece with her students. In 2023, Machado was named Affordable Learning Champion; she also received the University Senate Distinguished Faculty Award for Teaching.

Farheen Mahmood, a temporary faculty member and doctoral student in curriculum and instruction at Indiana University of Pennsylvania (IUP), has more than twenty-four years of experience in teaching, teacher training, and administration across Pakistan, Yemen, Qatar, and the UAE. Her research explores children's literature through postcolonial theory lens and innovative technology integration. Mahmood holds double master's degrees in education and teacher education and has received prestigious awards, including the Carter G. Woodson Award (2021) and the Julius P. Filcik Fellowship (2023).

Daniel J. Mallinson, PhD, is Associate Professor of Public Policy and Administration at Penn State Harrisburg and Director of the Penn State Harrisburg Policy Process Lab. His research includes policy process theory (principally policy diffusion and punctuated equilibrium theory), state politics, cannabis policy, and environmental policy.

Tami Micsky is Associate Professor and MSW Program Director for the social work program at Slippery Rock University of Pennsylvania. Dr. Micsky is a licensed social worker and certified thanatologist. Dr. Micsky has experience working in child welfare, grief support, volunteer management, outpatient counseling, and disability services. Her research interests include self-care and wellness in social work and higher education, grief and loss, community-engaged learning, and distance/online education.

Kelly M. Miller is President of Texas A&M University-Corpus Christi, having held various roles at the university, including department chair, dean, provost, and now president since 2018. President Miller received her Bachelor's degree in communication at Pittsburgh University and her master's and PhD in communication from Penn State.

T. Mark Montoya, PhD, is Associate Dean for Curriculum and Student Affairs and professor of ethnic studies in the College of Social and Behavioral Sciences at Northern Arizona University. Montoya's scholarship focuses on the US-Mexico borderlands, pedagogy, and first-generation student experiences. He is a Distinguished Teaching Fellow at NAU, a past president of the Association for Borderlands Studies, a member of the *Journal of First-Generation Student Success* editorial board, and a FirstGen Forward CatalystFIRST speaker.

Colleen C. Myles-Baltzly is a Professor of Geography and Environmental Studies at Texas State University, where she runs the Fermented Landscapes Lab. She's also a mother of three children.

Lizoon Nahar (D.Ed. Indiana University of Pennsylvania, 2025) is an Instructional Specialist at the Academic Center for Excellence at Florida State University. She has seventeen years of teaching experience. Her research focuses on innovative teaching techniques and technology integration. She holds a master's degree in zoology from the University of Dhaka. She has received several awards, including the Global Teacher Grant (2018), Julius P. Filcik Fellowship Award (2021), and Student Research Award (2024).

Maya Novak-Herzog is Assistant Professor of Political Science at Centre College. Her research explores issues of consent, Title IX, and the politics of sexuality. She holds a PhD in political science from Northwestern University—a feat that was greatly influenced by her lifelong journey with obsessive compulsive disorder.

Ronald Nyanzi is an instructional designer and doctoral student in curriculum and instruction at Indiana University of Pennsylvania (IUP) with more than fifteen years of teaching experience. He has provided IT support to the IUP's Center for Teaching Excellence and is working with the IUP Noyce Grant. Ronald's research explores artificial intelligence in education. He holds a PGD in IT and a master's degree in instructional design. He is recipient of esteemed awards such as the Fulbright-ILEP Award (2016), Dean's Merit Scholarship (2019), and Graduate Scholarship Award (2020).

Lillie Padilla is from Ghana in West Africa. She is Assistant Professor of Spanish at Sam Houston State University. She obtained a PhD and MA in Spanish linguistics at Arizona State University and a bachelor's degree in Spanish and sociology at the University of Ghana. Her research interests include Spanish language variation, Afro-Latinx representation, critical discourse analysis, and Spanish heritage language pedagogy.

Tara Parsons is Associate Professor in the Department of Justice Studies at James Madison University in Harrisonburg, Virginia. She is the coordinator of the Humanitarian Affairs minor and Director of The Nelson Institute for International and Public Affairs. Her professional interests include human rights, democratization, social movements, and using constructive dialogue for justice.

Summer Melody Pennell is a Senior Lecturer in Secondary Education at the University of Vermont. Her teaching and research interests are centered in equity and include English education, critical literacy, young adult literature, and queer theory, issues, and pedagogy.

Courtney B. Peters (PhD, University of Memphis, 2022) is Assistant Professor of Marketing at Samford University. Her research explores brand activism and ethics and impacts on consumers and society. She teaches principles of marketing, digital marketing, and content marketing, with a passion for mentoring students, especially first-generation college students. Dr. Peters is a wife, mom, and dog mom.

Gretchen Peterson is a Professor of Sociology at the University of Memphis. She received a PhD from the University of Arizona in 2000. Her primary research interests are in the intersection of the sociology of sports and social psychology. Her current research agenda focuses on adult recreational sports, particularly softball. She served as department chair at two different universities over a span of eleven years.

Leanne C. Powner holds a PhD in political science from the University of Michigan. She has coached hundreds of academics, including dissertators, for ten years. Find her online at www.leannecpowner.com or @leannecpowner.bsky.social for more practical tips.

Kaity Prieto, PhD, is Assistant Professor of Higher Education at the University of Southern Mississippi. Her research centers on the experiences of queer and trans students, with a focus on bisexual+ student communities and bisexual identity negotiation. She received a PhD in educational studies with a concentration in higher education and student affairs from The Ohio State University.

Rashna Wadia Richards serves as Associate Provost at Rhodes College. She has primary responsibility for matters of the academic budget, including faculty salary, equity structure, and administrative operations. She oversees faculty hiring, academic space and renovations, and student success, and she works closely with department and program chairs on their budgetary and staffing needs.

Ivanna Richardson is a trained linguist, working as an independent researcher in language reclamation, exploring mothering, and supporting voices of mothering; a mother of three, she lives in Montreal, Canada.

C. Kelsey Ryan is Director of the Center for Leadership Development at the University of North Texas. Kelsey received a BS in chemistry from Georgia Southern University and MS in higher education administration from the University of North Florida. With more than a decade of experience in higher education, Kelsey has seen the impact financial aid can have on a student's success in college. In her free time, Kelsey enjoys napping, traveling, and rewatching *Parks and Recreation*.

Jessica Salvatore is an experimental social psychologist whose research and teaching focuses on social stigmas, identity, and social (meta-)perception. She has published empirical work and research commentary in *Psychological Science*, *Sex Roles*, *Analyses of Social Issues and Public Policy*, and other journals, and previously served as associate editor of the *British Journal of Social Psychology*. She is a Fellow of Division 9 of the APA.

Dr. Melanie R. Savelli is a Professor of Communication specializing in mass communication and public relations. Her research and teaching focus on best classroom practices, inclusive pedagogy, and equity in higher education. As a disabled academic living with a chronic illness, she brings lived experience to her work educating others and creating awareness about the realities of chronic illness to foster empathy, support structural change, and advocate for scholars navigating similar challenges.

Austin Schutz (he/him) is an instructor of political science at Fresno City College who graduated with a PhD from the University of Alabama in 2023. He researches (1) political representation comparatively and in institutions of global governance, and (2) military coups. Austin is also comanager of the Coup Agency and Mechanism project (militarycoups.org).

Karen Sobel is a professor and Teaching & Learning Librarian with a focus on graduate education at the University of Colorado Denver. She holds a doctor of education (University of Colorado Denver), Master's degrees in Library Science and English (University of North Carolina at Chapel Hill), and a Bachelor of Arts in English (Penn State University). She directed her university's Center for Faculty Development & Advancement for five years. Her professional interests include career growth for mid-career faculty and motivations behind academic behaviors.

Rae Summers-Thompson is a PhD candidate in writing, rhetoric, and technical communication in the English Department at the University of Memphis. Her dissertation focuses on trauma-informed pedagogy for postsecondary composition instruction.

Jennifer H. Tatara (PhD, University of Memphis) is Assistant Professor of Marketing at DePaul University's Driehaus College of Business and Kellstadt Graduate School of Business. Her research explores consumer-based strategy, crisis management, and consumer neuroscience. Prior to academia, she worked as an associate broker at a leading global provider of risk management.

Kirsten L. Taylor is Dean of the Evans School of Humanities, Arts, and Social Sciences and the Charles A. Dana Professor of Political Science and International Affairs at Berry College. Her teaching and research interests include international institutions, global environmental politics and law, US foreign policy, and the scholarship of teaching and learning. She has coauthored textbooks on international relations and US foreign policy.

Lesley Thornton-Cronin is an art historian and Professor of Aesthetics at Humber Polytechnic in Toronto, Canada. She received a PhD from the University of Glasgow in 2016. Professor Thornton-Cronin's research interests include twentieth-century surrealism and its contemporary, Indigenized applications. As an undergraduate educator and in her research practice, she is committed to the decolonized teaching and learning of art history.

Dr. Gina English Tillis is a Research Associate with the Center for Research in Educational Policy (CREP) at the University of Memphis. She is an interdisciplinary scholar-practitioner who centers identities, cultures, and histories within urban educational policy, programs, and practice. She draws from community-based frameworks to engage in critical sociopolitical analysis of how education is shared equitably, accessibly, and inclusively in service of our community.

Dr. Claudio Villalobos Dintrans earned a BS in biological sciences from the Pontificia Universidad Católica de Chile, followed by a PhD in pharmacology from Wayne State University. He is currently a Health Program Specialist at the National Institute of Neurological Diseases and Stroke (NINDS/NIH). Dr. Villalobos also served as an associate group leader at PPD/Thermo Fisher Scientific and as an adjunct instructor in biology at Nebraska Wesleyan University before joining NIH/NINDS. His postgraduate work included positions at the University of California, Los Angeles, and the Universidad de Chile, investigating neuronal mechanisms of decision making and spatial memory consolidation. His most recent work has been published in *Cell Reports* and *Frontiers in Neural Circuits*, and he also writes about the politics of research funding and diversity in STEM.

Tera Warfield is a licensed professional counselor, educator, and researcher specializing in the psychological well-being of marginalized populations. Her work integrates clinical expertise with research-based strategies to address mental health challenges through a holistic and inclusive lens. Passionate about advocacy and education, she is committed to fostering resilience and empowerment by bridging theory, practice, and community engagement in mental health and wellness.

Crystal L. White, Assistant Professor of Educational Psychology and Research and Assistant Director of a mentorship network, is dedicated to fostering equitable learning environments and student success. With extensive teaching experience spanning K–12 to higher education, she passionately empowers diverse learners, educators, and counselors and leads research on identity, urban education, sociocultural justice, and hip-hop feminism. She employs culturally responsive practices and authentic mentorship, bridging theory and application through community-engaged initiatives and student-centered pedagogy.

Kelly Williams holds Master of Science degrees in educational psychology from Texas A&M University-Central Texas and in library science from the University of North Texas. She has spent most of her library career working in the technical services departments of academic libraries but recently made a change to outreach, reference, and instruction.

Zora M. Wolfe is Associate Dean of the College of Health and Human Services at Widener University. Her research focuses on developing and supporting productive learning communities within schools and classrooms, both within the United States and in developing countries, including how to use instructional technologies to enhance this work. She earned an EdD from the University of Pennsylvania while working full-time and parenting three young boys, the youngest born right before her proposal defense.

Irmak Yazici, PhD, is People & Culture Coordinator in the Nuffield Department of Clinical Neurosciences at the University of Oxford. She is a social scientist with a PhD in political science. Prior to this she was a lecturer at Stanford University and the University of Hawai'i at Mānoa for eleven years.